BONO

IN THE NAME OF LOVE

For Linda, Evelyn and Mollie

First published in Great Britain in 2005 by

André Deutsch
an imprint of the
Carlton Publishing Group
20 Mortimer Street
London W1T 3JW

A catalogue record for this book is available from the British Library

Hardback ISBN 0-233-00123-9
Paperback ISBN 0-233-00159-X

Typeset by e-type, Liverpool
Printed in Great Britain by Mackays

BONO

IN THE NAME OF LOVE

Mick Wall

André Deutsch

The publishers would like to thank the following sources for their kind permission to reproduce the pictures in this book.

Plate Section One:

Page 1: (top) Ken Welsh/The Irish Image Collection; (bottom) Paul Slattery/Retna UK; Page 2: (top) Steve Wood/Getty Images/Express; (bottom) Peter Gould/Getty Images/Image Makers/Keystone; Page 3: (top) George Chin/Redferns; (bottom) Ebet Roberts/Redferns; Page 4: (top) Ebet Roberts/Redferns; (bottom) Neal Preston/CORBIS; Page 5: CORBIS; Page 6: (top) Tim Mosenfelder/Getty Images/Imagedirect; (bottom) Neal Preston/CORBIS; Page 7: (top) Ebet Roberts/Redferns; (bottom) Bettmann/CORBIS; Page 8: (top) John Reardon/Getty Images/The Observer; (bottom) CORBIS.

Plate Section Two:

Page 1: (top) ShowBizIreland/Getty Images; (bottom) Nick Rogers/The Observer/Getty Images; Page 2: (top) Neal Preston/CORBIS; (bottom) Gerard Malie/AFP/Getty Images; Page 3: (top) Andrew Murray/CORBIS SYGMA; (bottom) Neal Preston/CORBIS; Page 4: (top) Timothy A. Clary/AFP/Getty Images; (bottom) Dave Benett/ Getty Images; Page 5: (top) Marcus Brandt/AFP/Getty Images; (bottom) Reuters/CORBIS; Page 6: (top) Michael Maloney/San Franciso Chronicle/CORBIS; (bottom) Alex Wong/Getty Images; Page 7: Richard Young/Rex Features; Page 8: (top) Carlo Allegri/Getty Images; (bottom) Corbis Images/Pascal Lauener/Reuters/Corbis.

Every effort has been made to acknowledge correctly and contact the source and/or copyright holder of each picture and Carlton Books Limited apologises for any unintentional errors or omissions that will be corrected in future editions of this book.

CONTENTS

PREFACE

I t's a cliché but no less true for that: for those of us who were there, whether in person (as I was fortunate enough to be), or simply watching on TV (as most of Earth's population seemed to be at one point), Live Aid was truly a day none of us will ever forget. And for all sorts of reasons, some shared, some not. Yet, when asked to summon up one vividly abiding memory from that day, we all reach for the same scattered handful of images: Status Quo kicking the whole thing off with 'Rockin' All Over The World'; the grand finale, where the flickering lights of the crowd outshone the stars now engulfed on the stage, interspersed with that heart-rending footage of the starving African child and mother relayed on TV to the strangely apt soundtrack of the Cars' 'Drive'; a visibly "tired and emotional" Bob Geldof yelling at the screen: "Send us your fuckin' money!" And, of course, that moment when Bono, of U2, descended, messiah-like, from the Wembley stage in order to "communicate better" with the crowd – and came a cropper.

Bono had done things like this many times before, of course: climbing the gantries, leaping from the stage, then returning to it, often with at least one audience member in tow; so much so, it had virtually become a feature of all the early-1980s U2 shows. Only this time, given the size of the photographers' pit that separated the audience from the massive Wembley Stadium stage, he couldn't quite manage it and what should have been a glorious moment descended into a lengthy, confusing interlude. Indeed, he took so long to persuade the security staff to allow him to pluck a willing if somewhat stunned-looking girl from the audience, then clamber back on stage to dance with her, that the band ran out of time and were forced to drop their planned third number, 'Pride (In The Name Of Love)' – U2's landmark song, at that point.

Afterwards, a distraught Bono apologised to his band-mates for "blowing it" yet it's still one of the moments we remember best from Live Aid. And not just for the cumbersome attempt at unorthodox audience participation, nor the impressively buffed "mullet" hairstyle he sported back then (amusing from this distance but absolutely *de rigueur* for any self-respecting mid-1980s pop superstar). We forgive Bono all that because we know at heart that, right or wrong, this is one rock star who actually means it. Yes, it's true. He really does believe that he – we – can make a difference. And right then – the Eighties, the most cynical, money-grubbing decade of the music business since the wild-west Fifties – sincerity and belief were commodities in laughably short supply. So much so that, all these years later, watching the clip over again on DVD, instead of laughing and pointing our fingers, for those of us who were there, there's still this secret desire, some lingering unexpressed hope, that this time he *will* make it back on stage in time for that third number. Because, whether we ever bought a U2 record or not, we all want to believe in Bono, or at least in someone like him. Someone straight with you, who doesn't just take the money and run but really does give something back; something even more precious than money: his time. Even if it occasionally makes him look foolish.

But it's not always easy to love someone so determinedly right-on or so deeply absorbed in their own role. Maybe if his group wasn't so astonishingly successful, it would be easier for non-U2 fans to believe in Bono more wholeheartedly. You would get to see the rough as well as the smooth. But U2 are the most successful band in the world, and have been for years. And so we are forced to confront this image of an absurdly rich and famous rock star as the ultimate, self-styled do-gooder. For a media-saturated public with little time to consider the implications of an African famine, the unchecked spread of AIDS or the implications of Third World debt, it's all too easy to dismiss Bono as some sort of cape-wearing crusader, the funky philanthropist constantly fighting the good fight on behalf of us lesser mortals, basking in the glory of all his good works. Maybe one of the reasons so many of us still recall his haphazard performance at Live Aid so fondly is because we got to see the cape flapping in his face for once. Proof that he was, after all, still human ...

As for so many of the artists appearing at Live Aid that afternoon, 13 July 1985 would prove a major turning point for both Bono and U2, though in a different way to most. Where Queen and Status Quo had effectively relaunched their careers off the back of the massive worldwide publicity their appearances had received, U2, already riding the crest of their fame as a rock band with integrity, musical chops and a pocketful of popular hits, had laid the second big plank for what would soon become a legend. The first had been their early breakthrough with straight-out-of-the-box hits like 'I Will Follow' and 'Sunday Bloody Sunday'. You didn't have to buy those records to see what lay behind them; to hear the extra effort being put in by all concerned. The second plank was Live Aid. From here on in, even if you professed to hate U2, you couldn't deny them their place at the big table, maybe not sat right next to Lennon and Dylan, but certainly in the same conversation.

Their timing had been immaculate. Live Aid, the biggest popular music event since Woodstock, was the perfect stage for them. Held simultaneously across two continents, Live Aid effectively wound the clock back to an era when bands and musicians thought they could change the world through their music and lyrics; demonstrating that the current, overpaid supergroups of the greed-is-good Eighties had a conscience after all. Having managed, against strenuous odds, to persuade a forty-strong group of the world's most egotistical pop stars to share a studio in November 1984 to record the original Band Aid single, 'Do They Know It's Christmas?' – with all monies from the sale of the record going to aid the millions of victims of the widespread famine then gripping

North Africa – then Boomtown Rats singer Bob Geldof's next plan was a sixteen-hour musical event to take place simultaneously in Britain and America and telecast to every country in the known hemispheres.

As a result, Live Aid would feature many of the biggest acts of the day – Queen, Status Quo, Led Zeppelin, the Who, David Bowie, Bob Dylan and Elton John, to name but a few; many re-forming especially for the occasion (and several collapsing in not so private acrimony afterwards). But one current band Geldof knew he *had* to have was the Irish quartet U2, *Rolling Stone* magazine's newly named *"Band of the Year"*. By then, of course, U2 were already well versed in the forbidden art of mixing politics with rock'n'roll, having already publicly backed the causes of both ecological pressure group Greenpeace, and Amnesty International, champions of prisoners of conscience. And of course it had been Bono who had delivered the chilling line in the original Band Aid song: "Well, tonight, thank God, it's them instead of you ..." Indeed, in Bono they had someone more than willing to use his fame, his charisma, to throw the spotlight on the oppressed and disadvantaged; the ones we thank God that we are not.

In fact, as soon as Geldof announced Live Aid, both Bono and U2 bass player Adam Clayton had hurriedly flown home from the States, where U2 had been touring, personally to offer their help on a practical, day-by-day basis. Many groups on the Live Aid bill were happy to give of their time that day – and to reap the resultant rewards of the worldwide publicity it garnered them. Already hugely successful in

Britain and America, U2 hardly needed to play that game, yet they were among the first to confirm they would appear. As if to underline the sincerity of their support, away from the spotlight, Bono and wife Ali later decided they would spend the month of September working as volunteers in Ethiopia; a fact which went largely unreported at the time, for which they were grateful.

Instead, on the eve of the event, the band chose to issue the following statement:

U2 are involved in Live Aid because it's more than money, it's music – but it is also a demonstration to the politicians and policy-makers that men, women and children will not walk by other men, women and children as they lie, bellies swollen, starving to death for the sake of a cup of grain and some water. For the price of Star Wars, the MX missile offensive-defensive budgets, the desert of Africa could be turned into fertile lands. The technology is with us. The technocrats are not. Are we part of a civilisation that protects itself by investing in life – or investing in death?

It was a good question; one Bono would return to doggedly over the next twenty years.

Live Aid's two main venues – London's Wembley Stadium (with a capacity of 72,000) and Philadelphia's JFK Stadium (90,000) – had been painstakingly prepared with identical revolving stages, each flanked by giant Diamond Vision video screens to help bring the action to those at the back of each crowd. Each site also carried events televised live via satellite from the other venue, as well as contributions from as far afield as Japan, Germany, Norway and the Soviet Union. Timing was of the essence: Geldof's idea for what he called a "global jukebox" meant that each band or singer would have just fifteen minutes to make their musical point as the stage on the other side of the Atlantic was frantically being readied for its next occupant. This "ping-pong" approach meant that, although performing at Wembley, U2 were introduced on stage live in Philadelphia by Jack Nicholson at 5.20 p.m. London time. The Oscar-winning star naturally gave them the big Hollywood build-up. "And now, to keep with the international and global feeling that we have, direct from London, a group whose heart is in Dublin City, Ireland, whose spirit is with the world, a group that's never had any problem saying how they feel – U2!"

As Bono matter-of-factly announced the first song, 'Sunday Bloody Sunday', Union Jack flags, Irish tricolours and several others all began to wave hectically among the already jumping 72,000 Wembley crowd. The song had first been heard as the opening cut of 1983's chart-topping *War* album and controversially addressed one of the most horrifying and bloody incidents of the Northern Ireland conflict. When U2 had first played the song in Belfast, where what became known as the Bloody Sunday massacre of January 1972 took place, Bono promised the audience there that night that they'd never play it again if they didn't like it. Fortunately, out of over three thousand people in the hall, only a small hand walked out, and the song went on to become one of their biggest early hits.

Two years on from its release, 'Sunday Bloody Sunday' was now recognised as a more universal plea for peace and under-standing, and therefore an appropriate number to open with at such an event. As Bono said: "Having a Protestant mother and a Catholic father I know how grey it is. There are no sides, and I think people know better now [and] I think we've contributed to that."

The singer hardly left time to receive the rapturous applause at the end of the song before stepping up to the mic to introduce himself and his cohorts. "We're an Irish band," he declared earnestly, addressing the viewers at home around the world as much as the Wembley crowd. "We come from Dublin City, Ireland. Like all cities it has its good and it has its bad. This is a song called 'Bad' ..." A stunning, largely improvisatory reading of one of the pivotal tracks from the previous year's million-selling *Unforgettable Fire* album, Bono used it as a musical platform to lead the band through snatches of the Rolling Stones' 'Ruby Tuesday' and 'Sympathy For The Devil', before segueing skilfully into a jazzy verse or two from Lou Reed's 'Walk On the Wild Side', which somehow slipped into the chorus of Reed's then more obscure 'Satellite Of Love' (in recognition, Bono later explained, of the fact that the event was being broadcast worldwide by satellite tech-nology; a remarkable feat in those pre-internet times).

Clearly, Bono, already well on the way to becoming one of world's great self-publicists, had decided Live Aid was a day worth leaving his personal stamp on. As a result, 'Bad' had already been extended to almost untenable lengths, the band – drummer Larry Mullen Jr, guitarist The Edge and bassist Adam Clayton – thundering away without ever quite knowing where Bono was really going with it. "The next thing we knew, he'd jumped off the stage," recalled The Edge.

On the day, the sheer magnitude of the event – still "the most extraordinary thing we've done" Bono stated, still giddy, a couple of years later – had made him "high as a kite on what was going on", he explained. Once on stage he had got carried away and managed to forget that each act was allocated barely a quarter of an hour to complete their set. "I thought it was just U2 playing. As a result we didn't get to do 'Pride'." He had ignored a "traffic light" system of lights giving the bands their countdown to vacate the stage, thus avoiding a logjam later in the day. He felt particularly foolish as David Bowie had also been obliged to drop a number from his set so that the famous Cars film clip, which inspired so many new donations, could be shown.

Of his unexpected and time-costly foray into the crowd, while it was true that he had wanted to make "some sort of gesture that included the crowd because they seemed as important to me as the people behind the stage", Bono later insisted that his initial reason for venturing off the stage was because he had seen "someone getting squashed down front and I was wanting to go down there" – jumping a full ten feet on to a platform intended for the dozens of TV cameras and press photographers, in an attempt to pull the girl out; later identified as one

Melanie Hills. Ironically, the favoured few who had camped out for tickets to get into the stadium were unaware of what was going on out of their sight line. But the worldwide audience glued to their television sets were transfixed.

That this literal tearing down of the barriers between artist and audience – an analogy for one of the things punk had originally tried to achieve a decade before – would be remembered as one of the defining moments of the day, was the furthest thought from Bono's mind at the time, he said. As it was, having been brusquely informed there was no time for another number, Bono grabbed a towel and stalked off stage, leaving the TV production team to fade out U2 and fade in the Beach Boys live from Philadelphia.

Though Bono's comedown after the event was considerable ("At Live Aid, the whole question of Africa and the idea that millions were dying of starvation brought back the stupidity of the world of rock'n'roll," he chided), he was lifted at length from his brief depression when everywhere he went people began telling him how the moment they always remembered best from Live Aid was U2; how, by common consent, Queen and U2 had been the unequivocal hits of the day. Newspapers reported that many thousands of people, in fact, went into record shops over the following days and weeks asking for something by "the singer that danced with the girl at Live Aid".

Live Aid would prove a watershed for both U2 and its most famous member in other ways, too. As the years passed, not only would Bono soon eclipse close friend and fellow Dubliner, Bob Geldof (who was later knighted for his work), as a political campaigner of true stature, he would manage both to retain his musical credibility and co-create some of the most successful music of the past twenty-five years. Many Live Aid acts found their record sales increasing exponentially in the weeks and months that immediately followed the show, and U2 were no exception, but no one could ever have accused them of exploiting the connection for that reason. The arc of their commercial graph had already begun reaching its apex long before Live Aid came along.

As such, the staggering success of, first the Band Aid record, followed by the even more staggering success of the concert itself, came as no real surprise to Bono, he said. "For Bob, the sight of little bits of black plastic actually saving lives was something of a shock," he shrugged. "He had always thought of pop music as something wonderful in itself, but nothing more than that. But I wasn't quite as taken aback by the success of it all. The 1960s music that inspired me was a part of a movement that eventually helped to stop the Vietnam War and there is no reason why contemporary music cannot have a similar importance."

Bono described how he later met a sculptor in his sixties who told him he had been so inspired by watching Live Aid that he had created a special bronze statue in commemoration of the event. "He described it all by saying that there was a different kind of energy coming off the TV set [that day]," said Bono. "The figure he was doing was of a man, a naked man, bent over, and he called it *The Leap*. He said to me he was trying to capture the spirit of the day, but the part of it he wanted was our part, the U2 piece. I thought to myself, if a person who's so removed from rock'n'roll can understand that, maybe it wasn't such a big mistake."

Bono, of course, has consistently been making leaps like that in the twenty years since Live Aid. Never happy confined to being merely one of the world rulers of music, these days he has become probably its most active campaigner for reform. In 2004, he lent his weight to South African Archbishop Desmond Tutu's Truth and Reconciliation campaign – where convicted murderers are forced to confront the families of their victims. Typically, Bono described it as one of "the most inspiring stories of the last fifty years".

While in South Africa, Bono also lent his support to the idea of an international AIDS/HIV vaccine initiative, which would have significantly cut the profits of the giant US pharmaceutical firms but made their vital new medicines more affordable to the poorest countries that needed them most. "They haven't been acting fast enough," he said. "In the United States this intellectual copyright was such a deal." Absurdly, the brand names of the products themselves were making their cost prohibitively high, he explained. "When we were bringing this up they said, 'You know we can't change this for anything. Once you do, the floodgates will be opened and intellectual copyright, including your music, pal, will be over,' and then something happened. There was an Anthrax scare and suddenly in Congress they passed a bill saying no intellectual copyright on the treatment for diseases." These days, Bono measures true success not just in record sales, but in saving human lives. A few weeks before that he gave testimony to the US Senate Committee on the need for increased spending assistance for Africa to tackle the AIDS epidemic. Still intent on ramming the message home, he then gave a speech to European Union development ministers in Dublin, putting his name to an open letter to the British Prime Minister, Tony Blair – along with over twenty other celebrities, including Helen Mirren and Jude Law – demanding increased aid to the poorest countries. "It's not really about charity at this point," he told reporters. "It's about justice."

Just as he saw no conflict in trying to bridge the gap between stage and audience at Live Aid, even when it cost him his grand finale, Bono still sees no problem in skilfully combining the roles of musical artist and political agitator: "What I want from music," he says, "are people who lay themselves on the line. People like John Lennon or Iggy Pop did that. Whatever you feel about their music, you do learn about them from it. If anything, that's where the divide lies." A line he has so far walked without too much fear of falling, it seems, even when he occasionally does.

In June 1985, a few weeks before the show at Wembley, Bono had talked about a conversation he'd had recently about his music with fellow Live Aid performer Elvis Costello, in which the bespectacled and notoriously spiky Costello had come up with a metaphor that could apply equally well to Bono's own attitude to life – then as now.

"He said to me, 'I'm ambivalent about U2, I love it and I hate it.' He said, 'You walk this tightrope that none of your contemporaries will walk – they're afraid to walk it – and when you stay on I bow my head, but you fall off it so many times.' There was no answer to that. We do fall off, a lot, and on stage I'll try for something and it won't work and ... but it might work and that's the point – it *might* work."

As a result, such is Bono's international standing these days that even U2's breaking-all-precedents decision to endorse Apple's iPod personal music system in 2004 brought not a shred of criticism, even from the more voracious sections of the media. While 2004 ended with Bono lending his name to something new yet familiar – a reprise of his role in the original Band Aid single – a twentieth-anniversary re-recording which featured the brightest young British stars of today, some of whom (such as white soul newcomer Joss Stone and boy band Busted) had not even been born when the phrases 'Band Aid' and 'Live Aid' first entered the vocabulary.

The tabloid press took great pleasure in engineering an "argument" between Bono and flamboyant Darkness front man Justin Hawkins, who allegedly butted heads over the decision as to who would sing the famous line, "Well, tonight, thank God, it's them instead of you". Hawkins was said to have claimed he had originally been offered the line on the new version, and accused his "rival" of pulling rank on him, claiming Bono was being jetted in to rerecord the line in order to avoid being upstaged. The "argument", if indeed that's what it really was, soon petered out, however, and, needless to say, it was Bono's line again when the latest Band Aid 20 – as in twentieth anniversary – version of the song was unveiled to the world via multiple simultaneous video screenings in December 2004. It seems not even "Sir Bob Gandalf" (as Joss Stone endearingly miscalled him) would have fancied trying to tell Bono he'd given his most famous line away to someone else.

Besides, the real arguments about Bono concern larger issues. The big question: what is it that makes him so sure that rock music, as he claims, "can help to change things, not in any melodramatic way, but certainly as part of a movement of positive protest. There are new problems and we need new solutions." His pledge to help come up with some of those solutions led, in 2002, to him becoming a co-founder of DATA (Debt, AIDS, Trade, Africa), an organisation that saw him link with Bobby Shriver and activists from the Jubilee 2000 Drop the Debt campaign, with a view to raising awareness about and sparking response to the two big crises swamping Africa today: namely, unpayable debts exacerbated by disastrously one-sided trade rules, and the – so far – uncontrolled spread of AIDS throughout the region, thanks primarily to an almost total lack of the right medicines and vaccines, or the necessary will or money to make them more widely available.

What is it about Bono that drives him to take his commitment to world reform to such intimidating non-musical arenas as the US Congress; co-writing newspaper editorials with billionaire Microsoft founder, Bill Gates, entitled: "Demand a better deal for the poor of the world in 2005"? "Only one of us is known for crunching numbers," Bono commented dryly at the time. "But we both believe that investments in human potential pay off many times over.

They have the power to end extreme poverty. But only if we learn to think big again."

That line "Tonight, thank God, it's them instead of you" clearly means more to Bono than just the pivotal moment in a song. It's become his credo: particularly, perhaps, as all other material goals in his life were apparently conquered so easily.

But how did it all begin? Where did it start? Who is it that Superman sees in the mirror when he takes off his cape at night? For the answers you have to search for the motivation behind his need to change lives and influence people, to challenge his own beliefs and ability to act on them. And for that you have to go back to his boyhood in Dublin, where he grew up in the Sixties and Seventies: a world he now recalls as poor but generally warm and loving – until one fateful day, when he was fourteen, something would happen that would change his life for ever, and, eventually, set him on the path that led to where he is – who he is – today.

CHAPTER ONE 1960–1978

aul David Hewson was born at the Rotunda Hospital in Dublin on 10 May 1960. He remembers Ballymun, the district he was brought up in but came to know best as a teenager, as a rough neighbourhood: "a high tower block area with gangs running loose". When his family had first moved there in 1960, however, Ballymun was still considered to be a modest suburb on the edge of the city, within jet engine noise of Dublin Airport. The high-rise flats wouldn't arrive until he was seven, as the Irish government sought to emulate the British and started knocking down the worst of the inner-city slums, shipping their residents into the gleaming new tower blocks with promises of a better future.

Paul was raised in a newly built semi-detached house at 10 Cedarwood Road, two doors down from Mrs Byrne, whose washing line flapping with damp underclothes he would later eulogise on the U2 song 'Shadows And The Tall Trees', considerately changing her name to "Brown" to avoid embarrassment. The boxy semis with three bedrooms and small front and back gardens that lined the surrounding streets were more or less identical and difficult to make your own,

but to the Hewsons they represented the suburban dream come true.

His parents, mother Iris and father Bobby, had both grown up in the considerably more urban Oxmantown Road area of the city. Bobby (born Brendan Robert Hewson), in particular, was brought up with a love for music inherited from his parents, who were both involved with various amateur dramatics groups as well as the local music hall. Music offered Bobby an escape from his humdrum job as a postal worker in which, again, he'd followed his father's footsteps at the age of fourteen – official school-leaving age in Ireland back then.

Iris Elizabeth Rankin came from a typically large Irish family of ten, and after leaving school, also at fourteen, worked for a small knitwear company as a book-keeper. She charmed Bobby when they started going steady at nineteen, but one major barrier stood in the way of their happiness: she was Protestant while he was Roman Catholic. "Mixed" marriages required special dispensation from Rome, plus a devout promise that any future children be brought up in "the one true church", on top of which the ceremony would also have to take place in a symbolically darkened church. For the headstrong Bobby, this was simply too much to ask, and so he boldly offered to marry Iris in the Protestant Church of Ireland instead, in August 1950 (though their union would, some years later, be blessed by a Catholic priest).

The couple's first child, a big healthy boy they named Norman, was born in 1952, eight years before Paul, when the

Hewsons still lived at 36 Dale Road in Stillorgan, south of the River Liffey. They had only bought and moved into 10 Cedarwood Road a matter of weeks after Paul's birth, the couple having been impressed with the area after Iris's younger sister Ruth had earlier moved there with her husband, Ted. Though hardly rich, the fact that the family now owned their own house, as well as being among the select few in their street actually to own a car, albeit a compact NSU, the Hewsons were considered reasonably well to do for the times. Though all their money would go on paying the bills and keeping the kids fed, they certainly weren't struggling in any practical sense.

Except maybe one. From an early age, Paul understood that he came from a "mixed" religious background: a major issue in the tribally drawn lines of 1960s Ireland. "I always felt like I was sitting on the fence," he would later confess, admitting he had no clear idea of whether he should be a Protestant or a Catholic, "working class or middle class". A situation hardly helped by the fact that Bobby would drop his wife and sons off at one place of worship (St Canice's Roman Catholic Church) every Sunday morning, then drive himself off to another, a fact Paul "really resented", he later confessed. On normal weekday mornings, Paul and Norman would take a ten-minute bus ride to the Protestant Asnevin National School, where they were both pupils, even though there was a Catholic school in Ballymun itself.

Paul's father was, he observed, "a very strict man, but I was one of those kids who was impossible to tie down". The two were very similar characters – bullish and always ready to fight their corner – and thus were often at loggerheads. Bobby, for his part, later described his argumentative young son as "a bloody exasperating child" and at one point even nicknamed him "the anti-Christ"! Paul had, in fact, been something of an attention-seeking baby who quietened down only after he'd bawled his head off for a couple of hours: because of this, Bobby would allegedly time his arrival home after a hard day's work to coincide with his youngest son's bedtime. As a result, as the boys grew up, the major bonds between the four family members became clearly defined: Bobby and Norman on one side; Iris and Paul on the other.

Compared to his bright, academically gifted elder brother, Paul seemed to his teachers and parents to spend most of the time in his own private dream world. Iris would watch with mounting horror as three-year-old Paul, playing in the garden, would lift bees on to his tiny fingers, chatting to them in that sing-song language only three-year-olds and possibly bees can understand, before carefully setting them back on to flowers again. When Iris scolded him and said that bees stung he didn't know what she was talking about.

Legend has it a fortune teller once told Iris that she would have two children one day and that the one whose name began with the letter "P" would go on to become famous in whatever he chose to do. It's not known whether Iris took the gypsy's word to heart when she named her younger child Paul, but it wasn't long before he began to show signs of fulfilling that prophecy. His introduction to the world of popular music and his first musical memory came, he says, at the age of eight. "I remember watching *Top of the Pops* and seeing this group called Middle of the Road singing 'Chirpy Chirpy Cheep Cheep'. I thought, 'Wow! This is what pop music is about. You sing like that and you get paid for it.'" Strange to relate then that he grew up almost entirely without a record collection, learning what he could from the older, now teenage Norman's cassette tapes of albums by artists like Free, the Who and Jimi Hendrix. In the warm summer months, he took to bicycling to and from school each day specifically so that he could stop off on the way home each afternoon and browse the city centre's record shops, listening to new releases while standing in one of the big wooden listening booths (the advent of headphones still being some years away).

During weekends and school holidays, the young Paul would often sit on a wall with his friends, overlooking the inmates of St Michael's Hospital, an old-fashioned "mental institution" which became the inspiration behind such early U2 songs as 'The Fool' and 'Electric Co' (a reference to electro-convulsive shock therapy). Another major influence around this time was William Golding's seminal schoolboy novel *Lord of the Flies*, which both frightened and fascinated him, he said.

When he was eleven, Paul suffered his own small version of the Lord of the Flies syndrome when he found himself cast as Piggy during an unhappy academic year at St Patrick's secondary school, where he never quite managed to fit in. It was a strictly run Protestant school, and apart from experiencing the usual problems in adjusting to being a small fish in a huge pool, he also compared it unfavourably with Norman's more prestigious school, the privately run Protestant Secondary. But his older brother had been bright enough to win a scholarship to the school and the normal fees that would have been involved in sending Paul there too were simply beyond the Hewsons' means.

Instead, Paul later admitted he'd spent the majority of the 1971–72 school year bunking off school, wandering around the centre of Dublin alone, frequenting the Grafton Street coffee bars, or simply "walking the streets". Bored and restless, he became recalcitrant and even those days that he did go to school were not good ones. He became embroiled in several unsavoury incidents, most memorably when he took out his frustrations on a Spanish teacher he strongly disliked, throwing dog turds at her from behind a bush as she ate her sandwiches in a city-centre park from which students were barred. "I was one of those kids it was impossible to tie down from the very beginning," he later said of these turbulent years. "People used to – and family still do – put up the cross [*i.e. make a cross sign with their two fingers*] whenever I came in." For a while, it seemed, he was taking that anti-Christ tag a little too literally.

A year of alienation and confusion finally ended when he became a pupil at the newly opened Mount Temple High School in Artane, the very place, in fact, where, fatefully, he would later meet the other future members of U2. Mount

Temple was the first co-educational comprehensive school in Dublin to be non-denominational, accepting students from both Protestant and Catholic communities, and Bobby Hewson decided straight away that it would offer his clearly troubled younger son a much-needed fresh start in secondary education. What was even better for a youngster of his age, both father and son agreed, in unison for once, was that Mount Temple encouraged a "relaxed" dress code that meant an end to the hated school uniform! Smart but casual, and, most crucially, individual. Paul immediately warmed to the place.

As a result, the contrast between the lonely, misunderstood figure that had haunted St Patrick's, and the newly confident boy that emerged at Mount Temple over the next couple of years could not have been more striking. His natural "gift of the gab" made him popular with most of the other kids at his new school, and he became a favourite pupil for the teachers that took those classes he excelled in, such as History, Drama and Art. It was also around this time that he became a keen chess player, playing for his town in community chess championships after being taught the rudiments at home by Bobby. Once the lure of making his own music had taken a grip, however, the chessboard was rarely seen again, the teenage Paul suddenly declaring it all too boring. The amateur dramatic scene would also appeal, the influence of the Hewson forebears shining through, perhaps, plus his own innate love of "showing off in front of people". But again it proved to be only a passing fascination, the final nail in the

coffin of any ambitions of becoming an actor being administered when he discovered that Dublin had no drama school,
as such, and that such a move would almost certainly mean
hoping to get a place at a college in London – a move considered unthinkable at that stage.

Musically, meanwhile, his budding tastes had moved on
from the Middle of the Road to Marc Bolan's T. Rex, who
dominated the pop charts throughout the early Seventies
with such Bono-approved hits as '20th Century Boy', 'Hot
Love' and 'Get It On'. Typically, his tastes were already broad
enough also to include a fondness for the earliest hits of
Welsh "white soul" singer Tom Jones. (Interestingly, 'Delilah'
and 'The Green, Green Grass Of Home', both story-telling
songs – a facet of nearly all U2's own best-remembered tunes
– were particular favourites.) He turned a disused school-
house at Mount Temple into a student disco to impress the
girls, naming it the Web and, in curiously prophetic echo of
the later U2 classic 'The Fly', restyled himself as a DJ character called the Spider, with self-proclaimed predatory
designs, he told the assembled throng of giggling adolescents,
on all the "female flies".

It was Norman who first introduced his younger brother to
the guitar, but after mastering the initial three chords the
attraction, as with chess and drama, quickly palled. There
were others better suited, he reasoned, to the endless hours
needed practising in the bedroom in order to master such an
instrument. Though Paul did admit that he was well up for
the "posing in front of the mirror" part, his gregarious nature

was never going to be able to reconcile itself to sitting at home on his own plonking away on an old guitar.

While the dynamic of the Hewson family frequently saw father and younger son at odds, Norman and his mother tried as best they could to remain a relatively neutral force. Most of the arguments came from the fact that neither Bobby nor Paul would ever back down, ending in an angry face-off when one or both would simply storm out of the room. One typically ludicrous but extraordinarily heated row erupted over whether the youngster should put his cake on a plate or, as he preferred, use a shelf by the fireplace for that purpose. With father and son firing verbal cannonballs at each other, the argument rumbled on until the early hours. It was already past two o'clock in the morning, and with Iris long since having retired to bed in tears, when Paul finally crumbled and admitted he was in the wrong ... only to come down to the breakfast table the next morning with a glint in his eye and declare: "I only agreed because I wanted to go to bed." On this occasion Norman sided with his parents: there were times when Paul was simply pig-headed and impossible.

On another occasion, the pair had such an almighty row that a furious Bobby, driven beyond the limits of his patience, got up and physically ejected his younger son from the lounge — only to find, when he himself next left the room, a strategically placed banana skin left underfoot, and Paul laughing from his vantage point halfway up the stairs. Despite all this, as a much calmer Bobby would later concede, "there was nothing bad in him; he was living in his own world and we were sort of superfluous to it". In a world of dysfunctional families, the Hewsons' was certainly solid enough to withstand the harsh winds of adolescence – and, having seen Norman grow up to become an intelligent, relatively placid and responsible individual, Bobby was prepared to weather the storm, as he saw it. Things would turn out all right for the boy in the end. He hoped.

Everything fell apart, however, when, on 10 September 1974, Iris died suddenly. It was the second blow in a month of emotional turmoil. She had been celebrating her parents' golden wedding anniversary, the day after which her father unexpectedly died. If that seemed a needlessly cruel card for fate to have dealt the family, Iris herself was then struck down with a brain haemorrhage while attending her father's funeral at the Military Cemetery in Blackhorse Road, Dublin, dying four long days later.

Confused, inconsolable, angry, for the next two years the teenage Paul Hewson roamed wild, using the loss as an excuse to behave badly. A spiked red haircut and outrageous Sixties jackets were among the outward manifestations. Rage and turmoil were the unseen badges piercing his chest. It had all happened so quickly, so unexpectedly, so unfairly. "There was the feeling of the house being pulled down on top of me because after the death of my mother it was not a home." Never at ease with his father, he now began to bicker and pick fights with his elder brother, too. "I think there's still blood on the kitchen wall."

Paul would later claim that he lost "two weeks of my life" he was so stricken with confusion and grief after his mother died, and that it was another two years before he "calmed down again" enough to try and search for a more realistic perspective. However, the long-term effects of that loss – that injustice – would haunt him for the rest of his life. Later landmark U2 songs such as 'I Will Follow' – their first hit, which symbolically opened their first album *Boy* – and 'With Or Without You' (their first Number 1 single in the USA) would allude to this unrequited desire for mutual unconditional love; the love only a mother could guarantee a son. In many ways it set the tone of an album that successfully encapsulated feelings of hope and faith, but underneath it also stood for deep loss and endless confusion. Or as Bono himself later put it, there is "real anger and an enormous sense of yearning" in those songs. His mother was there again, too, as recently as the dreamlike track, 'Lemon', from *Zooropa*, which Bono revealed had been based on his contradictory feelings about the then relatively recent discovery of some old cine footage of his mother wearing a beautiful yellow dress.

"The lyrical idea for 'Lemon'," explained close friend Gavin Friday, "developed out of an old home movie that Bono saw." Someone unknown to Bono had mysteriously approached one of his family at an airport one day in the early Nineties and advised them of the existence of the film, in which Iris and Bob both featured, apparently at some sort of family get-together where Iris can be seen dancing around in her 'lemon' dress. Watching it was an understandably eerie experience for Bono, who later admitted that his mother's death had come as such a blow he wasn't even sure any more if he could remember exactly what she looked like.

Indeed, it could be argued that the trauma inflicted on the teenage Bono – the same tragedy would also befall drummer Larry Mullen – has informed almost every aspect of U2; the source of that intangible extra something that gives them their unique sound: from the perpetually questing, almost pleading voice, to the baleful sound of the guitars, flickering church candles one moment, a furnace of hellfire the next; that sad, hopeful face Bono makes so easily on tracks like 'I Still Haven't Found What I'm Looking For' or the enigmatic 'One'.

But then, as he admits, music was what "saved" him from going completely under. Grief-stricken, lonely, and nursing a growing sense of injustice that would one day express itself on the world stage as a massive force for reform, he realised he could go one of two ways: back up again, or even further down. He wanted to get up, to reclaim his life, but at first he didn't know how to go about it. All he knew was that he desperately needed to discover other, less negative ways in which to channel his pent-up feelings. "When I was sixteen, I couldn't cope with the idea of getting a job, getting married, growing up and dying," he said. "I wanted more and I fought to break out of that rut. In the Sixties you had this love and peace movement where people were rebelling against the standards and the hypocrisy of their parents' lives, and they broke out of that. And I think they were right. I'm into that rebellion, it's just that that [Sixties spirit of] rebellion was diluted by escapism, through drugs."

Friends say the turning point came when Paul met and quickly became involved with another Mount Temple pupil by the name of Alison Stewart. Born in Dublin in 1961, Ali, as he always called her, was in the fifth year at Mount Temple when she first got to know Paul Hewson, alongside his new friends Dave Evans and Adam Clayton. With her long black hair and blemish-free olive complexion, all the lads agreed that Ali was a real stunner. But she had followed a succession of Paul's girlfriends, notably Zandra Laing and Maeve O'Regan; both huge passions while they lasted that had soon wavered once the novelty wore off. None of his schoolfriends would have guessed that Ali would even agree to go out with Paul, let alone end up happily married to him for the rest of their lives. Ali was seen as "a cut above" and Paul had already been rebuffed by her once when they met on his very first day at Mount Temple. But the attraction had been immediate for one side at least and over the years he'd never quite given up hope of winning her round eventually. Fortunately for him, they both shared a wicked sense of humour, and he saw that as the ace up his sleeve.

Finally agreeing to go out with him, they quickly became entangled in a typically stormy teenage love affair. Friends from those early days remember a lot of "arguments and fights" among the hand-holding and stolen kisses, and the relationship was volatile enough to break up – for good! – on more than one occasion, as when the newly punk-obsessed

Paul came to school one day in purple trousers and with a chain running from his ear-ring to his (apparently but not actually pierced) cheek. Ali was horrified.

Religion loomed large for both of them, as it did for most Irish kids, but not in any prescribed form – at least, not for Paul. Childhood experiences had taught him not to take the obvious route, as that would have meant "taking sides" – impossible as, technically, he belonged to part of both. Nevertheless, the hole left in his life after the loss of his mother meant her younger son needed to find something to help him make sense of what had happened, and what it meant to him in the world at large. Even before Iris's death, Paul had expressed an interest in the beliefs of the Plymouth Brethren, a locally well-known yet largely mysterious Protestant sect but, crucially, one with simple and unshowy rules.

Paul had first developed an interest in the workings of the Plymouth Brethren after he came into contact with their creed via the Rowens, a local family whose son, Derek, had been one of his closest childhood friends prior to going to secondary school. At the time, he had recently begun attending the school Christian Union, and in the summer of 1974 (shortly before Iris's death) had gone away for a fortnight to a camp in Criccieth, in north Wales, with the 'Bee Dees' – the Boys' Department of the YMCA, where he would occasionally attend bible study class.

Now, nearly two years on since Iris's death, still searching for some form of spiritual solace, Paul had sought out the Rowens once again. Gavin Friday's family home was also somewhere he would go often during this period, turning up at the Rowens' house one day and the Fridays' abode the next in the hope of being offered the chance to stay the night. As Derek Rowen would later recall, he was convinced that his friend was "calling round as much to be with my mother as me, I have no doubt of that".

Despite his understandable reluctance to embrace the broadest teachings of either the Protestant or Catholic Church, Paul was not unaffected by the evangelical wave that swept like a gale-force wind throughout Ireland in 1976. Despite his burgeoning fascination with the music scene, together with Larry and Dave (as The Edge was still known), as well as with Ali, he would, for a short time, find himself embracing Shalom – the Charismatic Christian group led by one Dennis Sheedy, and named after the Hebrew word for "Peace". Paul and Dave even went so far as allowing themselves to be baptised in the sea by full immersion – a required rite of passage into the sect – but their membership of Shalom would cause many strains within the earliest incarnation of what would soon become U2. Most notably with the sceptical Adam Clayton, who was not religiously inclined in any way, which we will come back to momentarily.

Musically, Paul's tastes had continued to grow beyond T. Rex, David Bowie and Tom Jones and become more eclectic. Like so many teenagers of his generation, in 1976 Paul's whole view of music had been turned on its head by his discovery of the first wave of new American 'punk' stars then making their mark on the scene, like the Ramones, Patti

Smith and Television, all of whom would release their astonishing debut albums that year. Meanwhile, on the British
mainland, there were equally obscure yet utterly fascinating
new bands like the Sex Pistols and the Damned, both of
whom also released their first singles in 1976 (the former
causing such a storm of protest over the inflammatory lyrics
of their debut single, 'Anarchy In The UK', it was quickly
withdrawn from sale by the band's own horrified record
label, EMI).

Paul didn't always like the music of punk – apart from a
handful of blissfully talented original artists, he decided that
most of the new wave, as it was quickly dubbed by the music
press, was made up of "fakers and copycats". Nevertheless,
the DIY ethos of punk – crucially, the notion that you didn't
need to be a skilfully adept musician to have something new
and meaningful to say with your music – made the whole idea
of forming his own band much more attainable. He may have
found the nihilism of so much of punk abhorrent, but its "hey
look at me" fashion sense was irresistible; the garish image
and deliberately provocative stance of the early British punks
suiting his constant craving for attention perfectly.

The fast emerging new wave was only one big influence,
however. Paul had also recently discovered Bruce
Springsteen, whom he later called "the Buddha of my youth",
and whose landmark 1975 album, *Born to Run*, told wide-
screen stories of American dreams that would be echoed in
later U2 albums, in particular, *The Joshua Tree*, their 15-
million-selling magnum opus to the American dream (as

longstanding an ideal in Ireland as it has been looked down on in England). As a poetry writer, Bob Dylan's lyrics also appealed, though his music was something he would not fully get around to exploring with any enthusiasm until he was much older, and had already got to know Dylan personally.

The question was how to take all this exciting new information and put it to work for himself. Despite his popularity at school, Paul's overall academic career at Mount Temple had been far from shining, covering enough of the bases adequately without ever really pushing forward in one direction for any concerted length of time. However, he knew he possessed enough innate intelligence to qualify for a university place, and an arts degree was said to be his for the taking – if he wanted it. As usual, it was left to his father to ask the really tough questions. Bearing in mind his son's tendency to drop things once the novelty had worn off, Bobby made it clear that continued funding for his education was entirely provisional upon his forthcoming exam results. As a motivational tool, it appeared to work, and Paul did well enough to secure the offer of a place on an arts degree course at University College Dublin. Bobby, initially delighted, was disillusioned to discover, therefore, just two weeks after Paul's enrolment, that his future there was already under threat. But the problem was an administrative error: the lad had failed his Irish Leaving Certificate exam – including an oral exam in Gaelic – and thus could not proceed, even though knowing the language was hardly a requirement for an arts course.

The prospect of returning to school to retake the accursed exam would have been enough to stymie the ambitions of most teenagers, who might have been more tempted to simply go out and get a job, at that point. But this was one argument Paul was never going to win with his father. Besides, being a year ahead of most of his schoolmates, he found himself not only welcomed back into the fold but looked on suddenly as something of a leader. With just the one subject on his academic timetable to worry about for the next twelve months, there was plenty of time, too, to pursue other interests. Most of the time, he and his friends would while away the hours together roaming the streets in a loose group that became known to the rest of the school as the Lipton Village. It was more than coincidence that this same little knot of friends would soon go on to produce not one but two bands, in U2 and the Virgin Prunes.

Paul described life in the Village as "an imaginary place, somewhere we developed in our imaginations to give us an alternative lifestyle as kids. We grew up studying people on street corners. We laughed at the way they talked and at the expressions they made. We mocked the adult world and agreed we would never grow up because all we saw was silliness."

It was 1977, and punk was now making headlines all over the world. As good a time as any, then, to be unconventional. But in an Ireland where contraception and abortion were still illegal, and where it was common to marry young, produce a large brood of children and settle into a cosy domesticity punctuated by a pub-centred social life (according to the brochure, anyway), alternative views were not so much discouraged as strangled at birth. The Village crowd, therefore, not only rejected the stereotypes, they resolved to become "born again" by choosing new destinies for themselves. Emblematic of this belief was their joint decision to change their very identities.

Regular Village member, Peter Rowen, younger brother to Derek, took on the name Guggi, and suggested that Paul might try the handle Bonovox, roughly translated from the Latin for "good voice" and stolen from a hearing aid shop called Bonovox on Dublin's busy O'Connell Street. A mouthful quickly shortened to just Bono (for the record, it is pronounced Bon-oh, and not Bone-oh, as often mistakenly announced by radio presenters). Fionan Hanvey, another local lad whose style of dress in the flamboyant Marc Bolan/David Bowie glam mode had earned him the nickname "yer man with the handbag", chose to be reborn as Gavin Friday (after Robinson Crusoe's Man Friday, as he was a good organiser). Later, when U2 would first start gigging as the Hype, Friday, Guggi and another Village regular nicknamed Pod would form a parallel group – the Virgin Prunes – with Dave Evans's older brother Dick (Village name: Dik) on guitar. Other exotically nom-de-plumed gang members included Strongman, Day-Vid, Pompous Holmes and Bad Dog. (Interestingly, although none of the other future U2 members was a proper Village-ite, Dave Evans also got given a suitably Village-esque name – The Edge – allegedly because of either his status as an outsider "on the edge" of things, or the strange shape of his head.)

This clannish behaviour could be viewed simply as childish escapism, of course, and no doubt a great deal of it was. But the moment of truth for all of them was about to arrive. As they entered their last months at school, faced suddenly with career and lifestyle choices they felt barely ready to make, things became even more manic. Paul and his friends' chief mode of transport in those days was a small car Guggi had bought with his wages from the family firm, having already left school. This, subject to a whip-round for petrol every so often, would take the Village-ites wherever they needed to go, which usually meant as far away from their own humdrum neighbourhood as the old car could take them.

Bobby Hewson's reaction to Bono's colourful new friends was predictably askance, if not downright hostile. When Bobby opened the door to Gavin Friday one night, he was shocked to see the most over-the-top of all the Village-ites dressed in a full-length dress. He kept his temper in check but roundly informed the boy that although the "head of the house" was reluctantly allowing him in on this occasion, it would be the first and last time. "Coming to get my boy looking like that!" he scolded. As for his son's own new nickname, years later he would tell the journalist Bill Flanagan that the very mention of the name Bono "used to drive me mad. I still will never call him that. I call him Paul. I've said to him on more than one occasion, 'Your mother christened you Paul, and Paul you are going to remain.' In fact, I think he gets annoyed if people outside [the family] call him Paul."

The story of how the earliest incarnation of U2 got together has been oft told; the catalyst famously being fifteen-year-old Larry Mullen's posted hand-written notice on the school bulletin board seeking would-be musicians to form a band. Larry had recently begun learning to play drums, but, as he discovered to his chagrin, unlike practising to play guitar or piano, it was virtually impossible to take his newly acquired skills any further without being able to play in an ensemble. Hence the search for other musicians to work with.

Laurence Mullen (who acquired his 'Junior' title in 1984 after his father, also Laurence, started receiving enormous tax demands in the wake of his son's newfound success) was born on 31 October 1961, and is the only member of U2 to emerge from what might be described as a conventional Irish Catholic background. He grew up with his family on the Malahide Road, in Dublin, with his parents and two sisters, Cecilia and Mary, and before graduating to Mount Temple had attended the Scoil Colmcille, where Gaelic was still the main language spoken. His first instrument had actually been the piano, which his sisters also played, but he soon became bored with it and was encouraged instead to take up drums by Cecilia, who kindly bought him his first drum kit in 1973 for £17. He took classes with a local teacher named Joe, and later Joe's daughter Bonnie. But his most effective mentors were arguably the likes of Slade's Don Powell, the Sweet's Mick Tucker and the double-drum punch of the Glitter Band – all of whom he followed with a passion via their regular Thursday-night appearances on *Top of the Pops*.

Far from discouraging the boy when he turned to another instrument, his father, a health officer in the Irish civil service, agreed with Larry, as everybody always called him, that forming a group was the only way for him to learn the drums properly – going so far as to permit his son, then just fourteen, to engender the neighbours' wrath by kicking up a racket on his drums at home. Early drumming practice was carried out with the bedroom windows wide open; sometimes crowds of kids from the neighbourhood would gather on the street below his window and Larry would play "requests" he'd learned from Cecilia's record collection. It was certainly more rewarding than playing for the Artane Boys Band, who drummed him out that very year for refusing to cut his luxuriant blond hair short. Like Paul, as a teenager Larry would also lose his mother – Maureen Mullen was tragically killed in a road accident, in Raheny, in 1978. Ultimately, however, the real reason Larry endeared himself so much to the singer was that he was someone who "made things happen". His note on the school bulletin board wasn't so much a promise, he said, as a confession that he felt he'd wasted his sister's money on the drums. Unless … could it be there were other pupils out there who felt they'd done the same on guitars?

Paul, one of "seven or eight" people who showed up in Larry's parents' kitchen for that first "audition", was seventeen and the oldest member of the putative band; a year ahead of Adam Clayton and Dave Evans, and two years ahead of Larry. His qualification for entry, he would later remember, was not so much his proficiency at the three guitar chords he'd mastered, but rather that he had the loudest voice.

"When we formed the group I was the lead guitar player, singer and songwriter," he later recalled. "Nobody talked back at first. But then they talked me out of being lead guitar player and into being the rhythm guitar player – and then they talked me out of being the rhythm guitar player and into just being the singer." Apparently, the next step was to talk him out of being the singer and into being the manager. "But I held on to that. Arrogance may have been the reason," he added with a straight face.

The band was quickly whittled down to five members – basically, the line-up as we know it today with the addition in the early days of a second guitar player, in The Edge's older brother Dik, before he left to join the Virgin Prunes. The four core members' interests in music were also usefully nurtured by the attentions of their teachers at Mount Temple, who even arranged for them to give their first public performance there, once they felt they were ready. In time-honoured fashion, at first the group played only cover versions, but using Paul's poetry – an occasional habit he had kept secret until then – as a basis, they decided to concentrate on trying to write some of their own material; a risky tactic in a country where the ubiquitous and hugely popular show-bands, playing conservative pop and dance standards, still ruled in Dublin's clubs and dancehalls. "At the start," said Bono, "we were criticised for using our own material, but we were making mistakes whereas established groups weren't. They were taking the safe way out ... The only way to go is to make the mistakes."

The new band's first ramshackle rehearsal in the Mullen family's kitchen attracted an audience of fourteen- and fifteen-year-old girls who kept climbing over the walls and looking in through the windows. "Larry just shouted at them to go away and then turned the hose on them," Bono laughingly recalled. "He's not interested in being a pop star. Larry likes to play the drums."

From the beginning, their stated aim, they told themselves, would be to produce music with the power of the Who and the sensitivity of Neil Young. "You know how on edge [Young] can be," Bono explained, "and we always wanted that." As they began to rehearse regularly, however, they began to develop an understanding of their own and from here on in the band's main musical influences would come from being with each other, bouncing their own ideas around, rather than paying too much attention to whatever was coming from outside. Even though it took them time to "really get it together musically," said Bono, right from the start "there was something there and I call it the spark. I called it something you *must* have. We've built on a spark, we haven't tried to put the spark in our music."

The punk-inspired new wave was, by then, gathering momentum and there was a general feeling of "not wanting to miss the boat". As Bono later recalled: "I remember thinking the first time we went into a rehearsal that a movement was going to emerge that would be a breakdown between flower power and the boot boy. I didn't really know what I was saying [but] it turned out to be punk rock."

Certainly, the early five-piece version of the band fitted the punk blueprint of thrusting have-a-go, non-musicians together and letting them loose on the public. "We were four people before we were four musicians. When we started out we couldn't play any instruments. We built the band around the drum kit but when we were on stage we were a shambles. It was like every night we'd want to break up, but then every morning we'd wake up and want to start again."

The Evans brothers had not actually been born in Dublin. In fact, Dave was born in Barking, east London, of Welsh parents, on 8 August 1961. (Later followed by a sister, Jill.) However, his father's engineering career took him to many different locations around the British Isles, which is how he came to be brought up in the Malahide suburb of Dublin, where his father had relocated the family when Dave was still an infant. A quiet, thoughtful child, who tended to stand in the background next to his more outgoing older brother, Dave bought his first guitar at the tender age of eight, for the princely sum of £1. In his case, far from the novelty wearing off, his interest in the guitar had grown into an obsession and he was already a pretty good player by the time, eight years later, he met Larry Mullen and was invited to join the band. Indeed, so good was he that, despite his protestations to the contrary, Paul knew he'd have to find somewhere else to fit into the group as he'd never be able to compete on the guitar with Dave. Brother Dick, born in 1959, was two years Dave's senior and also played guitar. Being a bit of an electronics boffin on the side, he had made his own instrument from a plan in a magazine.

Dave concentrated more on simply playing the instrument. A big hero in his early years and a huge influence on his later playing style was Irish guitar legend Rory Gallagher, who had first found fame in the group Taste before going on to enjoy notable solo success throughout the Seventies. Dave had the best of Rory's solos down note for note, and such party pieces would convince his new pals that he should be the lead guitarist of the band rather than his brother or any of the other hopefuls who had cheerfully responded to Larry Mullen's note (including future *Daily Telegraph* rock critic, Neil McCormick).

The brothers had been prompted to respond to Larry Mullen's request by Mount Temple's music teacher, Albert Bradshaw, neither brother having actually seen the note. A shy, reserved character who had taken time fitting in at Mount Temple, Dave's stated long-term ambition had been to go to university and study to become a doctor. Indeed, when finally deciding to get involved with music in a full-time capacity, he had first promised his parents that it was in fact a year out he was taking, rather than a huge career decision. A year would be long enough, he decided, to keep both the concerns of his parents at bay, and give him enough time to see if the band really was going anywhere. He could decide after that whether or not to return to his studies. "At first it was just amusement," he'd recall with a shrug, "it wasn't anything particularly serious, although we all had deep interests."

Like Dave, Adam Clayton had actually been born in England – in Oxford, on 13 March 1960. His father, Brian, was a pilot, and tended to get posted abroad for tours of duty. So as not continually to uproot him, it was decided Adam – one of two children, the other a girl, Sarah Jane – would go to boarding school; an experience he would later recall with no little disdain. He would always come home for the weekend, even if his parents were abroad, hated returning on Sunday afternoons, and was eventually expelled. (He did, however, persuade his mother to buy him his first bass in 1975, at a cost of £52, as an incentive to work harder!) After he fared no better at a succession of private schools, the Claytons decided they'd spent enough money on his education and he ended up at "the local comprehensive" – Mount Temple.

Unlike the archetypal "quiet one" bass player, as epitomised over the years by such famously stoic figures as the Rolling Stones' Bill Wyman and the Who's John "The Ox" Entwistle, the chain-smoking Clayton (who'd first met Dave at St Andrews Church of Ireland primary school in Malahide) was very much the rebel of the group, right from the outset. He had even managed to get himself expelled from Mount Temple, in March 1978, for a combination of relatively small but relentless misdemeanours such as defiantly drinking coffee in class (against the rules), wearing a kilt to school and streaking naked down the corridors (also, needless to say, against the rules). This may have made him a nightmare for the teachers but it lent him an almost instant cachet among the others; an infinite cool they could never hope to match. Most crucially of all, Adam had been in bands before, notably the strangely named Max Quad. To the other newcomers, this made his recruitment essential. Adam always looked and sounded as if he knew what he was doing, even when he didn't. He knew all the technical terms like "gig" (concert), "jamming" (playing spontaneously with other musicians), "demo" (making a demonstration tape of your songs to send to record companies and potential gig bookers) and "action" (the height of guitar strings from the fretboard of his bass). He had everything it took, in fact, to be a rock star bass player. The only snag – he couldn't actually play very well! "[Adam] had the only amplifier, so we never argued with him," Bono recalled. "We thought this guy must be a musician, he knows what he's talking about, and then one day we discovered he wasn't playing the right notes, not one!"

The possibility of being expelled from the band (as he allegedly had been from his previous outfit, for "sloppy playing") was clearly one Adam wasn't keen on exploring, so as well as now knuckling down to learn his instrument, he took on the equally vital task of acting manager. Organising school and youth club gigs, booking rehearsals (even if that meant just getting everybody together in the kitchen at Larry's for a pot of tea and a chat), even designing a band logo with computerised lettering to adorn a badge: all these things and more were all devised by the band's then long-haired fourth member. Amusingly, in January 1978, he placed an advert in a local newspaper claiming to be a big-time manager from London trying to contact this amazing band he'd seen playing in Dublin recently called the Hype, in the hope that local music biz figures would take note and seek out the group themselves; an enterprising tactic that, alas, provoked no interest whatsoever from either would-be Svengalis or record companies.

Not that the band was actually quite U2 at this stage. In the very beginning, they had called themselves Feedback, then changed it after a couple of months to the more fashionably new wave-sounding the Hype, on the advice of their close mate Steve Averill (aka Steve Rapid, who later became famous as the designer of all the U2 record sleeves from *Boy* onwards) because their original name (inspired by Adam's overloaded amplifier) was "out of line with the times". (Ironically, David Bowie had fronted a similarly named band in the mid-Sixties.)

The first Feedback gig had been held at Mount Temple. It was, Bono later recalled with only a trace of irony, "one of the greatest we have ever played. It was two years until we played another one like it." Word quickly spread among Dublin's small but passionate live music followers about a new teenage rock band that was worth a look, whatever it was called. As a result, they played one of their first concerts in a Dublin car park to an incredible 700 people, the makeshift power supply going on and off intermittently as they bluffed their way nervously around the stage. Suitably encouraged, they began to hawk their services around. By the summer they were increasingly in demand on the Dublin pub circuit.

Meanwhile, Paul was not the only band member starting to feel inspired by the excitement of punk. Earlier that year, Adam had stood there open-mouthed with astonishment as he watched the Clash tear the roof off at a packed Trinity College show; convinced more than ever as he caught the bus home that night that, inspired by the Clash's example, he and the Hype could make it too, he was hungry suddenly to make things happen. It was Adam's idea shortly afterwards to enter a school talent contest where their brief and decidedly un-punk set – comprising a Beach Boys medley, their version of Peter Frampton's 1975 soft-rock smash 'Show Me The Way', and a Bay City Rollers cover, 'Bye Bye Baby' – caused at least one teacher to exit the room mumbling underneath his breath (not to mention giving endless fun to all future journalists and biographers, even though, as Bono now insists, the Bay City Rollers cover had been "ironic"). They didn't actually win a prize that time, but their schoolmates' applause – as much, it seemed, for their sheer guts as their shambolic playing – was enough for now.

As the Hype, the music would become rockier, harder. The Boomtown Rats and Thin Lizzy, both bands from Dublin now hitting the headlines in Britain with chart-topping singles and albums, knew what it took to win over a crowd: you had to be loud and in their face; and you had to believe in yourself first, to give off that glow the way Rats singer Bob Geldof did; or at least try for some of Lizzy singer Phil Lynott's swagger. But while Lizzy and the Rats had blazed a trail for young Irish bands to dream of following, realistically, Bono knew those days were still a long way off for the Hype. Meanwhile, some of the more high-profile Village members that remained were inspired to form a band of their own. Called, sardonically, the Virgin Prunes, it featured the irrepressible Gavin Friday as (inevitably) the front man with Dik Evans, moonlighting from the Hype, supplying the musical backbone. Other members included Day-Vid (David Watson, vocals), Strongman (Trevor Rowen, bass), and Pod (Anthony Murphy, drums). With a confrontational attitude they christened "Art Fuck", there was little doubt that the Prunes were closer to the original hard-edged punk spirit than the more relatively mainstream-sounding Hype. As if to underline the point, Bono and the boys got their first real taste of success when they actually came top this time in yet another talent competition, winning the unheard-of sum of £500 when they travelled to Limerick on St Patrick's Day, 17 March 1978, to take part in the *Evening Press*-Harp Lager Talent Contest. Larry had seen the advert in the paper and immediately entered the band's name, then once they got there saw them come up against the equally accomplished East Coast Angels and a bunch of professional showband spin-offs.

The kind of songs that won them the cash and acclaim that night were mainly borrowed from others: Bowie's 'Suffragette

City' and the Stones' 'Jumpin' Jack Flash' were said to be particular highlights. But Bono was, as everyone would attest, "a great one for the gab", and The Edge no slouch with a solo, either, and the judges were won over by their sheer exuberance, not to mention versatility. "We had two sets," the singer later explained. "We played the unoriginal one first and then the original one to show people what we do ourselves."

On this occasion, they had showed up fresh from a gig at "Paddy's Punk Party" in Dublin and Bono's voice was shot to pieces. "We were a shambles," he recalled. "Especially [compared] with all these professionals and heavy rock bands. But I knew we had something. I knew the effect we had over an audience compared to the other bands with all their tight music and pompous playing. We made use of the fact that we were slightly fragile ... [just like] when we recorded our first demos and couldn't get a big sound; we had to work on the fragile sound."

By the end of 1977, there was also hushed talk in the Mullen kitchen of the possibility of a – whisper it – record deal. A few weeks after the Limerick talent show, impressed by what he had seen, CBS Records marketing manager, Jackie Hayden, who had been one of the judges in Limerick, had got in touch to offer them an evening of recording time at a CBS studio in Dublin, in order to try and make their first professional demo. Eventually, interest from CBS petered out – the band struggled to get the sound they wanted in the limited time available to them in the studio, and despite CBS A&R scout, Chas De Whalley, returning to Dublin to try and record the band again, going so far as to schedule a then aborted single, the impetus had been lost; the time taken to get to that point was simply too long.

By then, however, they had interest from other quarters. Strangely enough, even though it would be one of the few times the band would ever perform in Ireland's third largest city, the Limerick show had proved to be a turning point in other ways, too. Not only did they also get their first press mention, a favourable write-up courtesy of Bill Graham, then of leading Irish weekly music magazine *Hot Press*, but, through Graham, they were also introduced to the man who would help transform their careers: future U2 manager Paul McGuinness.

McGuinness, born in Germany in 1951, was some ten years older than Bono, the oldest member of the band, and as such his authority was unquestioned; not so much a father figure as one of those lucky uncles who always had a story to tell you of his far-flung adventures. As the widely travelled son of an RAF pilot, he had already lived a cosmopolitan life which had taken him to Hampshire, Malta and back to Dorset before his father's career finally allowed the family to settle in County Kildare. After failing to complete his degree at Trinity College – having "dropped out" to become location manager on the film *Zardoz*, starring Sean Connery – he had originally planned for a backstage career in the movies.

His first professional foray into the world of music had been with a then unsigned folk-rock band that took his fancy called Spud, who, in the space of a year under

McGuinness's untutored guidance, went from being complete unknowns to having a recording and music publishing contract. Though he then returned to the screen world, he had never given up the idea of repeating the experience – only maybe this time taking a band to the top of the tree. That was the dream, anyway. Then he was talking one day to a journalist friend named Graham, who had studied at Trinity with him, when McGuinness learned of an up and coming new band from Dublin who had already won a prestigious talent competition, thus attracting some interest from one of the big English record companies; little more was known about them. The sort of group, Graham concluded jokingly, that appeared ripe for someone of Paul's sort of experience to guide them through their next steps. Intrigued, McGuinness quietly determined to try and find out more about this group ...

Meanwhile, back in Ballymun, the Hype had now been renamed U2, taking their name from an American spy plane. But its appeal lay as much in its non-specific nature. It could also have the inclusive meaning of "you too", maybe even "you two", while to confuse matters still further it was also the name of a popular size of battery. The change of name, again at Steve Averill's urging, was also symbolic in other ways: they played the first half of a March 1978 gig at the Howth Community Centre, with Dik Evans still in the band, as the Hype, the second as the four-piece we now know as U2 (Dik having decided to throw in his lot full-time with the Virgin Prunes). Though they didn't know it yet, it seemed that, behind the scenes, the fates were beginning to conspire in their favour; the die was well and truly cast.

Things were suddenly moving fast. So fast, soon Bono would feel able to say goodbye to Paul for ever ...

CHAPTER TWO 1978–1984

Bono and the band recorded their first ever demo tape at Keystone Studios, in Harcourt Street, Dublin, in April 1978. Journalist Bill Graham later reported that this wasn't exactly the most trouble-free of sessions, even though they had now been playing together long enough to have learned how to please a pub crowd, "the band's inexperience showing up on what was a rush job". Graham added: "Their first numbers suffered as they were still getting the measure of themselves and the studio. It wasn't till later on that their real potential came through." However, that first session was, according to legend, cut short as Larry Mullen's dad turned up to take him home – after all, it was a weekday and there was school the next morning.

Graham was none the less impressed by a quartet whom he quickly sized up as "articulate, aware and hard-working individuals prepared to weigh up others' advice as they embark on their vocation ... Since they're currently studying for their Leaving Certs, U-2 [sic] won't be immediately around for inspection and further examination for another month or two. Even so, they're encouraging evidence that the flow of young bands hasn't dried up."

Bono himself felt that U2 stood out because they took themselves more seriously than most of the other young bands he had so far encountered – perhaps, he admitted, even a little bit too seriously at times. "But our crime was being *seen* to take ourselves too seriously," he concluded. "An interesting thing about self-righteousness, belief is so unfashionable these days. Whether it's belief in yourself or in something other … 'self-righteous', 'pontificating', these are the stones we throw at people who make it through."

One of their most memorable appearances that year came in September, when U2 played to their biggest audience yet – two and a half thousand Irish would-be punks in the Top Hat Ballroom – when they opened for London sensations the Stranglers. Regarding their first really high-profile show, they were left with distinctly mixed feelings after a nervous performance from them resulted in the more thuggish element of the Stranglers' notoriously partisan fans bombarding them with lighted cigarettes and some prolonged verbal abuse. True to form, however, afterwards, Bono shrugged the whole thing off, claiming not to be discouraged in the least. He had always believed the future of the band lay outside their native shores anyway, he shrugged.

"When we started," he later explained, "the only bands who were making any money in Ireland were the showbands who played other people's songs. Of course, at one time – when there was only Irish television – people didn't know what Gerry and the Pacemakers and the Beatles looked like, so they would see these guys in red suits and painted-on smiles and imagine that *they* were Gerry and the Pacemakers; that *they* were the Beatles. That was the tradition, and everyone rebelled against that."

If there was a positive to be forged from this, he went on, it was that same anger that would later be replaced "with a kind of affection, cos live music is bigger in Ireland than it is in any other country in the world – more people, per head of the population, go out to see a band and more people play instruments. So it's actually because of that tradition that the Irish are able to make money by being musicians."

The band would return to Keystone Studios – then owned by TV personality, Eamonn Andrews, presenter of the hit ITV show, *This is Your Life* – in November that year to record a second demo, this time under the watchful eye of Barry Devlin. Then the bass player with Irish Seventies folk-rock legends Horslips, Devlin would go on to produce and direct a number of U2's best videos in the Eighties, including 'Bad', 'A Sort Of Homecoming' and 'I Still Haven't Found What I'm Looking For'. Back in '78, the songs U2 worked on at that second Keystone session were all originals: 'Street Mission', an anthemic powerhouse that would end their first sets and was described back then as "a rock epic of spiritual longing"; 'Shadows And The Tall Trees', 'Stories For Boys' and 'The Fool' – all based, lyrically, on Bono's experiences and reflections as a child growing up in Ballymun. Afterwards, listening back to the tapes, Bono was inwardly relieved to discover that the band's sound had moved on considerably since their earlier, more stilted attempts at demo-making seven months before. With Christmas and a New Year just around the corner, Bono couldn't help but feel optimistic about the future; the first time he had allowed himself really to feel that way since Iris's death three years before.

Two weeks after the second Keystone session was completed, however, Larry's mother was killed in a road accident, a calamity which ended what until then had been a year of real hope in tragically bleak circumstances. Bono, still waiting for the wounds of his own maternal loss to heal, was not in any position yet to offer much comfort to his stricken friend. All he could do was tell Larry he knew how he felt.

Now acting as the band's manager, Paul McGuinness had meanwhile been working ceaselessly on the band's behalf, journeying to London and attempting to interest anybody in the music business who would give him five minutes of their time, waxing lyrical about his new charges, who were in ever increasing demand on the Dublin gig circuit, he boasted. Former music journalist, Chas De Whalley, who had recently begun working for CBS in London as their chief A&R scout, already knew the U2 manager reasonably well, and due to the interest the Dublin offices of CBS had already shown in them via Jackie Hayden, felt the least he should do was lend a friendly ear to the band's latest demo tape, which McGuinness had given him on one of his frequent trips. This was in February 1979, and De Whalley was initially unimpressed by what sounded, he later recalled, "like a thousand other wannabe new wave acts. It made no impression on my

jaded ears." Nevertheless, intrigued by tales of their enter-
taining live show (corroborated by the press clippings
McGuinness had shown him of their talent-contest win), De
Whalley decided to take a chance and fly over to Dublin to see
them for himself. CBS had just missed out on the Undertones
from north of the border, and De Whalley was determined
that the company would not lose out a second time.

What he did not know, however, was that McGuinness's
own position within the group had yet to be set in stone.
Despite their new manager's obvious enthusiasm and energy,
there was still, they later confessed, a certain reservation
within the band about his ability really to take them to the
very top – not least from Bono. Already the public mouth-
piece of the band, both on stage and in person, Bono had
persuaded the band to turn down an initial offer of a deal
from the Irish office of CBS after they had won the Limerick
contest. Now, it seemed, McGuinness was simply going back
to them. Surely they could have done that themselves? When
McGuinness attempted to drum up some much-needed
publicity for the band in the more prestigious UK national
music press – reportedly hawking the U2 demo tape to every
major rock critic in London, only to be met by blank-faced
indifference at every turn – he returned to Dublin with little
to show for his efforts, but a far greater understanding, he
later said, about the size of the task that lay before them if
they were to make it as a group. (In fact, the deal
McGuinness would later strike for the band with CBS, for
Ireland only, would turn out to be a stroke of genius, though

whether it was intended as such at the time it's no longer possible to say.)

Arriving in Dublin one warm June evening in 1979, De Whalley found himself being wined and dined by McGuinness, before being whisked to McGonagles nightclub, where the band was appearing that night. Embarrassingly, given the big build-up McGuinness had given the CBS scout about the band's popularity on the Dublin circuit, the attendance that night was low; many of U2's young fans were denied admission to the "over 18s only" venue. But despite the club being less than half full, De Whalley was impressed by the spirited performance the eager young band put on that night. De Whalley – already, as he later cheerfully admitted, somewhat woozy from all the free champagne McGuinness had been plying him with – had recently seen Shakespearean actor Ian McKellen (now Sir Ian) perform in the play *'Tis Pity She's a Whore*, and actually wondered if Bono had seen it too – and stolen all of McKellen's moves. "The way he moved through the songs was magic," De Whalley recalled years later in *Record Collector* magazine. "I hadn't seen star quality like this since the first time [I saw] Paul Weller and the Jam two years previously." As far as the dizzy but bushy-tailed CBS scout was concerned, "this guy [was] either going to be the next Sensational Alex Harvey or else he [was] going to be David Bowie".

For any band, the day their first ever record is released is always a special one: that hitherto unimaginable moment when they could actually put one of their own tunes on your record player, and the sudden legitimacy that fact now bestowed upon them. For Bono and U2 that magical day finally arrived in September 1979. Titled 'U2: 3', the limited-edition three-track single, released on the Irish CBS label, featured the three songs they now considered the best of the originals they were now including in their live show, with 'Out Of Control' the nominal A-side. Released in twelve- and seven-inch formats (the former being individually numbered from one to a thousand and now worth £600 a copy, should you be fortunate enough to find someone willing to part with one), the recordings were all the product of a particularly hectic August night in Dublin's Windmill Lane studios, with Chas De Whalley presiding over the production. The other two tracks were 'Stories For Boys', like 'Out Of Control' a live favourite, and – daringly – a new song obliquely titled 'Boy/Girl'.

Meanwhile, CBS's Dublin rep, Jackie Hayden, had conceived an imaginative tactic to try and get the record some much-needed exposure before it was even released. He took a tape of the three tracks to a pal named Ian Wilson, then producer of the Dave Fanning Rock Show on 2FM, the pop radio channel of state broadcaster RTE, and one of the most popular and respected shows on Irish radio. Wilson and Fanning agreed to air all three tracks on the show one night, then invite listeners to vote for the one they thought should be the eventual A-side of the forthcoming single. 'Out Of Control' won by a considerable distance, and Fanning's discerning audience would be vindicated when the track would go on to be rerecorded for the debut U2 album a year later, as well as becoming an enduring stage anthem on all their earliest tours.

The Windmill Lane session, from six in the evening until midnight, followed a free afternoon show the band had given on the other side of the city at the Dandelion Market, Gaiety Green, as part of the city's August Bank Holiday celebrations. Even though the band didn't get paid, the main attraction of playing these shows for Bono was that they allowed kids of all ages in to hear bands they would be too young to see on licensed premises, for tickets that cost between just 50p and £1, something else Bono very much approved of. The band was always well received, too, performing half a dozen such shows throughout Dublin in 1979.

The show had been an exceptionally good one that day, with three well-earned encores called for and wantonly supplied. Bono had been on top form that day, too, talking to the kids, cajoling them into singing along, giving his all as the band thundered histrionically through their brief but blistering set. As a result, Bono's voice might have been expected to have shown signs of wear and tear that night at the studio, given his usual refusal to hold back and keep something in reserve.

The singer immediately pooh-poohed such suggestions, however, when, on arriving at Windmill Lane, his first task was to lay down a guide vocal while the three musicians laid down the instrumental track. He would then be called upon to overdub his final, lead vocal performance. His microphone was actually placed in the studio control room, in order to prevent "spillage" into the rest of the microphones there to capture the guitar, bass and drums output as the band played together in the studio. As a result, De Whalley, seated next to him at the studio console, was amazed to find himself witnessing a complete Bono performance from the closest of quarters. "You wouldn't have known they were guide vocals by the way Bono went for them," he recalled in *Record Collector*. "He gave it the full Monty, arms flailing, legs pumping, willing his mates on the other side of the pale glass window to pull out all the stops. Which of course they did ..."

In De Whalley's opinion, the only real problem for the band in this first encounter with a big professional recording studio was Larry and Adam, who were "not the world's best timekeepers", as he diplomatically put it. As the drummer and bass player, Larry and Adam were the rhythm section of the band – the engine room – and while it was normal for a cooking live band to speed up and slow down, as the mood took them, laying down tracks in the studio requires an ability to do the same thing – in the same time and rhythm – over and over again, if necessary; a technical skill neither player was yet familiar with. De Whalley forced them to play 'Out Of Control' again and again until the song was of acceptable quality for release. Bono, almost inevitably, was quick to stick up for his pals and, according to later reports, was even ready at one point to stick one on De Whalley. "But Larry has had lessons from one of the best drummers in

Dublin!" he insisted to the nonplussed A&R man. "How can he be out of time?"

The resulting record, with all three tracks remixed by Boomtown Rats sound engineer Robbie McGrath before it was released four weeks later, was snapped up by U2's by now sizeable Dublin following. Bono was thrilled. He knew there would be a certain amount of demand for the record from the people who came to the shows regularly, but he could scarcely believe it when all thousand copies of the twelve-inch sold out within a day of going on sale in Dublin, thus ensuring the EP would enter the Irish chart a week later. Some copies made it on to the British mainland as imports, but this small step towards domestic "fame" wouldn't guarantee anything when they arrived for their first series of shows in London in December. Making a name for themselves in Dublin was one thing: a good start but no more. Now they would have to get used to becoming small fish again, but this time in a much bigger pond. As they were soon to discover, this was to be no overnight success story.

It had always been clear to Bono that in order to grab attention for the band outside Ireland, they would have to make it on "the mainland" first, starting with London, the heart of the British music business. Until they had accomplished some measure of fame across the water, they would never be able to say they'd truly arrived, no matter how many singles they sold at home. He also knew they would be starting from a disadvantage. Not living in England, they would not be able continually to slog away the way they had back home. Here their work would have to be done in quick-fire bursts, and they would be starting from the very bottom rung of the ladder. Not just unknowns, but unknowns from across the water.

As expected, their first, tentative steps towards establishing a reputation for themselves in London were followed by almost nobody: just nine people paid to see one of their very first gigs in December at the Hope & Anchor, one of the capital's leading pub-rock venues. As complete unknowns, they also found their unusual name rendered in many different ways, making it even more difficult for prospective fans to pick up on them. They were the U2s in Islington, where The Edge, already suffering a badly bruised hand through a minor accident on the way to Dublin airport, broke a string halfway through the set and the disconsolate band left the stage without returning, despite the fact that they knew at least one record industry A&R man was among the sparse audience. (This decision would cause Bono much retrospective soul-searching in the empty weeks that followed.)

The following night, at the Rock Garden, a small basement club in Covent Garden, they were billed as V2, but at least they played that night to a double-figure audience, though they conceded that this was almost certainly due to the fact that they were opening for a local all-girl group called the Dolly Mixtures. Rubbing salt into the wound, a subsequent review of the show in *Melody Maker* neglected even to mention them, let alone get their name wrong! Six days later, at the Bridge House pub in the East End's notoriously tough

Canning Town, they were billed as UR. Not that the dozen or so punters present seemed to care much either way.

Under the circumstances, the band might have been excused an identity crisis at this point and gone scurrying back to Ireland with their tails between their legs, never to be seen again. But, just as it seemed things in London couldn't get any worse, Bono was interviewed for the music weekly, *Record Mirror*. Considering it was his first major UK press interview, Bono came over in typically bullish fashion, informing the *Record Mirror* journalist that he intended to "take everything and break everything. I want people in London to see and hear the band. I want to replace the bands in the charts now, because I think we're better."

The band were understandably delighted when the article ran – yet more proof that they were moving in the right direction – but the impact it had on the numbers of people that turned up at their shows was negligible. People were still getting their name wrong. More bad news arrived when McGuinness informed them that the music publishing deal he had been on the verge of completing for them – and which they had been counting on the advance from to finance the cost of their London sojourn – had collapsed on the eve of departure, leaving family and friends to dig deep to fund the shortfall. Parents, pals and business associates came up with the necessary £3,000 to keep the show on the road. But not for long. If the trip to London was to reap any dividends at all, it would have to be soon.

Fortunately, their gamble finally paid off when McGuinness

was able to secure an opening spot for the band on a bill head-lined by then up and coming New York art-punk rockers Talking Heads, who were playing two shows at Camden Town's Electric Ballroom on 7 and 8 December. This time some of the music paper reviews did briefly mention the feisty Irish opening act, and, yes, they even got their name right. Better still, Talking Heads vocalist David Byrne was so impressed by what he saw that the offer for U2 to open for the Heads would be repeated in rather bigger venues a year later.

Despite these small but encouraging steps, the decision was made early on not to make London their base, even if things did take off for them there. Above all, said Bono, they felt it was essential to remain "a Dublin band". At the time, it may have seemed like a retrogressive move to make. If you really wanted to make it big and you didn't come from America, then London was where the action was. What hope was there for them if they wouldn't even live there? In retrospect, however, it may just have been the shrewdest move they ever made. By remaining in Dublin – in other words, by remaining as close to their real selves as possible – it helped them retain their freshness and energy, giving them a break from the relentless music biz grind. Familiar and protective, over the years Dublin would become the one place in the world where, if he wanted to, Bono could actually become Paul Hewson again.

Following that first, ill-starred trip to London, from here on in, it was decided, U2 would make raids across the Irish Sea and attempt to find a following; but only at the right times. This time they had returned home disappointed, yet strangely encouraged. They wanted to ensure that the next time they ventured to England it was under very different circumstances. With that in mind, the day before they had been due to board the ferry back to Dublin, Chas De Whalley had taken them into CBS's studios in Whitfield Street, ostensibly to record another single, more generally in the hope of coming up with something that would persuade his London bosses to sign the band up rather than continue to dither. Working on two new songs that De Whalley had identified – 'Another Day' (another anthem in the making which he saw as the A-side of their next single) and the poppy, light-hearted 'Pete The Chop' – both were committed to tape that same day. But although a small number of copies of the proposed single were eventually pressed up, De Whalley was still unable to convince his bosses in London to commit themselves to offering the band a long-term deal and the whole thing began to peter out.

Listening to those tracks today, it's easy to see what De Whalley was hearing that so excited him. The band's prolonged stint in London had sharpened up their performances and Larry, Adam and The Edge were now practically note-perfect. The problem this time was Bono, who had lost his voice after putting everything he had into all the London shows. Now, on the eve of his return to Dublin, he was completely exhausted. Copious doses of honey and lemon were administered, and the results were eventually to De Whalley's satisfaction. Bono had second thoughts, however, and phoned De Whalley the day before the tracks were due to be mixed to say that the band were unhappy with 'Pete The Chop' and, ultimately, would prefer neither track to see the light of day. In fact, a later version of the song was recorded for the B-side to 1983's mega hit 'New Year's Day', now retitled 'Treasure (Whatever Happened To Pete The Chop?)'.

Contrary to whatever Bono may have told Chas De Whalley, CBS went ahead and blithely issued the song, again in Ireland only, in February 1980, with a demo version of 'Twilight' on the B-side. Again, their fans in Dublin snapped up every available copy and, despite Bono's dissatisfaction, it is now considered a prized possession in the collectors' market. (Currently, a limited-edition picture-sleeve version of the single, complete with a postcard designed by Bono, will set you back some £350.) In a sad but telling footnote, when the London office finally passed on the band, a decision they would later come to regret several million times over, a frustrated and disillusioned Chas De Whalley parted company with CBS not long afterwards, "still astonished", he later shook his head, "by the company's inability to recognise U2's raw talent when it was right there under their noses".

More happily, the New Year had brought an immediate boost to U2's fortunes as the band accepted an invitation to perform live on TV chat show *The Late Late Show*, a veritable institution on Irish TV similar to the way the *Tonight Show* is in the USA. Deciding to play 'Stories For Boys' from their first three-track EP, as opposed to the new CBS single, the band veritably exploded on to the screen. Everybody back home remarked on how much they had all come on since they had returned from London. Their timing couldn't have been better, either. Just a week later, Bono awoke one morning to the astounding news that the band had won no fewer than five awards in the annual *Hot Press* magazine readers' poll! Amazingly, U2 had left signed and established rivals such as Thin Lizzy and the Boomtown Rats chasing behind them in almost every major category.

Despite the disappointment of the CBS deal collapsing, U2 clearly had something about them that the people liked. By dint of the deal the band had already signed in Dublin, CBS would continue to release U2's records exclusively in Ireland for the short term, at least. And Bono, for one, was convinced it was only a matter of time before they snagged the major recording contract they all craved. Not that Paul McGuinness was going to give them away too cheaply. Rumours now began to circulate that other big London-based record companies were slowly waking up to them – in particular, EMI Records, home of the Beatles and (briefly) the Sex Pistols. It came as a second significant blow then, when, by the end of February, it became clear that EMI had dropped out of the running. (Legend has it that one of their A&R men, who had agreed to come and see the band play at the Baggot Inn, excused himself halfway through the set – specifically so that he could return to his hotel room and watch the Specials on BBC TV's *Old Grey Whistle Test!*) On another occasion, McGuinness had managed to persuade a small handful of music publishing executives to come and see a show at Belfast's Queens

University. However, McGuinness found himself left with an uphill struggle to convince his guests that they hadn't wasted their time when a large crowd of hecklers in the audience began severely abusing Bono. "Stop fucking preaching and play, you can't fucking play!" came one typical cry. Never having faced such downright hostility south of the border, the band's usually loquacious singer found himself, for once, utterly at a loss as to what to say, visibly wilting under the relentless pressure of the partisan crowd.

Bono and U2 finally found the "home" they had been looking for when, in March 1980, they duly signed with Island Records. Owned these days by the giant Universal conglomerate of companies, back then Island was still the largest independent label in the UK (with Warner Brothers releasing all their product in the USA through their Elektra offshoot). Highly regarded for their long-term fostering of such unique and diverse talents over the years as Free, Sparks, Bob Marley and the Wailers, Nick Drake, and many more, Island would prove the ideal home in the early days for a band intent on sounding like nobody other than themselves, perhaps the hardest trick of all to pull off in the music biz.

The label's chief A&R man, Bill Stewart, alerted by the *Hot Press* awards, had journeyed to Dublin to see the band for himself a few weeks later. Knowing Stewart was coming and keen to make an impact, Bono and McGuinness hit on the ambitious idea of putting on their own self-promoted show at the two-thousand-capacity Dublin Boxing Stadium. Come the day of the show, however, the whole thing looked as if it was going to be a disaster. Fewer than five hundred tickets had been sold before the big day and as a last desperate resort, everyone with the slightest acquaintance with Bono, Adam or any of the band's family and friends was hurriedly press-ganged into turning up. As a result, when Stewart flew back to London he did so convinced that he had just seen something important. So important, in fact, that he returned to his office and told Island boss Chris Blackwell that to pass over U2 in favour of signing new romantics Spandau Ballet (who, ironically, would then be snapped up by CBS) would be the latter-day equivalent of turning down the Beatles. Recalling his epiphany some years later, Stewart wrote: "One bitterly cold night in February 1980, a shivering talent-spotter found himself in Dublin on what was beginning to look like another wild goose chase. The evidence of a pretty dire single and the urgings of a persistent but as yet unproven manager did little to lift my spirits. Suddenly in a burst of white light four slight figures pounced on stage, picked up their instruments as if they were soldiers seizing weapons and tore into their first song with a deafening roar. It was electrifying. It was the first night I saw U2."

Straight after the gig, Stewart had offered them a deal "in principle", shaking McGuinness firmly by the hand and promising he would be in touch again – soon. True to his word, having gone out on a limb over the band with Blackwell, the contracts were duly drawn up. All the band had to do now was sign on the dotted line. The wonder is that there wasn't a mad scramble to do so. The money, after all, seemed vast: £50,000 in advance, reportedly, on future earnings, plus a further £50,000 up front to help fund international touring. At Bono's behest, however, McGuinness had also managed to negotiate for them a greater degree of creative freedom than most contemporary record contracts afforded new artists in those days: U2 would deliver four albums over the next four years at a rate of one a year, all of which Island would accept "unseen" – i.e. the first time the label chiefs heard a new U2 album would be when it was already finished, so as to avoid any interference or "suggestions", an almost unheard-of clause for a new artist back then. The deal was actually signed in the ladies' toilets of London's Lyceum Ballroom, where U2 were playing on 23 March. It had to be the ladies' toilets, as this was the quietest place to do business that night.

The first fruit of the Island deal was to be the single '11 O'Clock Tick Tock' b/w 'Touch', recorded back at Windmill Lane over the Easter Bank Holiday weekend and released in Britain in late May. The song, a raucous, if surprisingly tuneful ditty, took its title from a note Gavin Friday once left on Bono's back door in Dublin. Using the title for inspiration, Bono had turned it into a song that had quickly become a highlight of the band's ever evolving live set.

In fact, its main feature, in retrospect, as with its successor, 'A Day Without Me', was The Edge's use of an echo unit for his guitar, a recent acquisition that allowed him to coax some remarkably compelling effects from his instrument, not least the wonderful use of sustain – the instinctive ability actually to use the echo of the ringing guitar chords as part of the rhythm – that would soon become his trademark. Musically, it was a watershed moment for the band: the actual birth of the classic ringing U2 sound as we now know it. As Bono once said, "When we started it was hard to get The Edge to play aggressively. He is a gentleman and he plays guitar like a gentleman." The echo unit, combined with a recently obtained Gibson Explorer guitar, had given him new scope to explore the guitar. Now The Edge could sound both aggressive and sensitive, all at the same time.

Unfortunately the single, which would not appear on the band's first album, failed to chart and, like their earlier Irish-only singles, is now considered a rarity item with a current market value of around £35 for a near-mint copy. Production on the single was carried out by Martin Hannett, the man responsible for overseeing the best work of other epoch-defining, early-Eighties British bands such as Joy Division and the Teardrop Explodes. This fact alone represented a huge step forward for the band in their own minds. That subsequent sales were modest was not yet an issue and '11 O'Clock Tick Tock' was now the centrepiece of the U2 set when they played their first major open-air festival in July, supporting Squeeze and the Police at the 'Dublin Festival 1980' in front of a 15,000-strong crowd at Dalymount Park.

Martin Hannett had also agreed to produce their second single for Island, 'A Day Without Me', but had to bow out at the last minute after being devastated by the news of the suicide of Joy Division singer Ian Curtis, on 18 May. Instead, the band went into the studio, at Chris Blackwell's inspired suggestion, with Steve Lillywhite, a young, fresh-faced Londoner then making his name as the producer for such critically approved artists as Peter Gabriel, Ultravox, Siouxsie and the Banshees, and XTC.

But if Blackwell and Stewart had been hoping Lillywhite might coax a hit out of their newest signings, the song the band wanted to record, 'A Day Without Me', an upbeat but mournful little number built around the theme of teenage suicide, was hardly the one to do it for them. Suffering the same uneventful fate as '11 O'Clock Tick Tock', Lillywhite later confessed that he'd never rated the song as a single, but had liked the band so much he wanted to try and do his best for them anyway. The feeling seemed to be mutual and it came as no surprise when Lillywhite was confirmed as producer for the first all-important U2 album.

Bono and the band spent all of August working hard at Windmill Lane studios with Lillywhite. The title of the first U2 album, *Boy*, had already been decided by Bono. In fact, both the title *Boy* and the album cover – a strikingly simple black-and-white photograph of a boy's face – had been in Bono's head for the past two years. The concept, he explained, revolved around youth and its primary features: exuberance, faith and disappointment. Still barely more than just callow youths themselves, for a band whose members' average age was still only twenty, these were more than just lyrical "themes" Bono had developed; these were real-life snapshots of life as it was for them back then. As Bono would recall: "I can remember as a child looking into the mirror and thinking, 'I don't look like that. It's wrong.'" A distortion of self-image, he seemed to suggest, which was "forced on you all the time, by [the media]. Strength, power – nobody's like that, but you're bombarded with all these images. The effect is total disillusionment with yourself, so you put on a mask and hide from yourself, from your own soul, what you've got to offer ..."

Released in Britain and Ireland in October 1980, *Boy* was big, brash and boisterous, full of loud guitars and impassioned lyrics – the truest, sharpest reflection yet of the band's burgeoning live powers. If you were Irish, two of the tracks on *Boy* had been heard before, albeit in slightly altered form: a splendidly revamped 'Out Of Control' had been the A-side of their first single the year before, of course, while the original demo of 'Twilight' had initially shown up on the B-side of the second single. More interestingly, freshly minted tracks like 'I Will Follow' were full of raw, raging, rampant energy, Bono's yelping voice ringing out like some pagan Celtic battle cry. The music press interviews that accompanied the album's release were every bit as up front and in your face. "I don't mean to be arrogant," Bono told one journalist, "but even at this stage I do feel that we are meant to be one of the great groups."

In retrospect, you'd have to describe such a statement as prophetic. At the time, however, such pronouncements were looked on with scepticism at best, downright contempt at worst. Nevertheless, everybody agreed that *Boy* had something. It would be a while, however, before the greater buying public would necessarily agree. Or at least, not in large enough quantities to see the album creep higher than a modest Number 52 on the UK charts – and even that small accomplishment took until August 1981, boosted by almost non-stop touring and the sudden publicity brought by their appearance that month at the prestigious Rock on the Tyne festival. In the States, where *Boy* was released through the Warner/Elektra deal in March 1981, the cover was changed at Warner's insistence because nervous executives were wary of any perceived paedophilic connotations to the image. As a result, instead of the classic sleeve originally designed for them by Steve Averill – featuring the innocent photo of a bare-chested, seven-year-old Peter Rowen, younger brother of the Virgin Prunes' Guggi – the US version of the album featured a comparatively – and deliberately – nondescript group shot.

Bono was exasperated by such narrow-minded attitudes but there was little he or McGuinness could do about it contractually if they wanted the album out there, and of course they did. Bono's mood soon lifted, however, when he began to read the mostly exemplary if sometimes completely off-beam reviews the band now began to pick up in the American press. The reviewer from the prestigious *Village Voice* magazine, based in New York's Greenwich Village, particularly amused him. "He wrote about all the fifths and ninths in our music and the most obscure chords and keys. He didn't realise we tuned down to E flat for my voice."

Back in Britain, however, they were about to get another

significant break – one that would help transform them from club-fillers into theatre-headliners in their own right – when they were invited again to support the now widely acclaimed Talking Heads, led by singer-guitarist and self-styled rock intellectual, David Byrne, at three important dates in London, in December. One year on from their Electric Ballroom pairing, Talking Heads had released *Remain in Light*, their most critically and commercially successful album yet, and U2 now found themselves opening for them for three nights at the more prestigious Hammersmith Odeon, followed by a further show together a few nights later at Paris's Baltrard Pavilion. It was a bill that pleased everybody, not least the several critics who attended the shows, and with Byrne and his newly expanded Talking Heads then approaching their creative zenith, U2's obvious proximity to the crown conferred on them a newfound credibility among the small but then still massively influential world of the London-based music press. Suddenly the Island Records press office was taking more calls about U2 than they were making – a welcome reversal of how things had been up until then. (The relationship between the two, on the surface, quite different bands would be further reinforced when they later came to share a musical co-conspirator in Brian Eno, the legendarily eclectic former Roxy Music star who had also helped Bowie conceive his trilogy of groundbreaking Berlin albums in the late Seventies: *Low*, *Heroes* and *Lodger*. Apart from producing a string of his own critically acclaimed solo and "ambient" albums, Eno had also worked with Talking

Heads from their second album on – from which would also spring the equally impressive 1981 Eno and Byrne collaboration, *My Life in the Bush of Ghosts* – before taking up with U2 in 1984 in time for their *The Unforgettable Fire* album and subsequent releases.)

December 1980 was to prove a landmark month for the band in other ways. Apart from the Talking Heads shows, it was also the month when John Lennon was assassinated, on 8 December, gunned down by a crazed fan, Mark Chapman. Just a few days before that horrifying incident, U2 had made their live US debut with a much-vaunted headline appearance at the Ritz Ballroom in New York; just a few blocks, in fact, from the Dakota Buildings where Lennon lived with his wife Yoko and young son, Sean – and outside which Chapman would, just three days later, shoot and kill the former Beatle.

The opening night of what had been planned as U2's first ten-date, major city tour of the States was designed to drum up press interest and make friends with as many bigwigs as they could at the numerous local radio stations that dominated the American record-buying market. All being well, the plan then was to return to the States early the following year, when they would begin their first major, three-month, coast-to-coast tour. They had originally pencilled in a low-key, warm-up date somewhere outside the city as a prelude to the high-profile Ritz show, where they knew all the New York music biz luminaries would be. But this had been cancelled at the last minute and so the band were forced to dive straight in. Bono said he didn't mind, he was happy just to be there in a city he had long dreamed of bringing the band to. But even his ability to stay cool under pressure was stretched to its limits, he later confessed, when he realised that all the seating in the balcony for the show had been reserved for the great and the good, including top New York booking agent Frank Barsalona, whose co-operation would be crucial for their future touring plans (and who had already, notoriously, turned down the Boomtown Rats), as well as several executives from Warner Brothers, whom they also desperately needed to impress if they were seriously to get behind their career in America.

Unfortunately, rather than the grand entrance they had hoped for, the band came on stage that night to only lukewarm applause. It seemed New York would need a little more convincing before bestowing its fullest blessing on this obviously self-confident but still utterly unknown new band from overseas. Most of the audience at the Ritz were regulars, the kind of people who were there every night because they loved the club, irrespective of whatever band happened to be playing there, and at first Bono struggled to involve them, unable to cajole more than a handful away from the bars and on to the dancefloor. Frustrated, he turned his wrath on the very people he was supposed to be trying his best to impress: the music biz execs and assorted hangers-on peering down from the balcony. "We've come to play for you," he shouted. "Get off your fat arses and dance if you want to dance!"

Barsalona later recalled that, undeterred by the stone-faced response this outburst provoked, Bono quickly got back to the business of helping the band communicate with the sceptical crowd, winning them over "song by song" until, finally, about three-quarters of the way through the set, the entire Ritz clientele was on its feet and dancing. Afterwards, a beaming Barsalona walked into the band's dressing room and told them the words they wanted to hear. He looked at Bono and said: "I give you my word, you are going to happen in America."

Making a band "happen" in America meant more than just a smile and a handshake, however sincere and well meaning. It meant touring there solidly for months at a time, as U2 would do throughout most of 1981. It also meant being away from home for quite unnaturally lengthy periods, something the young band had never experienced on quite such a scale before. Inevitably, this would bring a newfound pressure to life in the band. Splits and divisions began to appear sporadically within their ranks. Adam, being the only truly unreligious member, was often the lightning rod for this disruption. He would spend the long bus journeys up front with Paul McGuinness, in order to get away from the others, who would be seated at the back, often reading their bibles. Adam would try and avoid the subject but when the others started on about it he just couldn't help but clash with them sometimes.

As Bono recalled, things got so bad at one point in 1981 that the band might easily have broken up then. Their momentum was visibly building in America and the pressure of seeing the job through was starting to take its toll. It was as if, thought Bono, the band was being thrown some sort of last-minute test. Like, how bad did they really want it? Bad enough to put themselves through gruelling twelve-hour bus journeys just to play some half-empty college hall or backside of a club?

Bono's way of dealing with the stress of confronting the outside world each day was to turn his thoughts inwards once more. As he later explained, "I had less interest in being in U2 and more of an interest in other sides of me." The America he sought wasn't found at gigs or on tour buses, he decided. Instead, "whether I was talking to a Catholic priest in the inner city or a Pentecostal preacher, I was sucking up whatever they had to say. I was interested in that third dimensional side of me and I [suddenly] thought rock'n'roll was a bit of a waste of space … I thought, OK, U2 were good at being a band, but maybe we could be better at doing other things, real things like getting involved in the inner city or something. Not just pointing out the problems, but trying to sort them out." Instead, he claimed, the band couldn't even solve its own problems and was "teetering on the brink of collapse". Adam, in particular, he said, "was completely heartbroken about this". But concluded, more charitably: "I'm all right now, I've come to terms with being in a band … I think now this is what we do best."

Whatever had gone on between them off stage, Bono was certainly still throwing everything he had into the live act – arguably too much. "There was a gig in America when I threw Larry's drum kit off stage and had a go at the band," Bono later admitted. "And The Edge, who is my ideal – he's completely composed – he was so outraged he gave me a severe dig in the mouth. It was amazing! I've known him all my life and it was a really good dig in the mouth. That was on stage ... in front of Talking Heads and the B52s. I think they all thought it was part of the show."

But if he sometimes went too far, it was because Bono took his role as the visual mainstay of the band seriously. Like his boyhood hero, Bruce Springsteen, he wanted to be more than just a singer; he wanted to be a *front man*. The Edge was no conventional axe hero, either, but, said Bono, "a brilliant guitar player who completely understates it as a person. He pulls no shapes. He is a man of angles, he's got his chin and his guitar and the elbows and plays away and then humbly takes the plug out of the amplifier and goes home. My respect for him grows and grows."

A break in Nassau, accompanied by producer Steve Lillywhite, now more a friend of the band than just their producer, saw the group tempted into a busman's holiday when they decided on the spur of the moment to enter Compass Point studios to lay down a new number they'd been working up which they thought might make a good single. Entitled 'Fire', when it was released as a single in June, it may only have peaked at Number 35 in the UK charts, but it did afford them their first opportunity to appear on BBC1's *Top of the Pops*, then still the most watched pop show on TV. Boosted by this vital exposure, coupled with Island's shrewd decision also to release versions of the single with a special bonus disc of live tracks, 'Fire' became U2's best-selling record yet.

Typically, Bono would later play down the role that first *TOTP* appearance played in moving the band's career forward. "The miming was all over the shop and it was operatic in a way that TV will never understand," he grimaced. "The record company were really thrilled, but we went on and the single went down [the next week] because we were so bad." Certainly, the singer's choice of "sleeping bag shirt" and a determinedly "bad haircut" add an amusing dimension to old video clips of that performance now. Nevertheless, when they returned to the now familiar surrounds of Windmill Lane studios later that summer they did so in a mood of impatience. Whatever the merits of their TV performance, they had just had their first Top 40 single; the time to strike with their next album had come. They hurriedly recorded the remaining material they would need, then prepared to go back on the road again in America.

As they waited for the album's release, U2 celebrated the summer of '81 with an August festival show at Dublin's famous Slane Castle, on a bill that featured Thin Lizzy, the Seventies band that had helped blaze a trail out of Ireland for other bands, such as U2, to follow. In truth, however, Lizzy's best days were now behind them, their spirit broken by a combination of Phil Lynott's much-publicised drug problems and an audience left confused by a succession of lead guitarists that never seemed to last longer than an album. As such, although Phil Lynott and his crew were the nominal headliners, it was clear, walking among the crowd that day, that there were as many people there to see the up and coming quartet as were there for the more famous headliners.

Much as Slane felt like a triumph, Bono knew the real test for the band would come with the release of their second album, now titled *October*. Second albums were always notoriously "sink or swim", and had they buckled under the pressure of coming up with not just a credible successor but something even better than their fiery debut, U2 would hardly have been the first high-profile casualties to do so. First albums were simply unrepeatable: having spent years conceiving and road-testing material, most bands simply ran through their stage set for their debut album. The problem second time around is that all the best songs written over a period of years have already been used.

Bono and the band were determined that *October* would not suffer a similar fate. Appropriately released in the tenth month of 1981, exactly one year after its predecessor, to the immense relief of everyone involved, *October* proved to be U2's breakthrough album in the UK, for which they received their first silver disc, for over sixty thousand copies sold. Tracks such as 'Gloria' (an original Bono-penned anthem, not the Van Morrison classic) and the now familiar 'Fire' became immediate cornerstones in the new live set from which they were able to improvise and take their music that one crucial step further forward.

At first, however, it seemed that *October* might only replicate the modest success of *Boy*. Again, reviews were largely strong, but 'Gloria' would stall five places short of the Top 50 when it was released as their next single. However, things began to pick up when the title track, 'October', became the first U2 single to enter the UK Top 20, eventually peaking at Number 11. Why that particular song should have been their breakthrough, as opposed to any others they had released, was a subject Bono would later speculate on at length. There was a religious fervour to some of the lyrics, he seemed to suggest. Because of that, "A lot of people found 'October' hard to accept at first. I mean, I used the word 'Rejoice' [in the song] precisely because I knew people have a mental block against it. It's a powerful word. It's implying more than 'get up and dance, baby'." Even the title had a spiritual symbolism for him. "There is a very cold atmosphere in the world at the moment. We called our [album] *October* to reflect that, but also to suggest a revaluation. I do believe that there is a purpose to everybody's lives, if they yield to that purpose … I think that *October* goes into areas that most rock'n'roll bands ignore."

It has also since been suggested that 'Tomorrow' – along with 'Gloria' one of the standout tracks of the album, and not an arbitrary choice to start a vinyl side – was about Bono's mother, and it was interesting that it incorporated a traditional Irish instrument, as if in homage to a childhood memory, in the uillean pipes played by Vinnie Kilduff. The result is almost folk-rocky, and even the band making a typically crunching entrance halfway through can't spoil the effect. The singer himself admitted later that "when I listen to something like 'Tomorrow' it actually moves me".

On a more prosaic level, Bono also now recalls *October* as an album made quickly and under immense pressure. "I remember writing lyrics on the microphone and at £50 an hour [for the hire of the studio] that's quite a pressure. Lillywhite was pacing up and down the studio ... he coped really well. And the ironic thing about *October* is that there's a kind of peace about the album even though it was recorded under that pressure."

The album ended on a plaintive note with 'Is That All', a track improvised in the studio when the band felt they needed something suitably evocative to bring the album to a close. Looking back, it's easy to see 'Is That All' as an expression of the feelings of frustration and maybe even failure that Bono privately wrestled with and worked so hard with his bravura performances to conceal. With a guitar riff recycled from an earlier, unrecorded song, 'The Cry', the new title suggested that Bono was asking if all God required of him was to be a singer in a rock band ... a downbeat way to end an album otherwise brimming with purpose. Not surprisingly, it would be one of only two *October* tracks that would never be performed live, though the riff of 'The Cry' often made it into the live performances of 'Electric Co' from *Boy*.

Musically, the real key to *October* had been in using the studio to make the most of U2's basic instrumentation, layering The Edge's guitars to create a ghostly, eerie, yet at the same time strangely joyful sound. Integral to this was "fifth member" Lillywhite, who encouraged them to take technology to its limits. Working out how to reproduce the resulting sound on stage would be a bridge they could try and cross later. However, how much later remained to be seen, since the differences that had come to the fore during Stateside touring now seemed likely to rip the band asunder again. In May 1981, Bono had said: "Edge is the head of the band, I'm the heart, and Adam and Larry are the feet." One month after *October*'s release, with a twenty-date US tour already arranged, the quartet announced they planned, instead, to take a break from touring rather than promote the record. Would the head, heart and feet be detached from each other? Could the U2 story be over before it had really begun? Certainly, for a while there, it seemed that it might be so.

In 1987, Bono would reflect on the dilemma he felt he had been facing six years before. "Around the time of *October* we weren't even sure if we wanted to be in a band. I thought rock'n'roll was really just pure vanity and there didn't seem to be a place in it for some of the spiritual concerns in my writing. I felt like a fish out of water, the square peg in the round hole. But I've since realised that a lot of the artists who have inspired me – Bob Dylan, Van Morrison, Patti Smith, Al Green, Marvin Gaye – were [once] in a similar position. They all had three sides to their writing – sexual, the spiritual and the political. In our own way U2 have that same three-dimensional thing. That's why I'm more at ease [now]."

Behind the scenes, however, the key to what was going on was the band members' involvement in Shalom. With Bono pushing for answers, it seemed the group had been left in a position where they would have to make a decision: whether to throw in their lot with the band, or with the charismatic Christian group that held three-quarters of them in thrall. The way was led by two of their fellow Lipton Villagers, Guggi and then Gavin Friday, along with girlfriend Rene. As members of the Virgin Prunes, they had taken flak from within Shalom for the way they dressed and the "message" of their music. Deciding they were being unfairly scapegoated for daring to be different, they had now opted out. Larry was the first member of U2 to follow them.

The Edge, however, was a different matter. Bono has described him as "a really, really intense guy, he's got this incredibly high IQ, he's great at sorting out issues of worldly importance, it's just that he forgets the everyday things, like the chords of songs, where he is and so on". His spiritual beliefs too were so deep-rooted that for a week he was actually on his way out of U2. His change of heart eventually showed the way to Bono, too, who would trade charismatic Christianity for the likes of Greenpeace and Amnesty International, organisations that better reflected his new world view.

Of course, the dichotomy between religion and rock'n'roll – the "devil's music" – was one that had troubled many young singers long before Bono began grappling with it. Little Richard, the "Georgia Peach", regularly renounced rock'n'roll and all its rewards from the mid-Fifties onwards, even going as far as famously throwing his most ostentatious stage jewellery off the Sydney Harbour Bridge – only to return to play many more thousands of rock'n'roll shows over the course of his life. The late soul star, Sam Cooke, initially chose to record pop material under an assumed name rather than alienate the devout church following he enjoyed from his other work as a gospel singer. In 1988, Bono, who has struggled with religious issues all his life, swaying too far one way and then the other, added his own take on the subject. There simply came a point where he realised, he said, that, irrespective of your religious beliefs, "You don't join a band to save the world, but to save your own arse and get off the street. You want to play to the crowd rather than be *in* the crowd. I want to own up to this because people look at U2 and see all these pure motives – but we started off being in the band for the most impure motives." As a result, U2's music has constantly throbbed with the energy this paradox has created; the cross they have sought both to bear and burn, at different times.

Despite the air of uncertainty about the band at its start, the nearly aborted US tour of November 1981 proved, against all odds, to be a major triumph. No longer schlepping around the clubs and dives, they found themselves able to fill three-thousand-capacity theatre venues from coast to coast, establishing an audience for themselves that they would add to in early 1982 when they returned to open shows in venues up to five times that size for the then hugely popular J. Geils Band, coasting through a high-profile US arena tour off the back of their massive recent hit, 'Centrefold'. Spurred on by the challenge, despite the hoo-hah now surrounding everything the Geils band did, U2 duly succeeded in stealing away a few encores on several nights.

Meanwhile, March 1982 saw the release of 'A Celebration', a stop-gap single recorded between albums which reached only a disappointing Number 47 back home in Britain. With its references to Christ Church cathedral and Mountjoy, the song had an underlying Christian theme: every line Bono began by repeating the words "I believe in..." like a mantra. The band filmed a video for the song which portrayed them as "itinerant boys, traveller boys, the four horsemen of the apocalypse", but Bono admits now that neither this nor the song itself was really up to scratch, the whole thing put together hurriedly to please the corporate masters. "I remember thinking this will do: I don't remember thinking this is good."

The year of '82 also saw U2 catch festival fever, playing a number of huge outdoor shows that summer in the company of acts such as Peter Gabriel, Eurythmics and Simple Minds. Having played a couple of rapturously received pre-Christmas shows at London's Lyceum in December '81, the only time their UK fans would see them over the coming twelve months would be when they played a big outdoor show at Gateshead, in July, as special guests to headliners the Police. Held at an athletics stadium, it was a major event and one that saw Bono employ a stage trick for the first time. Plucking a white flag from the crowd while singing 'Electric Co', he scaled the side-stage PA stack and planted the flag atop it. "There's only one flag, and it's a white flag," he announced to the cheering multitude. Several thousand Irish fans had also flocked to see the band headline the RDS Hall in Dublin in January '82, turning the soulless agricultural "cowshed" into a seething, enthusiastic rugby scrum. Further gigs in Galway and Cork were their first at home for nigh on a year, and were received equally excitedly. They would also return to Dublin later in the year to play a fifth birthday party for *Hot Press*, the rock magazine that had given them so much vital support in the early days.

For Bono, personally, 1982 would also be remembered for the best of reasons, as it was also the year he and Alison married, on 21 August. The venue was the Guinness Church of Ireland at Raheny, the ceremony was modest, with no superstar trappings, and the families of both parties comprised the majority of the strictly invite-only congregation. In this, of course, Bono was following in his family tradition. Perhaps the biggest surprise was the best man – Adam Clayton. The selection of the man who "literally got me by the scruff of the neck and roped me into U2 when I didn't really want to be in a band" was symbolic. Bono was pledging his future to Alison, and at the same time affirming his kinship with the man who "believed in the band before anyone else did".

Over the years, Bono has not talked overmuch about his wife, who, he says, is more than happy to remain in the shadows, far away from the spotlight. On those rare occasions when he has spoken about her though, the extent of his feelings for his wife are clearly evident. "It's almost impossible to be married and on the road, but Ali is able to make it work. A year went by when I hardly saw her at all. I was coming in when she was walking out the door." The key, he says, is that she is "a very strong person and she doesn't take any shit from me".

After the wedding, the couple honeymooned in the Bahamas as the guests of Chris Blackwell. The Island supremo had offered them the exclusive use of Goldeneye, a house once owned by Ian Fleming of James Bond fame, and an idyllic setting in which to begin their married days together. Bono felt truly happy for the first time in years and, suitably inspired, it was at Goldeneye that the future single 'Two Hearts Beat As One' was written. "I don't write many love songs in a straight sense," Bono would later opine, reasoning that the world already had too many love songs as it was and certainly didn't need any more from him. "But in many ways I do think this is beautiful … it's a good song." His new wife would doubtless expect him to say nothing less, but it was true. Moreover, 'Two Hearts Beat As One' would demonstrate a new side to U2, a more tender, thoughtful approach, yet one that belied none of their inner fire.

As the Hewsons jetted off to the sun, The Edge was left behind in Dublin to work on ideas at home for the material that would make up their next album. As a result, with the exception of Bono's paean to marital bliss, the third U2 album would reflect more on the fact that, in Bono's words, "War seemed to be the motif for 1982. Everywhere you looked, from the Falklands to the Middle East to South

Africa, there was war." What better name, then, for an album concerned with somehow reflecting those times?

Released on the last day of February 1983, *War*, the third and most hard-edged U2 album so far, would not only prove, ironically, their biggest success yet, but would help establish an artistic-political stance that would become the thread of steel that ran through all their most radical future recordings. Featuring a newly married and suddenly heavily politicised Bono, this sounded like a far more knowing, streetwise figure than before; one who had emerged from travelling so much around America in these years, mixing with those – the Cubans, the blacks, the Irish – he would eulogise on potent new songs such as 'Refugee'. That and two other new numbers had actually been featured in the set which the band took around on a pre-*War* tour of Britain, Europe and Ireland in December 1982, before final mixing took place in the New Year. But the song that would be homed in on, both at home and abroad, as U2's most explicitly political yet was the rousing 'Sunday Bloody Sunday'. Bono's attempt to contrast Easter Sunday and the infamous Bloody Sunday incident of 1972, when the British Army opened fire on unarmed civil rights protesters in Belfast, in concert he was always careful to preface it with the words: "This is not a rebel song." Later, he would suggest that those people with axes to grind on either side of the sectarian divide had almost all missed the point of the exercise.

"A lot of those lyrics I'm very proud of," Bono explained,

"and I'm proud of them almost because they were written so quickly and so naïvely." 'Sunday Bloody Sunday' had been written "very, very quickly. But it's a big idea to take on. And, oh I don't know any more ... I've had enough bruises and scars not to want to take things head on in the same way any more."

Ultimately, said Bono, 'Sunday Bloody Sunday' was an intentional "slap in the face against the snap, crackle and pop" of most modern music, and he defied the critics to pass judgement on it. Interestingly, their UK record company, Island, were nervous enough about the potential of 'Sunday Bloody Sunday' to cause controversy that they persuaded the band not to issue it as the first single from the album, as they had originally planned, that honour now going, after much heated debate, to 'New Year's Day' instead – inspired by Lech Walesa, the charismatic leader of Poland's shipyard workers who launched Solidarity, the song's echoing refrain based on the Old Testament psalm of King David. (Fascinatingly, Polish authorities lifted martial law on 1 January 1983, just as the single hit the shops.)

Whatever the real message of U2's music, Bono was delighted (and quietly relieved) to discover that this more overt mix of politics and rock'n'roll had proved a winning combination. Not only would *War* outsell both their two previous albums put together, but both 'Sunday Bloody Sunday' and 'New Year's Day' would become their first big international hits. Once again, however, just as it appeared from the outside as though things could hardly be going better for them, the band was flirting with disintegration. The pressure of making the album had, as ever, cast all their relationships into the melting pot. Now things had reached boiling point again. As Bono later wearily recalled: "When we go into the studio we draw totally on our deepest resources and stretch them to the limit. If a band is going to be honest they've got to bring out everything, even the things that might frighten them."

The success of *War*, which hit Number 1 in Britain in its first week of release, and the inevitable return to the road soon straightened things out, however; Bono and the band were now simply too busy just keeping the ever expanding show on the road to want to keep pulling in different directions. The only major casualty appeared to be producer Steve Lillywhite, a notable absentee at this point. Lillywhite had long ago made it a personal rule that he would not do more than two albums with any group or artist, for fear that the creative relationship would grow too comfortable and stale. For the first time in three years, U2 would be forced to work with someone new in the studio. Concerned not to lose the momentum or "empathy" they had achieved together with Lillywhite, Bono instructed McGuinness to cast the net far and wide in the search for a replacement. At one time, Bruce Springsteen cohort Jimmy Iovine, who'd expressed a repeated interest in working with the band, was the strong front runner to land the gig. Less obviously, though just as keenly considered, was another American, Jimmy Destri, then keyboard player with the about-to-demise Blondie. Rhett

Davies, who'd made his name with the re-formed, Eighties line-up of Roxy Music, was another under serious consideration at one stage; while Sandy Pearlman, who had masterminded the rise of Blue Öyster Cult and superintended the Clash's controversial second album *Give 'Em Enough Rope* was also said to have thrown his hat into the ring.

In the end, the band admitted they didn't know what to do, and so agreed to a stop-gap measure: they would record one song, 'Refugee', with renowned Irish producer Bill Whelan, an old pal of Paul McGuinness's. A veteran of the contemporary Irish music scene, Whelan would, in fact, make a worldwide name for himself a decade later as the creator of the *Riverdance* phenomenon – the thought of Bono emulating Michael Flatley, an interesting one, to say the least – but the partnership, though enjoyable, never progressed further than that one track. Instead, within weeks, Steve Lillywhite, having re-evaluated his relationship with U2 and decided "to hell with it" and broken his own rules, decided to come back on board and the band collectively breathed a sigh of relief.

Bono admitted in January 1983 that the success of *War* – their first Number 1 album in the UK and, though he didn't know it yet, about to become their first major chart album in America, where it would peak at Number 12 – was hugely important, not only to him but to the whole band. But was it make or break? "I don't think so," he said. "More of a progressive build-up. We have developed the sound, taking it a stage further. It is far more rhythmic, with much more depth. *War* is our heaviest album yet, it will hit you right there. This band is having a go at all the blippety bop aural wallpaper we have rammed down our throats on the radio and the TV every day. I am personally bloody sick every time I switch on the radio of being blasted with this contrived crap."

It was, he felt, an album that was right for the times, a true product, as much as a reflection, of its environment. The fact that 'New Year's Day' actually made the Top 10 indicated, he said, "a disillusionment among record buyers with the pop stuff in the chart. I don't think 'New Year's Day' was a pop single, certainly not in the way Mickie Most might define a pop single as something that lasts three minutes and three weeks in the chart. I don't think we could have written that kind of a song." People, he concluded with a flourish, were "growing disillusioned with pap, with the wallpaper music and the gloss. It's as if someone has eaten too many [chocolates] over the last couple of years, and suddenly they're beginning to feel ill as they look at all the wrapping paper strewn around the room."

Criticism in some quarters that U2 had produced a stringently negative-sounding album, a collection of upbeat, angst-ridden downers, was strongly rebutted, though Bono did allow that the album title had been intended to "give people a slap in the face and at the same time get away from the coy image a lot of people have of U2". With a title such as *War* they could have taken the easy way out of putting tanks and guns on the cover: instead they gave it a child's questioning face. (This was in fact Peter Rowen from the *Boy* cover, this time a few years older and with his hands behind his head in what many interpreted as a gesture of surrender.)

Not so, said Bono. "A song like 'New Year's Day' might be about war and struggle," he insisted, "but it is also about love. It is about having faith to break through and survive against all the odds. Love is a very powerful thing. There's nothing more radical than two people loving each other. I mean, I'm in love and there is a lot of love in the album." He went on: "I think that love stands out when set against a struggle. That's probably the power of the record in a nutshell. The album is about the struggle for love, not about war in the negative sense. I would be failing if I made *War* sound like a gloomy album because it's not. I hope it's an uplifting record. Some love songs devalue the meaning of the word. Disco bands turn it into a cliché by tearing it down until it means nothing. The power of love is always more striking when set against realism than when set against escapism."

Certainly, if the songs on *October* had been more abstract, the lyrics on *War* are more challengingly direct, far more specific. "But you can still take the title on a lot of different levels," said Bono. "We're not only interested in the physical idea of war [but] on an emotional level. War can also be a mental thing, an emotional thing between lovers. It doesn't have to be a physical thing. There is such a thing as mental war. We're fascinated by all the different aspects and connotations."

What Bono didn't mention was that there had nearly been a war between him and Steve Lillywhite, who pushed the singer beyond his known limits, demanding take after take

until his throat bled. Guest musicians also made an appearance for the first time on a U2 album. At Lillywhite's urging,
Steve Wickham from In Tua Nua played violin on 'Sunday
Bloody Sunday', while the Coconuts, Kid Creole's vocal group,
supplied some background vocals. Towards the end of the
sessions, the band had found themselves one song short of
finishing the album, but with precious few ideas and time
running out. Finally, after several false starts, at six o'clock in
the morning, they finished '40', a song with which they would
close the majority of their live shows throughout the rest of
the Eighties. The Edge stood in on bass for the sleeping Adam,
as Bono, his voice now hoarse beyond recognition, put the
finishing touches to a song whose lyrics were lifted last-
minute from the Psalms. The plea from the opening track,
"How long must we sing this song", was repeated, but this
time it no longer sounded like an angry demand, it sounded
like a real prayer.

"Everyone else is getting more and more style-orientated,
more and more slick," concluded Bono. "John Lennon was
right about that kind of music; he called it 'wallpaper music'.
Very pretty, very well designed, music to eat your breakfast
to. [But] music can be more. Its possibilities are great. Music
has changed me. It has the ability to change a generation.
Look at what happened with Vietnam. Music changed a
whole generation's attitude towards war."

But if *War* was a huge step forward for the band – both
creatively and commercially – it still sounded like what it
was: the work of a clearly idealistic young band, and while

there were at least two of their finest songs on *War*, there was also what Bono would correctly identify as "a strident quality that was letting me down. I could see how it might have sounded like a finger pointing, and of course we've never pointed a finger at anyone, apart from ourselves. That voice was very angry. I didn't realise I was so tense."

It was time to take stock, maybe. Fat chance. Instead, 1983 found the band almost permanently on the road, most often in America. Their gig at the Red Rocks Amphitheatre on 25 June was famously filmed for broadcast on Channel 4's cool new Friday-night TV show, *The Tube*, and would also become, in time, the template for the band's first live album. In a sense it showed U2 at their bombastic best with more than a little stridency – but as history would have it, *Under a Blood Red Sky*, as the album would eventually be titled, proved to be a perfectly apt time capsule of U2 at their earliest performing peak.

The venue, a natural amphitheatre set between huge, deep red sandstone boulders two miles up in the Rocky Mountains of Colorado, proved the ideal backdrop for Bono and the band to put on one of their all-time, crowd-pleasing, down-on-one-knee, flag-waving, drum-beating, belligerently best performances. The nine thousand fans there that night gave the band every encouragement, not least because several days of unseasonably inclement weather had made it odds-on that the event would be cancelled. As it transpired, the torrential rain which had lashed down all day stopped just before U2 took to the stage, and the performance went ahead as planned. In 1999, influential US magazine *Entertainment Weekly* would rate this 40th in their list of 100 Greatest Moments in Rock, but for many U2 fans this spectacle has yet to be equalled.

The resulting eight-song mini-album, *Under a Blood Red Sky*, had to be 'retooled' in the studio quite considerably before it could be released, however. It was even alleged that music recorded from other concerts on the tour had to be called upon to replace music that had not recorded well at Red Rocks itself. But at a budget price of just £2.99 ($4.98 in the USA) it was an inspired move on several levels. Not only did it beat to the punch the bootleggers who had recently grown rich selling illegal recordings of U2 concerts, but at such a low price it gave an opportunity to new, undecided music fans to give them a listen. It also proved to be extremely profitable. Made for comparatively little, next to the costs of making a fully-fledged studio album, and released in November 1983, *Under a Blood Red Sky* would go on to become a triple-platinum item in Britain, where it reached Number 2 and sold over a million copies. While in the USA, fans put it straight into the *Billboard* Top 30 at Number 28. Suddenly, the band was making real money. Not just thousands – millions. The only real expense had come as a result of Bono's decision to include a snatch of Stephen Sondheim's 'Send In The Clowns' during his live rendition of 'Electric Co' – an unintended but expensive error that cost them $50,000 in copyright fees when a court case resulted: later copies of the album had the expensive lines removed, while the whole show appeared on video – *sans* Sondheim – in July 1984.

British U2 fans had also enjoyed a twenty-eight-day tour from the band in February, after which the live single 'Two Hearts Beat As One', Bono's love hymn to Ali, made a disappointing Number 18: all the fans, it seemed, already owned *War* and, with a live 'Sunday Bloody Sunday' single out of the equation in Britain, having only recently been a hit there, there were few uncommitted purchasers. But the States was definitely in U2's sights and, after Red Rocks, they moved on to the last leg of their US tour in high spirits. They'd been headlining and selling out ten-thousand-capacity arenas this time round, and Bono was delighted when Bruce Springsteen himself arrived to see what all the fuss was about at their show in Philadelphia.

However, an incident at Los Angeles Sports Stadium on 17 June drew a line under Bono's flag waving for good. It was typically during 'Electric Co' that he would now start climbing speaker stacks, scaffolding or whatever was available to plant his white flag, hanging on grimly to his radio microphone all the while. But on this occasion there was a fight in the audience and someone tore the flag from his grasp. He stood on the balcony behind the stage and commanded it to stop – or he would jump. It didn't stop. He jumped ...

The world stood still as, from twenty feet, the singer plummeted towards the audience. Bono the rock god had suddenly turned into the all too mortal Paul Hewson. No matter that the crowd broke his fall, he had been brought up short. And what was worse, the rest of the band knew it too. "They took me aside backstage and said, 'Look, cut it out. You're the singer in a band, you've just got to get up there and sing. You don't have to remind the audience that U2 are stars to be worshipped – they already understand.'"

Another painful lesson learned ...

CHAPTER THREE 1984–1989

The unanticipated scale of the success of their live album, *Under a Blood Red Sky*, bought U2 the precious time they needed to step back and reassess the group. Bono knew that if their success had been hard won, capitalising on it with a new studio album that somehow trumped what was, in essence, a live compilation of all their best-known songs up to that point, would be harder still. Moreover, *War* had been an album that dealt with inner and outer conflicts; reflecting both the frightening developments of the outside world – from the ongoing conflict in Northern Ireland, to Prime Minister Margaret Thatcher's decision to send British forces into battle with Argentina over the disputed dominion of the Falkland Islands – and the ongoing tensions within the band, epitomised by Bono's hair-shirt angst and Adam's party animal instincts. Unique circumstances, Bono felt, that could scarcely be repeated, certainly not with the same impact. And impact was now the name of the game for U2 on both sides of the Atlantic – a fact demonstrated when *Rolling Stone* magazine voted them their Top Rock Act of 1983. "We broke up the band after

War," Bono later revealed. "We literally broke up the band and formed another band with the same name and the same members. That's what we did."

War had undoubtedly been one of the early Eighties' most strident musical statements, and the film and album of the Red Rocks show had more than ably demonstrated that U2's music took on a whole new dimension when they performed it live. There would be an established running order of numbers in the set each night which would get tinkered with at the start of a tour then more or less stay the same for the vast majority of the shows. With so much spontaneity within the band, however, it's fair to say that no two U2 shows were ever quite the same. Capturing that essence on their more manicured records still remained elusive, however, and it was this that would become their main musical preoccupation as they prepared to enter the studio again. Releasing a live album had also, Bono decided, cleared the way for something new to emerge from the band. He described *Under a Blood Red Sky* as "the full stop at the end of a sentence; we are beginning a new paragraph". An exclamation mark might have been more appropriate. Following up *War* was not going to be as straightforward as that.

As Bono later revealed, "It was really difficult, that period after *War*. It was awful. I was a madman. You know what they do to terrorists in Northern Ireland? They put brown paper bags over their heads, they put them in rooms where they can't stand up or sit down with their legs stretched out, they keep the light on twenty-four hours a day so they don't know what time it is or whether it's night or day." That, he suggested, was how he could come to feel after so long on the road, building empires. Out there, lost somewhere on the road, he said, it was too easy simply to lose track of yourself, too. "You walk out on to a stage, you give of yourself for an hour and a half, and the applause that comes back is uplifting, but sometimes it's anonymous. You leave the venue and I need to talk to people afterwards, I need for that applause to be personified in some way so I can get a grip on what's been going on. But if you don't, you end up going back into this empty space which is your hotel room ... a bit like the guy with the paper bag over his head."

In many ways, said Bono, *War* had also been a reaction to the excesses of the then ultra-fashionable "new romantic" movement, as championed by the new generation of colour Eighties mags such as *The Face* and *Blitz*, that liked to mix music with fashion, as exemplified by new, early-Eighties UK chart acts such as Duran Duran, Culture Club, Spandau Ballet and Adam Ant. Because of all that, Bono claimed, "We stripped our sound to bare bones and knuckles and three capital letters, W-A-R, and we put these prime colours in." Nevertheless, he realised in retrospect, that in taking such a forward stance, he had allowed himself to become categorised and caricatured as surely as Simon Le Bon or Boy George. "What upsets me," said Bono, "is that when people see U2 they see only 'Sunday Bloody Sunday' and the guy with the white flag. They don't see 'Drowning Man', which was on the same album. There is another side to U2. Sure, we arrived with a placard in our hands – and bold placards – but that's not *just* what U2's about."

The key to their next step, broadening their musical base, was the start of their relationship with Brian Eno and his Canadian cohort, producer, writer and multi-instrumentalist Daniel Lanois. Because of his background working with people such as Roxy Music, John Cale, David Bowie and the intensely cerebral Talking Heads leader, David Byrne, to name just a few, Eno was seen by Bono and the rest of the band as the ideal candidate to help bring to their music what at the time he characterised as "a more European sensibility", as opposed to the arena-friendly, US-centric attack sound that had reached its apotheosis on *Under a Blood Red Sky*.

Daniel Lanois had produced fellow Canadians Martha and the Muffins and was an up and coming figure in the studio world who would later work – at Bono's instigation – with Bob Dylan. Still then largely unknown, however, outside the small circle of musicians and studio heads he had already impressed, Lanois was delighted to be in the frame for working with such a big-name band. Eno, however, initially turned down the offer. Already famous in his own right and having no need to take jobs simply for the money or prestige, he later recalled how Bono and the band "nagged me so much that [eventually] I listened to some of their own material". However, as he later confessed, "It didn't inspire me particularly." In fact, said Eno, he was "mystified by their reasons for even wanting me. But once I met Bono I knew I had to work with him." There was, said Eno, simply "something about"

Bono that made you want to believe in him. "He talked about the band in a way that I hadn't heard anyone doing in a long while, and so, on that basis, on the basis of curiosity, I agreed to work with them."

For Bono, apart from the allure of working with someone who had helped coax some of their best work out of Ferry, Bowie and Byrne, working with Eno would be a huge opportunity, he felt, for the band really to stretch their music and experiment with it. They already had a defining "U2 sound", as instantly recognisable on the radio as that of the Beatles, the Pistols, Springsteen or any of the greats. What, Bono wondered, might Eno, a master of lateral production thinking, do with such a rich palette? Meeting to discuss how they would approach the album, Bono was immediately struck by Eno's unique perception of the band. Surprised to hear Eno describe his fondness for gospel music, he was further intrigued when Eno told him he could see parallels in the heart-swelling intensity of gospel with the sort of cathartic, mushroom-cloud effect U2's best songs seemed to be striving for.

It certainly gave the young singer food for thought. As he later mused: "People talk about the spirituality of U2, and I realised that was part of everyday life in black music. Indeed, Jimi Hendrix was the wildest rock'n'roll performer; and Janis Joplin would have loved to be black." He realised that Eno had been right and that even "though we weren't rooted in black music, there was something in the spirit that was similar". Bono had always felt that there were at least two important sides to U2. First, "the energy and the atmosphere. With Steve Lillywhite, it was always the energy that was showing, but now Brian Eno [was] helping bring out the atmosphere again." The last year had seen Bono and his band get "a little bit lost", he admitted. Working with Eno and Lanois, though, "represents a return to our initial aims".

Another new element Eno's involvement in the creative process helped bring out that had previously remained hidden was a capacity to take their foot off the pedal momentarily, to step back in a more contemplative style, adding whole new layers to their music, making it infinitely more engrossing, more inclusive, and far more convincing than the finger-pointing sound of old. As a result, the album they made together, *The Unforgettable Fire*, found Bono and U2 diving into whole new soundscapes, previously unexplored areas of the musical map they hadn't even realised existed before. Or if they had, they hadn't known how to get there – until Eno and Lanois came along to give them directions. Contradictions were encouraged – while the sound became more polished and satisfyingly rounded, it still allowed certain numbers to arrive sounding almost unfinished or only half-formed. A good example was 'Elvis Presley And America', which, with Eno's encouragement, Bono later claimed, was literally written and recorded in five minutes. "Eno just handed me a microphone," Bono recalled with a smile, "and told me to sing over this piece of music that had been slowed down, played backwards or whatever. I said, 'What, just like that? Now?' He said, 'Yes, this is what you're all about.' So I did it and when it was finished there were all these beautiful lines and melodies coming out of it. I said, 'I can't wait to finish this.' He said, 'What do you mean, finish it? It *is* finished!'"

With Eno's encouragement, Bono's lyrics began to lose their didactic edge and become more abstract and poetic again. Not everybody in the band was convinced at first by these developments, sometimes mistaking spontaneity for the merely slapdash, but Adam Clayton, for one, made clear that he was as enthusiastic as Bono about seeing where such experiments led. "Understanding Bono's lyrics has never been particularly important to me," he said in a rare interview in 1985. "I go with my instincts and if Bono is singing and it doesn't sound right, then I'll consult him about it. But if the whole thing fits as an image, I don't even listen to what he's singing, I listen to what I'm hearing in my head, which is something completely different."

In keeping with the "clean-slate" approach Eno and Lanois had helped usher in, rather than book a return to Windmill Lane studios, as had originally been the plan, with the old studio about to undergo a major refit anyway, it was decided, instead, to set up base at picturesque Slane Castle, the two-hundred-year-old home of Lord Henry Mountcharles, the grounds of which he allowed to be used to host outdoor concerts every summer. On the surface, it may have looked like a grand move to make for a band so concerned with staying connected to the realities of street life. From Eno's point of view, however, the ancient castle was a wonderfully "atmospheric" choice of venue in which to work together for the first time.

Situated some thirty miles outside Dublin, the band would have to bring all the facilities they needed with them. Unfortunately, the mobile generator they'd brought in to power the portable studio they'd hired kept blowing up. At such times, the delights of working al fresco, as it were, could seem paltry, and they would later revert to Windmill Lane to finish off many of the tracks begun at Slane. But by then they had what they wanted, for when the equipment had worked properly at Slane, some great, one-off moments were captured there.

Meanwhile, with the four albums promised on their original contract with Island all now safely delivered, it was time to negotiate a new deal for the band, and Paul McGuinness was beavering feverishly away behind the scenes to make sure the rewards U2 received were commensurate with their newfound worldwide success. Now bargaining from a position of considerable strength, McGuinness was able to secure a lucrative new contract from Island that dwarfed the original. The bottom line: a deal for the next four U2 albums, for which the band would reportedly receive $2 million in advance, plus a healthy hike in their present royalty rates, now raised to almost double their original cut. As before, the albums would be accepted by the label unheard, but with the chief execs now having no right of veto on any of the product, either. It was also agreed that three videos would now be made to promote each album, at Island's expense: with a start-up budget of

$75,000 per video, rising on a sliding scale as the years passed. And, buried among all the small print, a clause of major new significance in terms of Bono's future finances, whereby the band would now own the publishing rights to all their original songs, past, present and future. As a result, the moment the twenty-four-year-old Bono put his signature on the new contract, he and the other three members of U2 were all now millionaires. Make that multi-millionaires.

Such an outlay comes with its own inbuilt pressures, of course. Not least a sense of renewed expectation; the dread feeling of the bar, already dauntingly high, being raised just a crucial few inches higher. U2 now had huge ambitions to fulfil, great things were expected of them. The success of their next album would be absolutely crucial to all their plans. Privately, however, record bosses in London and America admitted they were nervous about the new collaboration with Eno: they were sure it would be fascinating, but would it provide the necessary hits?

Fortunately, the fourth U2 album was blessed with a song that would become one of the finest, most inspiring, not to mention hugely successful singles the band would ever release. Its title: 'Pride (In The Name Of Love)'. The most outstanding track from an album overburdened with precious jewels, 'Pride …' was a new landmark for U2 in the same way 'Sunday Bloody Sunday' and 'New Year's Day' had been on *War* – the song that really stepped things up and took the band's music into a whole other realm. Inspired by the work of assassinated civil rights activist Dr Martin

Luther King, as witnessed at an exhibit the band had paid a visit to in the Chicago Peace Museum, The Edge, for one, rated it "the most successful pop song we've ever written: you listen to it and you understand it almost immediately".

Bono, too, immediately accorded 'Pride ...' a special place in his heart. As he said, it was a one-off. "We've done very few songs," he mused at the time, "normally we just make music. It's very different from the rest of the album though – there's nothing on there as straight as this." Indeed, he said he thought the rest of the record "totally devoid of the tricks and techniques of rock'n'roll – which is why it's foxing half the USA even as we speak."

Whatever the fans or critics thought of it, ultimately, said Bono, he saw *The Unforgettable Fire* as "very unlike a billboard or an advertising slogan", and much more like "a beautifully out-of-focus record, blurred like an impressionist painting. These days we are being fed a very airbrushed, advertising man's way of seeing the world. In the cinema I find myself reacting against the perfect cinematography and the beautiful art direction – it's all too beautiful, too much like an ad."

U2 may have tired of war, but that didn't mean they were now shirking reality. Certainly, Bono's lyrics, when they were direct, were still ready to tackle the gloom head on, as with the darkly hypnotic 'Wire' and its evil twin, 'Bad', both tracks riven with stark images of drug abuse and self-loathing. As Bono explained at the time: " 'Wire', for me, is an image of a hypodermic needle. That's its subconscious value to me. I'm intrigued that, often, imagery that is for me subconscious, is actually quite conscious to other people." He went on to tell the story of an acquaintance of his that the song had had a very direct effect on. "A guy, somebody in the music business in London, came up to me in the Portobello Hotel and told me he had nearly died last year. Three cardiac arrests, three overdoses. He got involved in Narcotics Anonymous and [is now] sorting his life out. He told me that our music was a real soundtrack to a change in his life. And – this completely bowled me over – he knew everything I was on about on *The Unforgettable Fire*. He knew what 'Bad' was about, he knew all the feelings, he knew what 'Wire' was about. He knew the two songs that were related directly to what he'd been through. As abstract as they were …"

Even the title of the album was inspired by an atrocity, its name taken from a painting Bono had come across in a Chicago museum and had become transfixed by: a startlingly graphic piece of work depicting the American nuclear attacks on Hiroshima and Nagasaki in 1945 – the ultimate expression of hate and war. To the general public, however, *The Unforgettable Fire* was just a cool title and when it was released early in 1985, it entered the British album chart at Number 1. 'Pride (In The Name Of Love)' had already reached Number 3 in the UK singles chart, and an already booked Australian tour followed hard on its heels – too hard, as it turned out, since a writer's block which held up Bono's lyric writing had led to them delivering the tapes to Island late in August 1984, just a few short weeks before they had to hit the road or be hit by swingeing financial penalties from the tax office. It never came to that, of course – but recording *The Unforgettable Fire* had clearly left them feeling exhausted, and they hadn't even started the tour yet. The Edge, in particular, seemed to be suffering some sort of mental hangover. He became forgetful, distracted, and claimed not to be able to remember some of their oldest songs. So thoroughly expunged from his thoughts had their previous music been while he'd been working on the new album, one story, possibly apocryphal, actually has The Edge sending a roadie out in Sydney to buy all the old U2 albums so he could relearn the songs! Meanwhile, so rusty had the others become that it was said a rendition of 'Gloria' on some of the early dates was played in two different keys: the band rather uncharitably blaming "tone-deaf" Adam.

Though it was the start of their biggest, most important world tour yet, they had not even had time to rehearse any of the numbers from the new album, due to the close shave in recording, and so to begin with they were forced to play a bowdlerised version of the show they had performed for the previous *War* tour, augmented by occasional new songs, as and when they learned them while practising at sound-checks. Hardly the most auspicious of circumstances in which to launch your biggest assault yet on the world at large, backstage the atmosphere was now fraught with anxiety. Unsatisfied with the standard of their performances generally, ironically, the tour really came to life only

The Rotunda Hospital in
Dublin, where Paul Hewson
was born in 1960.

Bono performing in
Dublin, 1979.

Two of Bono's music idols:
Marc Bolan of T Rex from
the UK (above) and Bruce
Springsteen from the US (left).

An early photo of U2 shows Larry Mullen, Adam Clayton, The Edge and Bono (1980).

Bono and Adam Clayton on stage in 1981.

Bono with his wife, Ali,
in the 80s.

Bono in 1983.

Top The Edge (left) and Bono performing in San Bernadino, California, 1983.
Bottom U2 on stage in California, on tour for the album *War*.

Steve Lillywhite.

Bloody Sunday,
Londonderry, Northern
Ireland, 30 January 1972.

At Live Aid, Wembley, 1985, Bono clambers off the stage to try and reach the audience.

Live Aid performers in July 1985 included (from left) George Michael, Bono, Paul McCartney and Freddie Mercury.

following an incident at one concert where a furious Bono stopped the show after he saw violence break out in the cheap seats at the back. Pointing at the perpetrators as he called a halt to the music, he thundered: "We do not have violence at U2 gigs. Not ever. Enough!" Remarkably, it worked: the shamed perpetrators returned sheepishly to their seats, and the show rolled on, only better than before. Louder and more rowdy. More in the moment again. The tour had finally begun.

By the time U2 had left Australia behind to begin a European leg headlining sold-out ten-thousand-seater arenas in Germany, Italy, France, Belgium, Holland and Switzerland, they were now clearly a worldwide phenomenon. Four of their albums were now dominating the charts Down Under. Meanwhile, having already sent *The Unforgettable Fire* to Number 1, a new generation of U2 fans began buying both *Under a Blood Red Sky* and *War*, both of which were now back in the UK Top 50. While in the States, *The Unforgettable Fire* had entered the charts at Number 47 with a bullet. Six weeks later it was nestling like a snake in the belly of the US Top 10. Nevertheless, Bono still detected a certain backlash from both people in the biz, and certain fans themselves, who had assumed until then that U2 were the future of stadium rock and were unwilling, or unable, at first, to trust their new musical direction. Bono recalls being accosted for this by more than one disgruntled critic in America. "They went, 'What are you doin' with this doggone hippie Eno album?'" he laughed. But, he added, more seriously, "We owe Eno and Lanois so much for seeing through to the heart of U2."

Mainly, Bono said, he thrived on the more genuine feedback he got on the album from outside the magic circle of the music biz. For example, at one point on that year's US tour, he had joined in with a demonstration at Columbia University, a hunger strike protesting against the apartheid regime in South Africa. "I went down there and found that 'Pride ...' was on the tape they were listening to in their sleeping bags in the pissing rain, and that gave me some encouragement. That's not why you set out to write a song – but if it has an impact on another person's life as much as it's had on your life, well, I'm pleased."

Bono was also pleased to find that many of U2's fans, inspired by his rhetoric, had now been getting involved in more direct political action. "Things like famine relief organisations and anti-nuclear movements," he said. "People just feeling, 'Yeah, I'm going to find my place in this.' That's their place, off stage."

Just before leaving Dublin, Bono had accepted an invitation from Bob Dylan, no less, to return to Slane Castle where Dylan was playing a huge outdoor concert, and actually get up and sing with him. The number Dylan had suggested Bono join him on was 'Blowin' In The Wind', the classic anti-war anthem from the Sixties, originally made famous by Peter, Paul and Mary, and one of the big encores that Dylan routinely ended his shows with. Bono readily agreed, nodding when Bob asked him if he knew the lyrics. In truth, however, Bono hardly knew the words at all, and even though he asked for a lyric sheet – hastily scribbled out for him by his friend Neil McCormick – once he was jumping around on the Slane stage, striking poses, he had hurled it to the wind and improvised his own words – mainly, from what could be discerned in the crowd, about the ongoing conflict in Northern Ireland. Dylan, still trying to stick to the actual lyrics of the song, looked across at his guest star perplexed as he leapt about the stage shouting about war and injustice. Arguably, Bono had stayed true to the song's purist spirit, and the crowd – if not a seemingly nonplussed Dylan – roared its approval.

Afterwards, however, the veteran minstrel admitted he had to admire "the kid's guts" in getting up there and just busking the whole thing. Most artists, invited on to the same stage as the master, would have wilted under the glare. Not this one. Oh, no. Dylan was intrigued. In fact, sharing the stage at the Slane show would prove to be the first step towards what has turned out to be a long, mutually respectful friendship between two men seen by many, perhaps not entirely coincidentally, as the spokesmen for their respective generations.

The follow-up single to the barnstorming 'Pride ...' was the title track, the equally rousing, some would argue even more thought-provoking, 'The Unforgettable Fire'. Released in Britain in April 1985, it eventually reached Number 6. Bono was unabashed. A hit was a hit whatever number they gave it, he argued. But a Number 1 single was still an unfulfilled ambition, even if he didn't always like to admit it. A string of high-profile British dates had been completed at the end of 1984, and included pairs of sold-out London shows at the Brixton Academy and Wembley Arena, as well as several equally hothouse shows around the rest of the country. And, of course, in between times, Bono and Adam had represented U2 by agreeing to appear on a "strictly one-off" charity single that Boomtown Rats singer and fellow Dubliner, Bob Geldof, had written with Midge Ure of Ultravox, entitled 'Do They Know It's Christmas?'.

The year of 1985 would for ever be remembered for Live Aid, of course, and not least Bono and U2's part in making it such a historic occasion. Against all odds, the event, master-minded by the tireless Geldof, was an unqualified success — at the final count, the original Band Aid single had raised in excess of £8 million, with the Live Aid concert raising over £60 million. Typically, however, Bono was not content to rest there and in September that year, just a few weeks after his performance at Wembley, he and wife Ali flew to Ethiopia's northern province of Wello, where they worked anonymously for a month with various aid agencies. "In the end we received more from the Ethiopian people than we could ever give," he said afterwards.

He also took part in the "Sun City" charity single later that year, to raise money for Artists United Against Apartheid, an organisation headed by Bruce Springsteen guitarist (and future *Sopranos* TV star) Steve Van Zandt. The "Sun City" single also gave birth to an album, for which Bono wrote and

co-sang the song 'Silver And Gold' – a bluesy, rootsy departure from the typically more austere U2 sound, and, though
nobody knew it yet, a pointer for the next direction Bono was
to take the band in. He described it at the time as "the first
song that I've ever written from somebody else's point of
view. U2 songs are always from my point of view, but this is
a departure into the third person." It was also, as he pointed
out, "the first blues-influenced song I've ever written, and I
play the guitar with my foot miked up, the way that old
bluesmen like Robert Johnson used to do. And I'm hanging
the sides of my guitar with my knuckles to keep the rhythm.
As the song goes on the tempo keeps getting faster and the
mood more and more intense."

It certainly does. The theme – the story of a man (possibly
Nelson Mandela) imprisoned for the colour of his skin, and
an old boxer down on his luck. Or as Bono would have it, "a
prize fighter in his corner being egged on by a trainer. It's a
sport that I've found increasingly interesting over the past
year. I find a lot of aspects of it very sordid, a bit like cock
fighting, or something, but the image was very powerful for
the song." Nevertheless, he admitted that he had found the
song hard to write, if for no other reason than, as he only
half-jokingly said, "because our record collections started in
1976 with Tom Verlaine, Patti Smith, the Clash and the Jam.
'Silver And Gold' was my desperate attempt – and I wrote it
in two hours – to write a song that belonged to a tradition. I
was writing it about South Africa, about a man who was at
the point of violence, which is something that fascinates me."

Even before Live Aid, the scale of U2's American success had already hit Bono when he and the rest of the band found themselves marooned on the twenty-second floor of the five-star Parker Meridian Hotel in Boston. His message over the phone to the local radio station, WBCN, sounded like a hostage reading a note: "There's a lot of people downstairs, I can't walk out on the street because people are pushing against us. So, as I say, I'm on the twenty-second floor, in this hotel room, and I wish I was on stage. I don't like this waiting around."

The on-tour level of comfort improved, however, when a turboprop Vickers Viscount airliner was hired to allow U2 the privacy and convenience of organising their own itinerary rather than conforming to airline flight times – and having to stand in too many queues being gawked at by slack-jawed passers-by. The Stateside tour of early '85 had climaxed on All Fools' Day, 1 April, with a major show at New York's fabled Madison Square Garden. On their first headline date at the venerable old arena, they won rave reviews worldwide thanks to the bevy of journalists Paul McGuinness had triumphantly flown in from all over the world to see it.

The Garden had provided the stage for some of the best in the biz – from Frank Sinatra to David Bowie via Bob Dylan and Led Zeppelin – and Bono was imbued with a sense of the history he was about to become a part of as he and the band ran on to the stage that first time. In the dressing room afterwards, his back arching with pride, Bono was visibly moved by the occasion, feeling, he said, as though he were representing not just U2 but the place they had come from. "For an

Irishman to be standing on that stage means so much," he said, his voice cracking with emotion, "not just for us but for all Irishmen ..."

By the time the world tour finally wound up in Florida some five weeks later, Bono estimated that U2 had played to over half a million people in eight months, an astonishing figure to the boy from Ballymun. A final, celebratory show, held in Dublin's Croke Park that summer, saw fifty-five thousand people – a respectable international rugby or football crowd – gather to fete the homecoming heroes. After that, one, brief, final appearance doing three songs at Live Aid should be a doddle, they reasoned ...

But if we all now remember the band that day, how they spent the weeks and months that immediately followed it was less widely reported. Given that they had just spent the best part of a year working and travelling almost non-stop, not unnaturally the band largely opted to return to their abodes in Dublin and close their doors firmly behind them. Which is what they all, barring the eternally restless Bono, basically did for the next four months. Three of the members of U2, Bono included, were now happily domesticated. Larry Mullen had settled down with long-time partner Ann Acheson, though the couple would not start having children together until the mid-Nineties. By contrast, Dave "Edge" Evans had married Aislinn O'Sullivan, whom he'd met at a U2 concert in 1983. They were overjoyed to see the safe arrival of their first daughter in 1985, with whom dad was now besotted, and there would be two more daughters between then and 1989, though the couple would separate the following year. Adam, the easy-going, secular sinner to Bono's restless, tortured saint, was still happily living the bachelor life to the full.

Meanwhile, in the small amount of time he spent at home, even when he was off the road, Bono had now begun fully to explore married life with Ali. They had recently moved into the exclusive Dublin suburb of Howth, where Thin Lizzy's Phil Lynott lived, in a picturesque little cottage they had rented. But if the Hewsons might have expected the occasional visit from their illustrious new neighbour, they were sadly disappointed. The first rock superstar Southern Ireland had ever produced was fast sinking into a drug hell of his own devising and, in January 1986, died in hospital after his heart gave out. The ever compassionate Bono would later admit that it "really bothered" him that the pair had lived so close to each other for two years, yet remained so distant. Unaware of Lynott's plight and thus not in a position to help avert the tragedy, Bono still wrestled with feelings of guilt in among the sorrow.

"I would see him everywhere else but on the street [where we lived]," he once recalled. "Every time I saw him, he'd say 'Why don't you come down for a bite?' And I would say, 'You have to come up for a bite' … Every single time. And I never did call down and he never did call up. That's what came back to me. I never did call up."

One newfound group of friends Bono did find time to call upon in late 1985, however, was Clannad – aka the multitalented Brennan family from Gweedore in Donegal. Clannad had found themselves unlikely chart climbers that year after enjoying a massive hit with the single, 'Theme From Harry's Game', aka the theme tune of the epony-mously named hit TV show of the time. In the wake of that success, they had invited Bono to duet with singer Maire Brennan on the track 'In A Lifetime'. The result was a Top 20 hit in early 1986. (It also reached Number 17 when reis-sued three years later.)

Bono loved his life in Dublin with Ali, but he also yearned to be out there in the world, doing something more with his life than merely sitting around at home, however luxuriously appointed. By November, he was regularly visiting Larry Mullen's new house, also in Howth, where he would begin writing the first new batch of songs he'd attempted for a year, in order to kick-start the process of beginning the next U2 album. Thankfully, Bono found the bones of several new tunes, key lyrical phrases, coming to him easily. Nevertheless, once recording sessions with the rest of the band officially began they would extend halfway into 1986.

Encouraged once again by Eno, unlike previous albums, initial recordings for *The Joshua Tree*, as the new album would be called, took place not in conventional studios but in various, hurriedly equipped rooms at either Larry, Bono or Adam's homes. Once they had the loosely recorded frame-work down, they returned again to the familiar environs of Windmill Lane studios, where the tracks were overdubbed and the final mix completed. This new way of working clearly stimulated their creativity. Bono, in particular, found a new freedom outside the conventional studio environs. "During *The Joshua Tree* myself and Edge would be up at six o'clock in the morning, then Adam would drop in just writing songs and playing records," he recalled. "A lot of the songs were recorded in Larry's spare bedroom or Adam's living room," he continued. "When the red [studio] light is on we often don't respond to it. When we're just left to be, left to make music our own way, well … some of the tracks are almost like demos. We had to fight to make them work and there were a lot of songs left over. It could have gone off in a number of different directions We wanted the idea of a one-piece record, not a side-one, side-two thing."

It all sounded remarkably straightforward, yet the sessions at home and later at Windmill dragged on for months. In June, U2 were forced to interrupt recording, to fulfil a promise they had already made to join forces with the Band on a six-date US tour to mark the twenty-fifth anniversary of Amnesty International. So high was Bono and U2's Stateside profile now, that the tour proved a huge success, eventually raising over $4 million in audience donations, as well as almost doubling Amnesty's US membership overnight.

Flying back to Dublin that summer, Bono went straight from the airport to the studio, where work continued with the album until the end of the month. The end result, however, was well worth the extra effort – an album so broad in its scope yet so personal in its visions, an album so advanced on anything they had ever attempted before, musically, lyrically, spiritually, it would become one of the cornerstones of the Eighties.

On the surface, there were enough songs on *The Joshua Tree* to suggest that the band had not lost its overtly political edge – most emphatically on the panoramic sweep of the Zeppelinesque 'Bullet The Blue Sky', which reflected angrily on Bono's recent trips to Nicaragua and El Salvador and his first-hand experience of the cold dead hand of totalitarianism. But with The Edge discovering Hendrix for the first time as a guitar player and Bono indulging his newfound passion for American roots music and gritty prose writers like Flannery O'Connor and Raymond Carver, all of the material on the new album had a far earthier, more organic "live" feel.

Swathed in suitably moody and magnificent black-and-white shots by auteur rock photographer Anton Corbijn, the album title was taken from a hardy tree found only in the dry desert lands that separate California and Mexico – which Corbijn had cleverly suggested using as the dramatic backdrop for all the photos. As a result, not only did *The Joshua Tree* sound better than any previous U2 album, it also looked better. Produced once more by the Eno-and-Lanois team, and released in March 1987, it was immediately acclaimed as the finest, most mature U2 collection yet. It would also become their most successful, topping the charts in Britain and becoming their first Number 1 album in America as well as more than a dozen other countries, eventually selling a staggering fifteen million copies worldwide. Record stores in the USA opened at midnight to satisfy the incredible demand that now existed for all new U2 product. When *The Joshua Tree* immediately went to Number 1 there, it sparked a record-buying frenzy that propelled all five previous U2 albums into the US Top 40, a situation that had veteran industry observers harking back to the Sixties heyday of the Beatles for the last time they had seen anything like it from a "British" band. To give some idea of the exponential rise in sales, *The Unforgettable Fire* had sold around six million copies at the time its successor was released two years later; *The Joshua Tree* would sell nearly three times that amount in less than half the time. As Larry Mullen reflected in typically down-to-earth fashion, the success of *The Joshua Tree* was "not bad for a bunch of yobbos from Dublin ..."

They also became the first Irish group ever to score a Number 1 single in America with another of the album's standout tracks, 'With Or Without You', which spent three weeks at the summit in 1987. The video for 'With Or Without You' was shot on a Los Angeles rooftop, with more than a tip of the hat to that famous scene in the movie, *Let It Be*, where the Beatles climb up on the roof of Apple to blast out a spontaneous rendition of 'Get Back' and others, before being 'detained' by the police for their trouble. As a reference to the last group to dominate America's charts, the symbolism was obvious. Meanwhile, in April '87, U2 become only the third rock band in history – after the Beatles and the Who – to appear on the cover of *Time* magazine, under the emphatic headline: 'U2: Rock's Hottest Ticket'.

'With Or Without You' ("a great single ... a classic forty-five!" claimed Bono, immodestly) reached Number 4 in the UK. The follow-up single, 'I Still Haven't Found What I'm Looking For' was another Top 5 success and the band's second US Number 1. The third and final single from the album, 'Where The Streets Have No Name', was yet another huge hit on both sides of the Atlantic, reaching Number 4 in Britain and Number 13 in America. As a result, in the States, only Michael Jackson's *Bad* album would outsell *The Joshua Tree* that year, while back in Britain, Bono was astonished to be told the album had sold an amazing 250,000 copies in its first two days on sale – exactly the sort of welcome back Bono had secretly hoped for in those long, sometimes confusing months spent in the studio. Ten years on from that shambolic yet fateful "audition" in Larry's kitchen, Bono could look back on a decade of seemingly unbroken success. No, it had not been easy – what was? – but at the end of it Bono and U2 had completed their first decade together on a previously undreamed-of high.

The icing on the cake came when they scooped their first ever Grammy awards – the US music biz equivalent of the Oscars – winning both the coveted Best Rock Performance by a Duo or Group award for 'I Still Haven't Found What I'm Looking For' and Album of the Year for *The Joshua Tree*. Bono, as outwardly relaxed and inwardly coiled-up as ever, quipped from the stage: "It's actually really hard carrying the weight of the world on your shoulders, and, uh, saving the whale, and, uh, organising summits between world leaders and that sort of thing. But we enjoy our work ..."

Whatever the awards represented to each member of the band, whatever the huge material gains they also made, the overriding joy Bono took from the astounding success of *The Joshua Tree*, he said, was that he truly believed it was an album, more than any of the others, where he had finally said what he really wanted to say. "Certainly for me, as the word writer in the band. In a way, it doesn't need me to do the interviews to explain it." Nevertheless, he did attempt to explain how his songwriting methods had changed. "I used to think writing words was old-fashioned, so I *sketched*. I wrote words on the microphone. For [the songs on] *The Joshua Tree* I felt the time had come to write words that meant something, out of my experience." He concluded, somewhat enigmatically: "On this record, I'm interested in a lot of primitive symbolism, almost biblical. Some people choose to use red, some people choose turquoise. Some people like lavender. I like red."

Layers within layers, words that sometimes had more than one meaning ... this was now Bono's stock in trade as a lyricist. He still reflected directly on the world around him, but he also allowed himself to take a sideways, more impressionistic perspective on things, too. Like his new friend, Dylan, Bono considered his songs almost simplistically direct, while others could only listen sometimes and ponder. Even the title, *The Joshua Tree*, was, mused Bono, "the sort of record title you'd expect to sell three copies of". Named after "the oldest living organism in the desert", according to Larry, the title also gave its name, said Bono, to "a very odd town on the edge of the California desert. A lot of the psychedelic writers came out of there." It was even said that country star Gram Parsons was buried in the desert out there by a roadie friend, after dying from an accidental overdose in a motel room at the Joshua Tree Inn. There was a Parsons-like connection, too, in that the album was dedicated to a recently departed friend: Greg Carroll, who had joined the U2 entourage in New Zealand on the *Unforgettable Fire* world tour, before becoming a full-time member of the backstage team as Bono's personal assistant. Tragically, Carroll was killed in a horrendous car crash, at home in Dublin, during the recording of the album. Bono was absolutely devastated. "We haven't, and I don't think we ever will, get over his loss," he said sorrowfully. "And he died doing me a favour. I don't know what to say. He was one of those guys you say is too good for this world. He further made 1986 the most paradoxical year in our lives. That's why the desert attracted me as an image. That year was really a desert for us, it was a terrible time."

Those who knew his personal history appreciated Bono's point when he drew a parallel between the death of his friend and the equally unexpected loss of his mother all those years before. "Death is a real cold shower and I've had a lot," he said. "It's followed me around since I was a kid and I don't want to see any more of it."

Maybe so. But that hadn't stopped him travelling to El Salvador, then in the death grip of a totalitarian regime intent on killing and imprisoning its poorest people. This was where he wrote 'Bullet The Blue Sky', by his own admission, "out of fear, using very primitive imagery. Because Salvador looks like an ordinary city. You see McDonald's, you see children with school books, you see what looks like a middle-class environment until you go twenty-five miles out of the city and see the villagers and peasant farmers dead on the side of the road … or 'disappeared'."

Another political storyline for a song – 'Red Hill' – had emanated from closer to home with the much-publicised national miners' strike that threatened to bring down the Conservative government in Britain in the mid-Eighties. "I wrote the words to 'Red Hill' about a year after the strike [finished]," Bono recalled. "What particularly interested me, aside from the politics – because you can get bogged down in that – was the breaking down of relationships and what the strike had done to people's sex lives. Literally, you know, men and women couldn't relate to each other through losing work and losing belief in themselves."

Amid the lyrical angst and musical pyrotechnics, more than ever before, a strong gospel influence could now be heard in the music. In this context, 'I Still Haven't Found What I'm Looking For' became a hymn of despair and hope intertwined by powerfully evoked, if barely glimpsed dreams. "The spirit in which we recorded it was akin to the idea of a gospel group," agreed Bono. "We wanted to capture a moment, the feeling of a room and people being in a room, which is essential to gospel music. Eno was a real ally in this. He listens to more gospel music than anything else."

The sheer variety of moods and music now in evidence was something Bono believed harked back, above all, to the previous decade. The greatest bands of the Seventies may have sunk into musical over-indulgence at times, but they were lucky, in that they had lived through and come to epitomise an era when rock had been less afraid to test itself and experiment; when rock had still been important in people's lives. "The lack of inhibition of the Seventies," said Bono, "though it can go wrong, is right to a point. In the Eighties, people are so claustrophobic and won't make mistakes, and yet a lot of these young bands see themselves as part of the Seventies rock'n'roll tradition. They want to get away from this feeling of we-can't-play-guitar-like-that. The answer is, you can do what you like. That's what *The Joshua Tree* is about. There's electric blues wound up in 'Bullet The Blue Sky', or a simple piano piece. We were feeling bound up as well, in U2, with this sound we'd developed. We didn't want to go down in the A–Z of rock'n'roll as a band with [one] sound. We wanted to leave some songs ..."

Critically, the album took no prisoners, either, and for once Bono found his work universally acclaimed even by those magazines that had previously proved impervious to U2's charms. In the *NME*, leading writer Adrian Thrills claimed that *The Joshua Tree* was "the strongest and most complete LP they have ever released ... the 'Boy' of their debut has now surely emerged from the shadows as a man." *Rolling Stone* in the States topped even this when their annual readers' poll saw U2 beat Bruce Springsteen to the prestigious Artist of the Year award – an accolade the Boss had previously laid claim to for several years running. In the same poll, U2 also won the top spots in the categories for Best Album (*The Joshua Tree*), Best Single ('With Or Without You'), Best Band, Best Live Performance, Best Songwriter (shared equally by the group) and Best Album Cover (*The Joshua Tree*).

With the biggest album of their lives to promote, inevitably, when U2 hit the road again in 1987, it would be the start of their longest, most successful world tour yet: 110 dates that would keep them away from home for over a year, and at the end of which they would have played to over three million people and grossed an estimated $35 million. It was quite a responsibility for the four young Irishmen, still just in their mid-twenties, to shoulder, to fulfil, with the numbers of people on the tour, now relying on them for their livelihoods, running into the hundreds. More than that, there was something bothering Bono less easy to explain. Success was exciting, thrilling, inspiring. Mega-success on the scale U2 were now enjoying it, however, that could also be gut-wrenchingly frightening. Everything suddenly became magnified so that the smallest thing could spark trouble. When, early on, the band had been forced to cancel a concert for the first time in their career, after Bono lost his voice in the dry heat of an outdoor show in Arizona, some saw it as an omen. It was as if neither Bono nor anyone else in U2 could actually believe what was happening to them. As though they were simply waiting for something to go wrong; willing it, almost. When the plane carrying them across the Atlantic had been struck by lightning, it was seen as yet further proof that their luck was about to run out. That time, though, Bono merely laughed and brushed it off as "God taking a photograph" of their frightened fellow traveller in first class, the film star Sophia Loren.

As the tour wound on, relatively trouble-free, and their success continued to grow beyond anybody's wildest dreams, Bono would find new reasons to worry. Of chief concern in one interview was that the mega-success of *The Joshua Tree* would attract a new, less understanding, more mainstream audience. The kind "that is just into big bands like the Stones and Queen and aren't really a partisan audience". While that almost certainly was the case, fortunately for Bono, neither he nor the band seemed to lose their hard-core audience who, rather than being turned off by seeing the band "discovered" by so many new people, entered into the spirit of the thing and saw it, instead, as simply a triumph for good music. As Bono said: "We found out there was still a U2 audience, people who had been to the first gigs, people that had bought *Boy*, people who were growing with us, changing with us. I only hope they will be with us next year."

The feeling of making history was now palpable and, determined not to let the moment pass without comment, the band arranged to have what was now going on for them documented in some form. Not merely to reflect on their success and the huge changes it had wrought in their lives, but something that showed clearly just how far the band had moved on since the days when Bono tried to scene-steal by swinging from the stage gantry.

For those of us fortunate enough to find ourselves at some of those *Joshua Tree* tour shows, the experience was unlike any other to be had in rock at that time. Here was a band even more popular than Duran Duran or the Pet Shop Boys, who rocked as hard as the Stones and Led Zeppelin at their satanic Seventies peak. This sort of band wasn't supposed to exist in the Eighties – even Bono's hair was now unfashionably long, and The Edge's guitar solos were now stretching to dexterous lengths of Hendrix-ish proportions. Yet there they were all the same, Bono grabbing a spotlight and shining it into the faces of the audience during 'Bullet The Blue Sky' … The Edge striking his non-conformist poses, as his guitar weaves sonic spells … this was way beyond punk or the new wave or whatever was supposed to be going on in the *NME*. This was old-style rock theatre brought to its modern, raw, yet sophisticated apotheosis. It was breathtaking.

Plainly, U2 was now a different proposition from the band depicted thrusting away earnestly in *Under a Blood Red Sky*. Phil Joanou, the man behind so many of their videos, was therefore invited to shoot them in live action at indoor arenas across America. It was decided early on that all the footage would be filmed in black-and-white, in keeping with Anton Corbijn's stark cover pictures, and in dramatically sharp contrast with an earlier outdoor show shot in colour at the

Sun Devil Stadium in Tempe, Arizona. Extra live and back-stage footage would be filmed later on in the tour at Dublin's Point Depot. The main idea, explained Bono, was to do something more than just filming another live show. "That's what big rock bands do," he chided. "They take the money and run." Instead, U2's tour film would take the form of a travelogue, an open-ended documentary that would, in Bono's words, chart their "lyrical, spiritual and emotional exploration into the heart of America".

A great idea on paper, the realities of suddenly having to accommodate a travelling film crew on the tour would cause no little trouble or confusion for manager McGuinness, who had the task of making sure the film-makers got the access they needed, while at the same time ensuring that the band actually got some time to themselves each day – or, at least, every other day.

Musically, the band had now – perhaps predictably, given their contrary natures – decided that their next move would be, as Bono put it, to create "the sound of four men chopping down *The Joshua Tree!*" But if that, admittedly offhand, statement could have been read as a sudden detachment from their current fascination with the authentic sounds and sights, the real stories behind modern-day American culture, the truth was quite different. "I'm not just interested in America *now*," explained The Edge. "I'm interested in what has happened to America since the 1950s, during the rock'n'roll age. The character of Elvis is interesting from that point to follow, where he went and what happened to him."

For Bono, this interest extended beyond more traditional American roots music like blues, country and gospel. What he was looking for now, he said, was to get as far away from the sort of fire-and-brimstone imagery that had proved so effective from *The Unforgettable Fire* onwards and had now, he felt strongly, reached its definitive conclusion with *The Joshua Tree*. Just the thought of trying to "top it" made him feel weary to his bones, he said. "For years I had been writing all these words which I could never use for U2. I could never fit them into songs. They were words with harder edges." Now, in the wake of the dizzying success of *The Joshua Tree*, "I was in a sense looking for a new U2 where I could feel free to use these words."

The next album would have to reflect all these feelings, he insisted. And so was born the idea for *Rattle and Hum* – a part-live, part-studio double-album comprising snatches from the US *Joshua Tree* tour and a clutch of new original tunes mixed with some of the best of the old Americana in which they had been immersing themselves in those few quiet moments on their private plane. When considering material for the new album, Bono revealed how he had tried to come up with something that didn't leave him feeling outside of what he called "the rock'n'roll tradition". He recounted the story of meeting American R&B singer T-Bone Burnett in New York, at the sessions for Steve Van Zandt's Artists United Against Apartheid album. Bono recalled with faint embarrassment how the grizzled legend had "played me a song and then handed me the guitar and asked me to play one of mine". Not knowing what to play, it was the first time Bono realised that, "in that sense, U2 is more like an orchestra than a rock'n'roll band. You can't just sit down and strum 'The Unforgettable Fire' or 'Bad' ... As far as I remember, I turned the guitar over and just beat the back and sang a song or two." It was a moment that afforded him a valuable insight, he said. It was "this feeling of wanting to be able to write songs in the traditional sense that led to songs like 'Silver And Gold'", and the later direction of the new songs on *Rattle and Hum*. "I want to reveal the dark side as well as the light side of who I am."

With the title taken from a line in 'Bullet The Blue Sky', the idea was to release both the *Rattle and Hum* album and the accompanying, similarly titled, documentary film simultaneously. The world premiere of the *Rattle and Hum* movie took place in Dublin in September 1988. Tickets sold at £50 apiece, with all the proceeds going to a charity for the homeless. Even though only eight hundred people could be admitted to the screening, a seething throng of some five thousand massed outside the cinema, waiting to glimpse the band arriving in their limousines that night. Typically, and with just minutes before the film was due to start, the band suddenly materialised, not in limos, but standing on the street between the cinema and the Gresham Hotel next to it. For the next ten minutes they entertained their jubilant fans with renditions of 'When Love Comes To Town' and 'I Still Haven't Found What I'm Looking For'. They had an unexpected treat for the fans outside at the end of the show, too, when, as soon as the screening had ended to rapturous applause, the band re-emerged, again as if by magic, outside the cinema, to busk their way through 'Angel Of Harlem' and the Ben E. King soul classic 'Stand By Me', Bono improvising the majority of the lyrics as he'd only ever paid attention to the chorus before.

Despite going down extremely well on the night, however, press reaction to both the album and the movie-doc was muted, to say the least. In the giddy aftermath of the mega-success of *The Joshua Tree*, it had seemed that nothing could possibly go wrong for U2 ever again. Now, however, just when Bono least expected it, the U2 backlash began in earnest.

Never intended as any sort of auteur vision of life on the road, the loose meandering feel of both the *Rattle and Hum* film and album seemed to confuse those critics who had been waiting, perhaps, for the next big musical statement from the band. Instead, what they got in the film was a vibrant, colourful, warts-and-all hotchpotch of live sequences – all excellently shot and well worth the price of admission – and a lot of informal off-stage meanderings, some of it worth repeat-viewing, most of it not. Well-intentioned, if gnawingly naïve in some respects, as a target for the critics, it was like a red rag to a bull. The band were ridiculed for the sequences when they busk on the street or try to hang out with genuine blues legends like B. B. King, but most of all, it seemed, just for their sheer audacity in embarking on such a vainglorious scheme.

Although several Hollywood studios had expressed an interest in funding the project, the U2 members and Paul

McGuinness had clubbed together and put up the money to make the film themselves, in order to ensure total artistic freedom. In retrospect, however, as Bono would later privately admit, this may have, ironically, proved to be the fatal flaw of the film. The first time in his career that Bono had had to face serious criticism from his peers, in 1993, with the benefit of five years' hindsight, he admitted that even he now found *Rattle and Hum* a hard film to try and sit through. "Maybe we just weren't paying attention," he mused. "The whole thing was just throwaway to us, in the best sense of the word – not just the movie, but the record. That showed us just how powerful the media are. We genuinely believed it was a record about being fans of rock-'n'roll. And we put a bit of Johnny Cash there ['When Love Comes To Town'] and a song about Billie Holiday here ['Angel Of Harlem'] to kind of show we were just fans. It was so obvious to us. Maybe we didn't understand how successful we were and that it looked like we were hanging out with these guys so, by association, that we were one of the greats. We never saw it that way."

The *Rattle and Hum* album, released a few weeks after the film, in October 1988, was no less freewheeling, and just as crossly received by sections of the press. Which is a shame, because *Rattle and Hum* is a fine U2 album. You can measure it against *The Joshua Tree* and call it retrogressive, and there's no doubt it was a step sideways. Bono's point was: that's all right, too. You don't always have to have all the right answers. Sometimes it's OK simply to sing and dance and enjoy the moment. Fortunately for nervous record company executives all over the world, U2 fans by and large ignored the dire warnings of the critics and immediately sent *Rattle and Hum* to the top of the charts again on both sides of the Atlantic. Indeed, despite the poison-pen letters that continue to appear in the music press whenever the album is mentioned, within five years of its initial release, the *Rattle and Hum* album had sold more than eleven million copies worldwide.

As if further to stick one in the eye of the ponderous critics who had taken such delight in pooh-poohing the whole project, *Rattle and Hum* would also provide Bono with his long-desired chart-topping British single. Built on an ancient Bo Diddley beat beefed up by futuristic-sounding guitars and howling lone-wolf vocals, the storming 'Desire' may not have been the most original-sounding offering U2 had ever presented, but it connected immediately. The song's sparse, basic sound was deliberate – it was, in fact, a demo recorded "in five minutes", Bono admitted. "We nearly chickened out of [releasing] it but we didn't."

The subject matter, Bono explained, was "blind ambition ... the ambition to be in a band. You don't join a band to save the world ... we started off through just being bored at school. We didn't want to get a job in a factory or work for the government. We didn't want to be schoolteachers or join the army or whatever. People get in bands for all the wrong reasons, not the right reasons."

'Desire', which peaked at Number 3 in the States, hit the top in Britain in October, deposing a rerelease of the Hollies' hoary old Sixties hit, 'He Ain't Heavy, He's My Brother' (now resurrected for seemingly the thousandth time as the music to a TV ad) and frustrating Phil Collins's equally backward-looking Sixties revival hit, 'A Groovy Kind Of Love', taken from the Great Train Robbery film, *Buster*, in which Collins starred. Save for Bon Jovi's predictably formulaic 'Bad Medicine' single, U2 were the only rock representatives in that month's listings, but in terms of an advertisement for the forthcoming album 'Desire' more than did its job; a second single, the infectious, soul-tinged 'Angel Of Harlem', would also make the Top 10 later that year.

The option of a straight-ahead double live concert album, Bono explained, had been deliberately avoided with *Rattle and Hum*. "The double live LP has been exciting over the years, but with very few exceptions it's a pile of crap and basically a cash-in by big fat rock bands – to extort more money from their fans. We felt that if we were going to put out a soundtrack to a film we'd better put out something more interesting. So we came up with *Rattle and Hum...* It's just our way round the problem."

Five of the songs for the album had been recorded at the legendary Sun Studios in Memphis, where the likes of Elvis Presley, Jerry Lee Lewis, Roy Orbison and Johnny Cash had recorded some of rock's earliest and most seminal sides back in the Fifties. "It was a totally mind-blowing privilege to be playing there," said Bono, ever the fan. "In fact, I'm embarrassed to say this, but I saw this old microphone in the corner and I asked the producer if I could use it, and he said: 'Elvis used this mic but it doesn't work now.' So I said: 'Are you sure?' So he plugged it in and it worked! It really did work! And actually – this sounds like total bullshit, but it's the truth – 'Angel Of Harlem' was recorded singing through Elvis's mic! I only wish I could sing like Elvis," he added with a stubbly smile.

Being in Memphis, Bono and the band had also felt obliged to pay a visit to Elvis's Graceland mansion, where they did their best not to act like Spinal Tap. Then later that same evening, they arrived at Sun, where they stayed from 7.30 until the not so early hours of the morning. Playing specially hired instruments, as they hadn't brought any of their own with them, the legendary Memphis Horns – stalwarts of countless classic Sun sessions – were among the extra musicians who also took part in the sessions. While entering the studios, Bono is reported to have said reverentially: "There would be no U2, there would have been no Elvis, if there hadn't been a Sun."

Ultimately, said Bono, *Rattle and Hum* was always supposed to be an album "made by fans – we wanted to own up to being fans. And we thought rock'n'roll bands just didn't do that – we all know they are, but they don't do it. The Rolling Stones did it on *Exile on Main Street*, sort of, and it was kind of a role model [for *Rattle and Hum*]. But we wanted to go even further and have pictures because there's people out there who probably don't even know who Billie Holiday is or who B. B. King is. We thought of it as, 'We have this thing, U2. Now let's just put it aside almost and let's just get lost in this music.'"

In cutting loose from those aspects of their past they had once viewed as essential apparatus, Bono accepted that U2 were now making what may have seemed like unnecessary demands on their audience, but he had more faith in them than that, he said. He described a typical U2 record buyer as someone "into the where-to-next kind of approach. They're one step ahead of us in some ways. Rather than have to lead the audience around by the nose, we get the sense that they're right behind us every step of the way. We thought if we stripped away the U2 sound completely, if we immersed ourselves in gospel music, country, soul ... we're bound to shake off at least fifty per cent of U2 fans: they can't cope with this. But they really could. We might have the most elastic audience when you think of what we've gone through in the last five years. As long as the songs are good they'll go with us all the way. When we start writing shit songs then I'll know it's over."

Having already presided over the production of *Under a Blood Red Sky*, their first US-recorded live album, Jimmy Iovine had been the natural choice to produce the live tracks on the new album. It also made sense, Bono reasoned, to have someone on board who understood the roots of American music, given the decidedly retrospective, not to say reverential, musical stance *Rattle and Hum* was to take. There wouldn't be an official tour to promote the album – the film was intended to do that, winning the members of U2 some much-needed off-road time to attend to their private lives before they completely withered on the vine – but many of the new songs it contained would be played live in the autumn of 1989 when the band completed what they dubbed the Lovetown tour of Australasia and Europe.

Instead of consisting of separate live and studio albums, as might have been expected, *Rattle and Hum* interspersed live cuts and new studio songs, including, unusually for a U2 album, a couple of cover versions. The band had been playing many different cover versions on stage over the years, either whole songs or snatches interpolated into U2's own compositions – most famously, as at Live Aid – and the track selection here continued in that stage tradition. The Beatles' 'Helter Skelter' kicked off proceedings – a daring choice given its Charles Manson mass-murder connections (not to mention the almost impossible task of trying to emulate that frenzied rhythm) and not one even U2 were able to pull off entirely convincingly, it has to be said. Followed by the album's only really cringe-making moment, when they recklessly attempt Dylan's 'All Along The Watchtower', cranked out more in the fashion of the famously explosive Hendrix cover than the physically frail, acoustic original – and adding little to it. But then that was hardly surprising, given what Bono had to say about it later. "What other band in our position would learn the chords five minutes before they went on stage, play it live and record it?" he asked.

Three recent songs, 'I Still Haven't Found What I'm Looking For' (recorded live in New York with the New Voices of Freedom gospel choir), 'Pride (In The Name Of

Love)' and a hair-raisingly ferocious 'Bullet The Blue Sky' were also featured in scintillating new live versions, while 'Silver And Gold', Bono's first de facto solo track, was subsumed into the concert repertoire and interpreted in typically blistering U2 style.

Aside from 'Desire', the song most U2 fans now associate with the project is 'When Love Comes To Town', which also featured, rather wonderfully, the guitar and vocal talents of B. B. King. Cut live on the killing floor at Sun Studio in November 1987, all that was missing from the session was the legendary bluesman himself. Unfortunately, King, as ever, was gigging and so added his own contribution in a different studio some time later. Nevertheless King's band supported U2 that same month at Fort Worth, Texas, stepping up to perform the song with the headliners, and the *Rattle and Hum* film contains footage of both the soundcheck rehearsal and the performance itself. When it was released as the third single from the album in April 1989, the song would reach Number 6 in Britain, as well as becoming another sizeable hit for them in the USA and the rest of the world. Its biblical allusions even earned praise from King himself. "How old are you?" he asked Bono in mock amazement. When Bono asked why, the guitarist replied: "[Because] they're heavy lyrics. *Heavy* lyrics."

Another of the new songs, 'Love Rescue Me', was actually co-written by Bono with Bob Dylan, pursuing the relationship first struck on stage at Slane Castle and about to bear fruit again when Dylan decided to take Bono up on his suggestion of working with producer Daniel Lanois (resulting in the critically acclaimed *Oh Mercy* album in 1989). Recounting the story of how he and Dylan came to work together, Bono recalled how he had been staying in Beverly Hills and, after a sleepless night dreaming, had a call simply inviting him over to Bob's house in Malibu.

"I woke up with an awful bleedin' hangover one day," he said, "and I had [the melody to 'Love Rescue Me'] in my head. Some of the words were in my head at the same time and I thought, 'Oh God, do I have to write this down now?' I just wanted to go back to bed. But I couldn't avoid it, so I wrote it down." He also noticed in his frazzled state that, unusually, the start of the song "sounded like a Bob Dylan song. I thought maybe it *was* a Bob Dylan song – signs of megalomania in that too." Later, talking with Dylan at his home, Bono, still unable to get the song out of his mind, came out and asked him straight. "I went up and said, 'This isn't one of yours, is it?' And he [listened and] said: 'No, but you know, we could write it now.' So we wrote it."

As far as the film of *Rattle and Hum* went, Bono laughingly admitted he'd abandoned any stray thoughts of impending matinee idol status the moment he saw the early rushes. "I thought I looked like Robert Wagner until I saw myself on screen," he joked. "The idea for the film was that the director, Phil Joanou, would make us all look like movie stars. The deal was that we'd all look like Montgomery Clift ..." Nevertheless, he felt Joanou had done a more than passable job, whatever the critics had to say about it. "We needed someone robust enough to stand life on the road, the whole lifestyle. Phil had to be capable of being locked up in a flight case. We responded to him in the end and he prised the best possible film out of us. One thing I didn't like about Phil Joanou though – he was better-looking than me!"

The presence of the iconic 'Sunday Bloody Sunday' – one of the most affecting clips in the film – was also down to Joanou, Bono confessed; the singer having originally been staunchly against its inclusion. "I stand by everything I said [in the song lyrics] because it was the truth. It was the way we felt, on that day, on that night," Bono explained. However, he was "not sure that we'll ever play that song again. That's the way I feel about it [now]. I've just about had it up to here with 'Sunday Bloody Sunday' as a song and the weight it carries."

The real and abiding problem with *Rattle and Hum*, as Bono had earlier hinted, was that, in trying to portray themselves as fans of American music making pilgrimages to the "shrines" where rock was first forged, U2 ran the risk of being seen to rank *themselves* among the great and the good. Probably just as well then that their trip to Elvis Presley's Graceland mansion was edited out of the finished film ...

Despite the self-deprecating, philosophical face Bono would put on the critical mauling *Rattle and Hum* had received, there's little doubt that the criticism he received personally for the project cut Bono far deeper than he'd ever care publicly to admit. In fact, it would be nearly another three years before any more of any substance would be heard from either the man or his band. Whether right or wrong, Bono understood that the criticism meant they would be wise to go no further in that direction, and that whatever U2 did next it really would have to be better than anything they'd done before. Above all, it would have to be something *different*.

Nevertheless, he looked forward to the turn of the decade with a cautious optimism, he said. There was simply "something in the air" even if he couldn't yet put it into words. A feeling made more palpable, he later recalled, by the collapse of the Berlin Wall, in November 1989. Witnessing this momentous occasion in the story of the twentieth century, the band felt so moved by the television pictures they were watching at home in Dublin that they actually caught the last flight into East Berlin to join in the street celebrations. Led by Bono, they spent most of the trip checking out the ancient Trabant cars and noting the only station where trains had been allowed to move between East and West: the ominously named Zoo Station.

Suitably inspired, when the band returned home to play their final show of the *Rattle and Hum* tour on New Year's Eve, 1989, at Dublin's massive Point Arena, Bono announced at the end of the show that he and the band would not be seeing the audience "for a while". Amid a hale of boos and cheers, nobody quite knowing what to make of this latest declaration of intent from the charismatic front man, he motioned for silence and continued. "We have to go away and dream it all up again," he announced enigmatically. Then the band, eager perhaps not to prolong the moment or invest it with too much meaning, thundered into the final song and

Bono said no more. Inevitably, the press took it as a hint of an imminent split in the group, and though they continued to deny it publicly, in some ways, that's exactly what it was.

The next day, Bono recalls waking up at home in bed, thinking he should be looking forward to the start of a whole new decade – and realising, suddenly, he had absolutely "no idea what to do".

CHAPTER FOUR 1989–1999

By the end of the Eighties, U2 were now a major hit band all over the world, Bono their instantly recognisable poster boy. Nowhere was their success more clearly demonstrated, though, than in America. The critics, both in Britain and America, may have had a field day knocking spots off the *Rattle and Hum* album and film, but in 1989 the readers of *Rolling Stone* were near-unanimous in their overwhelming approval, voting both Bono and U2 top in no fewer than nine of the most high-profile categories in their annual poll: Artist of the Year, Best Band, Best Album, Best Album Cover, Best Single ('Desire'), Best Producer (Jimmy Iovine), Best Male Singer, Best Drummer and Best Bassist. They would have made a clean sweep on the honours, only The Edge narrowly missed out, coming second in the Best Guitarist category, the accolade going instead to Eddie Van Halen.

The work they had been obliged to put in, though, to make it happen – the endless, back-breaking tours, stretching back to 1981 – had slowly taken its toll. The sights and sounds of the road had long since shed their novelty value, even for the magpie-eyed Bono, to whom the States had represented a land of opportunity and wonder for as long as he could remember. The years spent away from home, however, helping build the U2 empire, had left him tired and feeling empty, a shell of his former self. As he later said, "If you spend too long [on tour] in America you get sick of the constant hard sell. The first thing I do when I get home is to order a pint of Guinness and listen to some traditional music … doing this helps remind me of what normal life is all about. I'm not from the limo/private jet/luxury hotel type of world that has become part of the territory with U2 [now]."

But if the band had truly been sucked in by the US music machine (to be spewed out fat and bloated at the other end, as some of their detractors had suggested), they would surely never have thought of pulling a stunt like using that most unusual of US icons, Germanic sex therapist Dr Ruth, to announce the release of their next album, the adventurously titled *Achtung Baby!*, live on television and radio throughout the United States – what's more, on the grounds, they claimed, that they considered it their sexiest record yet! The message was clear: while U2 were happy to dance with the corporate bigwigs of America, they preferred to do it to a tune of their own choosing. The new album would also see a radical realignment of the band's musical direction, and rather as David Bowie had done thirteen years earlier with Brian Eno, they headed to Hansa Studios in Berlin, situated next to the fabled Berlin Wall (the remains of which were still then very much in evidence and as earlier eulogised by Bowie on 'Heroes'). Bono arrived with the band in Berlin, ready to record their first album of the Nineties, in a mood of cautious optimism and what he called "a totally open mind about where we go next".

With Eno now wielding more influence than ever, the new album's clanking European electronics and eccentrically treated voices and instruments would echo throughout their next three albums. Rather than try to clone their biggest sellers, as most major bands would have done at this crucial moment, U2 preferred instead to look on their wealth of earlier hits as now liberating them from having to repeat themselves, so that they could now finally make the music they wanted, as devoid of commercial constraints as they had ever dared themselves to be in the studio. "We couldn't care less about the success of our records at this point," said Bono defiantly. "We've had one LP [*The Joshua Tree*] that sold so many records that we don't have to worry about things like that again. We didn't even worry in the first place, I must say. But we certainly don't worry now. We're just after music …"

In essence, the new album, explained Bono, would represent "a new start" for U2. "Things move in shifts. I mean, there's another record that belongs with this, just as *Rattle and Hum* belonged with *The Joshua Tree*. I know that record, I can hear it in my head. And we have notes, we have songs already for our next record as it happens. There's more where that came from. So I can see further down the road."

The singer also noted that in the past the building Hansa Studios now occupied had been used at different times during the Second World War as a ballroom by both the Allies and the SS. He still shivered at the thought, he said. "[But] when we went in there we asked ourselves: 'Are there still any demons in the room?' We had the sense that if there had been any demons, music had driven them out." He added: "I think fear of the devil leads to devil worship. And I don't want to give fascists the power over you to the extent you might be afraid to go into a building where they once were. You should take these icons and change them."

Bono had started writing the songs that became *Achtung Baby!* during a break with Ali in Australia. Staying at their own private luxury apartment in Sydney, even in that most cosmopolitan of cities Bono found himself subject to the kind of interpersonal surveillance that would inspire some of the album's dark, edgy mood. Though, as ever, he was still prepared to see the funny side, too. He talked of a woman living in the apartment opposite that "I used to watch when I'd come in at six, seven in the morning. She was overweight, had a punk haircut, and used to get home around the same time I did. I made up a whole life for her – that she ran a punk club, that her parents financed it for her. I started watching her through a telescope. We excuse a lot in the name of reconnaissance! One night I was watching her and I happened to look two windows above her. There was another woman with another telescope watching me! I was *furious*! I was so offended, I jumped up and called her a bitch and pulled the curtains shut."

The Edge's marriage to Aislinn sadly came to an end during this period, and it was put to Bono that his friend's heartbreak over his recent divorce must surely have been the inspiration for some of his own contributions to the material on *Achtung Baby!*. He didn't deny it. "Oh, there's lots of stories in there, by no means only [The Edge's]. In fact, it's the story of just about everybody I know. People are desperately trying to hold on to each other in a time when it's very hard to do that. And the bittersweet love song is something I think we do very well. It's a tradition, and Roy Orbison was probably the greatest in that tradition."

More happily, Larry and Bono's own marriages still appeared rock-solid. Indeed, Bono and Ali became proud parents for the first time on the singer's twenty-ninth birthday, on 10 May 1989, when their first child, a beautiful baby girl they named Jordan, was born in Dublin's Mount Carmel Hospital. No concert, however big or important, no amount of record sales, had ever matched the thrill Bono now felt every time he looked at or even thought of his tiny daughter. Deciding their present home was too small to bring up a brood, Bono hired a private helicopter at a reported £300 an hour to help him and Ali look for a new home. Their eventual choice was a nine-bedroom mansion of Victorian style in County Dublin, an area long popular with pop and film stars in Ireland.

Bono was well aware of the fact that he was now a rich man, and the way this information was received by certain sections of the public. However, he delighted in the fact that, as he said, "From all the flak we get from the middle class, we still have a huge working-class audience ... I think [ordinary] people feel, 'well, it's his business'. And they know we pay taxes and they know we make a lot of money for the country anyway. I mean, I don't mind paying taxes, though I try to pay as little as I can, obviously – I prefer to equally distribute my wealth."

He continued: "I think I've said before that I always felt rich. When we were growing up in the Lipton Village gang, some of us had money, some of us didn't. I didn't notice. I was being supported by my mates, by Ali, by everything. But I'm not stupid. I know how to make money, and probably have some sense in that area, but I'm not interested in it for its own sake and never have been. You know, my old man laughs at me – he finds it hysterically funny, cos I was never interested in money. He thinks this is evidence of God's sense of humour because I'm not that way."

Though the Hewson family was now growing – a second daughter, Memphis Eve, would follow in July 1991 – Bono still refused to leave himself out of the firing line when it came to his new lyrics. For example, one of the new songs he had written called 'Acrobat' was, he said, "a song about hypocrisy – my own hypocrisy as much as anything. That's what we started on *Achtung Baby!*. It was just to get into the politics of your own heart and start with that."

The pressures of fame even got to Adam, who with his bachelor lifestyle was, perhaps, the one most aware of and vulnerable to the constant public attention that he and his band-mates now received wherever they went in the world. Now resident in a "fortified mansion" in Rathfarnham, south

Dublin, far away from prying eyes, Adam disappointed all his friends when he was busted in a Dublin car park for possession of nineteen grammes of cannabis. He'd always been the band member singled out at customs for special attention as he looked the most obviously "rock star-ish" of the quartet, but on this occasion he was able to get away with it by donating £25,000 to charity and thus avoid a criminal record (which could have proved problematical for future US tours).

Not that a sum of money like that would prove to be a problem for the newly minted bass player, especially after Paul McGuinness had secured another good record deal for the band. In 1993, four years after Island boss, Chris Blackwell, sold his famous label to the multinational PolyGram conglomerate for £200 million, U2 secured a reported $60 million for six more albums at a generous 25 per cent royalty, an almost unprecedented sum for an artist now, let alone fifteen years ago.

However, neither Bono nor his wily manager was as happy about a book published that year by former Eire international footballer turned sports journalist Eamon Dunphy. Bono and the band had long been besieged by requests from book publishers in London and New York to write their own official band biography, but had so far resisted, partly, they said, because they simply didn't feel enough of the U2 story had actually unfolded yet for it to make a really conclusive book, and partly, they confessed, because they couldn't think of a writer who might be able to tell their story in a truly empathetic way. Dunphy, a generation older than the band but from the same grass roots in Dublin, seemed like an inspired choice at the time it was first proposed to Bono and the band. But they soon came to change their minds.

In fact, having agreed to collaborate with Dunphy on what was hoped would be an officially sanctioned biography, to be titled *The Unforgettable Fire*, the two sides were to fall out so spectacularly that McGuinness was moved to tell the press: "We intensely regret doing this book." Undaunted, Dunphy laughed all the way to the bank with an estimated £250,000 advance, while the finished book itself – a dense read for most fans, which spent too long on the socio-polit-ical context of the band's music rather than either the band or the music itself – still went on to become a worldwide best-seller.

In the extended break they had taken in the lead up to recording *Achtung Baby!*, U2 had also put some time and no little effort into an intriguing and, briefly, fruitful side project they called Mother Records: a small, independently run label outlet aimed specifically at encouraging emerging Irish talent. As Bono explained, before Mother Records, if you were a new band in Ireland, "there was nothing or nobody you could turn to for advice. Obviously people like Bob Geldof and Phil Lynott, God bless him, were there to help you out if they could, and I remember Adam ringing Phil up one morning at about eight o'clock and asking him something about a recording contract! But that was it! Hopefully now people don't feel that same lack of help and that same pressure to leave the country before they're really ready for it."

Always ready to put their money where Bono's mouth was, Mother actually did quite well to begin with, and some of its earliest signings were impressive new Irish outfits like In Tua Nua, Cactus World News and, most noteworthy, the Hothouse Flowers – all of whom released first singles on Mother that would prove to be stepping stones to major-label contracts for all of them and a more realistic chance of international fame. As with all such ventures, however, the band-run label soon lost momentum once U2 began slowly to reassemble. Not that Bono had actually had any misplaced visions of creating an Apple-like monolith, as the Beatles had. As he explained in February 1988: "It's not meant to be a record company or a label that brings out stuff regularly and ties bands to contracts or anything like that. It's just a bit of a leg-up in that really early period when most bands here [in Ireland] can't even get a single out. If a record company then comes along after that and signs up the group, then fine."

Another couple of fascinating musical interludes occurred on the way to making the new album, including one track, a movingly tender reading by Bono of the bittersweet Cole Porter classic 'Night And Day', which was dedicated to an AIDS charity fundraising album called *Red Hot and Blue*. The band also agreed to supply the music to accompany a stage version of Anthony Burgess's celebrated novel *A Clockwork Orange* (famously turned, in 1972, into the apocalyptic Stanley Kubrick film of the same name). Although the Royal Shakespeare Company was involved, however, this didn't prevent Bono and U2 receiving the sharp end of author Burgess's tongue; he strongly disapproved of the choice of music and made no bones about saying so in the press – comparing U2's efforts disparagingly to Beethoven, his own choice of soundtrack. Forced to respond, a nonplussed Bono simply shrugged and said he thought the septuagenarian author should "stick to writing – that's what he's good at".

One thing Bono did have to agree on, though, was that what U2 were really good at was making music – not cover versions, however inspired, or even stage-show music, but their own kind of music: rock'n'roll plus all the usual complications. As such, the troubled gestation period between the end of the *Rattle and Hum* tour in Dublin, in December 1989, and the arrival in the shops of *Achtung Baby!* almost two years later, once again brought the band almost to the point of throwing in the towel and breaking up. The Edge, in particular, was once again experiencing great difficulty trying to reconcile the band's more outspoken songs with his own deeply held religious beliefs. With what he saw as the largely self-inflicted wounds of his recently collapsed marriage still raw and open, he explained how that, for him, the worst thing about being away on the road for so long "is coming home and spending two months trying to pick up the threads of the life you had before you left. You spend a lot of time finding normal life very weird."

So weird, in fact, that he had already considered leaving many times before – only to change his mind or be persuaded back at the last minute. Would that be the case again now, though? Or would he finally carry out his threat to quit? Bono didn't know. But he did try to counter the troubled guitarist's threats to leave by letting The Edge know in no uncertain terms that he would "break the band up" if he did leave. The Edge drew his breath and sat back down – for now. He just wanted to do the right thing, he just didn't know what it was any more. As a result, as he later admitted, "the magic just wasn't there for a long time". There was a view, unspoken in the studio yet none the less palpable, particularly during the earliest sessions in Berlin, that if the new music the band was now determined to create failed to reach the high standards of *The Joshua Tree*, this would be The Edge's last album with the band.

Little wonder then that the album's release in November 1991 was accompanied by four deep exhalations, and as usual it was left to Bono to put the collective sigh of relief into words. "I just can't believe that we've finished the record and that it's out," he shook his head. "That's what's amazing to me, because we've been working on it for about a year and you forget that when it's out people are going to be listening to it in the kind of way they are. It's been really amazing to hear people singing the songs and getting lost in the music. I really love that, it's great."

At manager Paul McGuinness's insistence, the entire *Achtung Baby!* sessions had been blanketed by a total press ban, a decision Bono was happy to comply with. As he later explained, "We thought everyone was just sick and tired of hearing us talk, so we decided that we wouldn't [talk] … not until we figured out what we wanted to say. We just didn't want to do interviews, basically, because it was the predictable thing to do, and also what happens is you finish an album, and immediately after you've got to go off and start explaining yourself – and that's just the wrong moment to do that," while you're still in the studio making the album, "because you're so wrapped up in it".

Unfortunately, much to Bono's chagrin, a recording of some of the early sessions from *Achtung Baby!* was later smuggled out of the studio by shadowy persons unknown and immediately bootlegged – a hugely frustrating state of affairs that a clearly miffed Bono likened to "having your [private] notebook read out. That's the bit I didn't like about it ... There were no great undiscovered works of genius, unfortunately, it was mostly gobbledegook." He did retain enough of his sense of humour later to reflect, however, that there were, in fact, "a few bits and pieces on that bootleg that I actually liked, when I got a copy". He confessed that "I had to go out and buy one, of course, myself. The thing about bootlegs is ... the only thing that can piss you off is if people are charging a lot of money for something that isn't very good, and that was maybe the story [here]."

Undeterred – McGuinness had looked into it and there was precious little they could do about it anyway – the band soldiered on in Hansa with an increasingly excited Eno at the controls. As a producer and artist in his own right, Eno may have professed to being beyond such cares, but even he was delighted at how fascinatingly fresh so much of the new, more experimental material was turning out to be. One of the most transcendent moments in the studio came with the recording of the album's standout track, the enigmatically titled 'One'. Beginning life as "just a doodle" on The Edge's guitar, by the time Bono and the band had worked their magic on it, 'One' was arguably the most intensely moving track U2 had ever recorded, a beautiful, haunting refrain that builds into a bonfire of pure, nailed-to-the-cross passion and emotion. Indeed, one of the great dichotomies of what would come to be seen as a huge artistic leap of faith for the band was the fact that both 'One' and the album itself would prove so popular. So much so that, unusually, the band would eventually allow the record company to release no fewer than five singles from the album, all of which would become substantial hits. To wit: 'The Fly', which reached Number 1 in the UK, 'Mysterious Ways' (Number 13), 'One' (Number 6), 'Even Better Than The Real Thing' (Number 8) and 'Who's Gonna Ride Your Wild Horses' (Number 14) – overwhelming testimony to the all-round strength of the new, so-called more 'difficult' material.

With the UK singles charts now featuring an increasingly high turnover of hits, the decision to delete the first *Achtung Baby!* single, 'The Fly', after just three weeks on sale in British shops – and at a time when it was still riding high in the Top 10 – was a tactic intended to overcome over-exposure, claimed McGuinness. Or as he put it: "To get it out of the way for the next one." Nevertheless, there were more than a few critics who disagreed with what they saw as such chart-

manipulative tactics and the band found themselves accused of cheap exploitation. Bono, for his part, tried his best to see both sides of the argument.

As he pointed out diplomatically, "We're in a really great position in a way because we can get away with things that bands not at our level can't get away with." Not just deleting singles quickly but actually influencing the way radio is broadcast. "It might be something like just releasing 'The Fly' and actually making American radio stations play it because it's the new U2 single. I mean, sometimes small things like that can actually make a difference and it's good fun just challenging the accepted way of doing things."

His attitude in these matters, he maintained, was a prosaically simple one. He and the band would gladly do anything they felt comfortable with to draw attention to their work and to make it a success. Or as he only half-jokingly put it: "Whatever it takes to get that bastard to Number 1. And that's what it's about, it's [about] abusing your position, that's what it is." Though he claimed that having it on release for just three weeks was not his idea but the record company's, it was, he insisted, "a really good idea". He continued: "I don't know, I just think that is a cool thing to get away … and that's our job, to abuse our position to get stuff on the radio that wouldn't normally get on the radio."

Or as he told Radio One's breakfast show early one morning in 1991, "We've had some help [with the album] and we're very pleased with it. And it is cool that you're playing [the single] and all the people are playing our records. We don't expect to get played at seven-thirty a.m., and the fact that we are I think is good – not only for U2, which it's very good for, but for the BBC because they don't look as asleep as they might do," he added.

The ominously be-shaded Fly character, first glimpsed in the dizzyingly fast-cut accompanying video to the single, would also now become Bono's new, more ambiguous stage persona: the Fly – a mysterious, amoral stage figure, or as Bono put it, someone who "needs to feel mega to feel normal". He went on to explain how "one of the lines that didn't make it into the song was that *taste is the enemy of art*. There's a point where you find yourself tiptoeing as an artist, and then you know you're in the wrong place. It's like you have a rule book, but you don't remember where you got it. And along with that being true of the music, it can become true in a wider sense. I felt like I didn't recognise the person I was supposed to be [any more], as far as what you saw in the media. There's some kind of rape that happens when you are in the spotlight, and you go along with it."

The band chose Leap Year's Day – 29 February 1992 – to launch their first Stateside tour for four years. The opening night of the tour, held at a modest (by U2 standards anyway) six-thousand-capacity arena in Lakeland, Florida, also premièred the new stage show: a postmodern patchwork of zigzag lighting, flashing images on screens and rotating mirrors. The Zoo TV tour, as it became known (in oblique reference to East Berlin's creepy Zoo Station), would also break with established U2 tradition by playing just a single night in each city – where, in the past, they would have played multiple nights – before moving on to the next, all pre-show publicity being kept to a strict minimum in order to maximise the sheer surprise of the new show itself. Not that this proved any barrier to selling out the venues: Lakeland, for example, had sold out within a matter of minutes.

Once the earliest reviews and pictures were published, the demand for tickets went through the roof. Word quickly spread of U2's stunning new show, hitting its wall-eyed audience with a bombardment of non-stop sounds and images, inviting fans not just to accept passively what they were being served, MTV-style, but to question, be challenged ... even to participate. This, the band seemed to say, was a multi-media concept taken to its fullest extent; the perfect antidote to the antipathy-as-art muse of the 'nu' seen-it-all Nineties generation X-ers. "This is technology we can abuse," Bono laughed. "Therefore we can make rock'n'roll into something new, instead of trying to pressure it, instead of trying to put a glass case around it."

The first objective, he said, had been simply to try and knock down people's preconceived ideas of what U2 was about – no easy job after more than a decade in the public eye, and particularly in the aftermath of the critical mauling their last album had received. In an effort to do just that, Bono had already made a point of distancing himself and U2 publicly from the prevailing philosophy of the Eighties. "When the Seventies were over the consensus of opinion was: let's just enjoy rock'n'roll for what it is – but with a wink.

Let's enjoy rock'n'roll with a sense of irony and trash. But I don't feel part of that."

Of course not. But, as he was now busy discovering, by inventing different stage characters, he could indulge in that very thing – even if it would come, initially, as something of a shock to both longstanding fans and critics alike. Showing a positively Brechtian sense of theatre, Bono also now set about altering his image. As the Fly, he would have his long brown hair retooled each night into a shiny black coif, don a leather jacket, pull on a pair of wraparound shades, and become the cool phantom hoodlum: part Jim Morrison, part Lou Reed. As the new decade unfolded and the next two U2 albums would continue to explore the theme, the Fly would be developed into first the Mirrorball Man, an ironically compelling "tribute" to tele-evangelists all over the world, then Mr MacPhisto, a gold-lamé-suited cross between the Devil, replete with pointy red horns, and decadent, Vegas-era Elvis with more than a touch of metaphorical burger-and-fries thrown in for good measure.

As Bono later reflected, "What we did with [the Zoo TV tour] was, again, just a way of stopping me being placed as one person because you have to accept the bold type and the caricaturing that goes on when you become a big band and have fun with it and create these alter egos. I mean, we weren't parodying at all, you know, these were other sides of myself. The snake oil salesman, the Devil, the Fly, the Mirrorball Man, it was also a way of sending out decoys in a way, because, deep down, I'm still a really nice guy … Honest."

And of course, whatever metaphysical musical games Bono felt he was now able to indulge in, both in the studio and on stage, the hard-won political savvy remained firmly intact. But if Bono's political earnestness had once seemed in danger of turning U2 into a caricature, this newly revealed sense of humour delighted fans and critics alike, adding a knowing laugh, however hollow, to the grim emotional pain so much of the album's songs dealt with. Indeed, humour – both black and white – would become the new, sexed-up Bono's on-stage calling card. Performing in Detroit on the Zoo TV tour, in March 1992, he actually stopped the show at one point to call Speedy Pizza on his satellite phone and order ten thousand pizzas to be delivered to the arena! "Deep pan or thin crust?" he asked the delighted but barely believing audience.

McGuinness's shrewd new tactic of making U2 tickets hard to come by also had a knock-on effect in that it meant the audiences they were now playing to each night were all highly motivated and receptive. While it was reported elsewhere that, in the middle of a deepening world recession, other established American stadium acts such as Dire Straits and Genesis were having trouble filling seats, U2 were blissfully bucking the trend. Absence had definitely made the heart grow fonder, it seemed, and with a show quite unlike anything they had ever presented back in the earnest Eighties, U2 were now playing to the biggest audiences of their career.

The original idea for Zoo TV, Bono revealed, had come to him "at the end of 1989 – literally, on New Year's Eve, the turn of a decade", at the final concert in Dublin. "It was a radio concert that went out all across the Soviet Union, and Eastern Europe. And we printed, in Soviet magazines, the covers to the bootlegs [we knew] they were going to make from the concert. I think five hundred, or you know – some ridiculous amount of people – five hundred million people tuned in. At that moment we got the idea for Zoo TV. I love this satellite thing. I love beaming across borders. That's what U2 is about."

Certainly, all manner of mixed messages, sounds and signs were being pumped out on banks of screens that flanked the stage as the Zoo TV tour proceeded across North America. Behind the band, provocative poses from band heroes such as Lou Reed, Elvis Presley and Public Enemy would be routinely flashed up on to the screens. Built around them: shapes, samples and sounds all jumbled together to create a live experience like no other in rock at that time. Even from the best seats of the house, right in front of the stage, you could never be *quite* sure that what you were seeing was what was actually happening. So much so that on one occasion, when roadie Stuart Morgan helpfully offered to deputise at the last minute on bass for a suddenly ailing Adam Clayton, hardly anybody in the audience even noticed, and U2 minus 1, as they jokingly referred to themselves that night, pulled off the show without missing a beat.

In Bono's view, it was simple: "Zoo TV gets its energy from turning a stadium into a living room with TVs [and] with very personal songs on a huge PA. Metal guitars, dance grooves, trash art, something for all the family, something to annoy everyone. The more contradictions the better. It's like having one hand on the positive terminal, the other on the negative – that's the energy of Zoo TV."

It was a fitting description. The first leg of the tour having ended to unanimous press acclaim in Vancouver at the end of April, the band returned home exhausted to Dublin, to regroup and be with their families for a few short weeks before setting out on the next stage of the gargantuan tour. It all began again in June when they performed at a Manchester benefit concert protesting at the environmental damage that would be caused by the foundation of a second nuclear reprocessing plant at the already notorious Sellafield site in Cumbria. The plan to import nuclear waste from around the world for this second plant to reprocess would, it was widely believed, increase by ten times the radioactive emissions already emanating from the site. In an irresistible show of bravado, Bono stopped the show that night while he pulled out his trusty sat-phone and actually tried to get then Prime Minister John Major on the line. When his request to speak to the PM was repeatedly refused, he asked the startled switchboard operator at 10 Downing Street if he could leave a message: "Could you tell him to watch more TV?" he deadpanned. The audience roared with delight.

They later followed this up in even more dramatic fashion by joining a hard core of protesters in a planned landing from the sea by dinghy, before symbolically leaving several black-painted drums – said to contain mud from Ireland contaminated by its discharges – at the high-water mark. The protesters had earlier collected over three thousand signatures supporting their stand at the site and had defied a last-minute court order to make their anti-pollution protest, clad dramatically in radioactive-protective suits and masks.

"We live one hundred and thirty miles from Sellafield, in Dublin," Bono explained to the large media throng that had assembled to witness the protest. "It's a lot further to Downing Street, as you might have noticed. It doesn't smell right here. It's pretty absurd that we have to do this – we're a rock'n'roll band. But Sellafield Two increases radiation by one thousand per cent. Someone has to do something. I didn't know that the Irish Sea was the most radioactive stretch of sea in the world. It is absurd that a rock'n'roll band such as this had to do anything to bring the facts out."

For a moment, he seemed lost for words. Then he gathered himself. "Sellafield Two," he continued, "will be an environmental disaster, and it would appear that it is also an economic disaster. The Germans are considering pulling out, even the British government is considering pulling out. They have spent two billion pounds of British taxpayers' money on Sellafield Two already. It will take another billion to see it through. We are asking the people of Britain to stop and think, to take this seriously, as it affects us all. We have a chance for the first time right now to impress upon the British government the madness of opening Sellafield Two."

The Rolling Stones may have once famously claimed that "It's only rock'n'roll", but Bono was determined that U2 would continue to use their music and their fame to promote change. Rather than link with a political party as Paul Weller, Billy Bragg and their well-meaning but naïve Red Wedge companions had once done with the old Labour Party of the early Eighties, Bono would ensure that U2 presented the facts as they saw them for their fans to ponder upon for themselves, regardless of political or religious allegiances. As The Edge confirmed, "The important thing is to give people information so they can make up their own minds."

November 1992 also saw U2 perform live in Central America for the first time. Bono had privately visited the Central American countries of El Salvador and Nicaragua, where human rights were less than universal, back in the Eighties. Playing there would have been unthinkable then. Now, in a new, supposedly more democratised age, there was at least an opportunity there, decided Bono, to do something. "Whenever people talk about our music having messages, it makes me feel like a postman," he mused. "As the writer of the words, I write about things the way that I see them. I never set out to change the world, just to change my own world. Rock'n'roll is a noise that has woken me up and it's good if, along the way, it wakes other people up too. But I feel we mustn't fall asleep in the comfort of our messages. Also, Edge can say more about the struggle in El Salvador with his guitar than I can with words."

On stage, Bono's new-found showmanship was now further enhanced by an exotic belly dancer, hired specifically to cavort with the dreaded Fly on a catwalk as the band spun through 'Mysterious Ways'. As well as the slogans and images being back-projected, half a dozen wildly painted Trabant cars, liberated from East Germany, also now hung over the audience and became something of a running joke among the band and road crew. As ever, Bono's jokes had a serious side too, resulting in the now famous on-stage phone call, at Wembley Stadium, in August 1993, to Salman Rushdie – the British author then in hiding after Iran's notorious Ayatollah Khomeini issued his famous death-sentence *fatwa* against the writer, whose 1988 novel, *The Satanic Verses*, had caused such outrage in the fundamentalist Muslim world that it inspired bloody, violent protests. As Bono continued to speak with Rushdie on the phone, the audience was astonished to see the author himself actually stroll out on to the Wembley stage before them. Then the two dropped the pretence with the phones and simply stood there embracing each other warmly at the front of the stage. It was Rushdie's first major public appearance since the *fatwa* issued against him five years previously. As such, Rushdie would later credit both Bono and U2 with helping him take what he would see, in hindsight, as the first major step towards his public rehabilitation. As a beaming Bono, still dressed as the Fly, said afterwards: "We're just as serious about what we do now. We're just pretending not to be."

He certainly found plenty of black humour in the situation. "You've got to remember," Bono smiled, "I was dressed as the Devil, so *The Satanic Verses* just seemed right, I guess." Then he added, more seriously: "It was more important than that. Salman Rushdie's position is more than just as a standard [person]. The idea of freedom of speech, something we just accept as a given, isn't so in a lot of cultures. Particularly with rock'n'roll music and rap groups, I think it's very important that people have the right to be able to say whatever they want to say even if I don't like it. So Salman Rushdie's dilemma is closer to rock'n'roll than you might think. Plus, I think he has behaved with enormous grace under pressure, and with humour and wit." Not to mention, he concluded mischievously, "It must have scared the shit out of him to be on stage at Wembley Stadium with the Devil!"

There were other matters of a more serious nature to discuss backstage that night as well. The month before, there had been an important meeting in the dressing room before a show in Verona, Italy, between Bono and Bill Carter, an American film-maker who had just returned from working in a relief camp in Sarajevo, the war-torn Bosnian city in the former republic of Yugoslavia that had recently become besieged by the Serbs. Inspired by what he had just heard, during the concert, Bono told the crowd about an "underground" dance club the Bosnians had built in Sarajevo, where they played rock'n'roll music to drown out the sound of the bombs that were slowly destroying their city piece by piece, it seemed, night after night.

After the show, Carter told the band more about the terrible situation now gripping Sarajevo. They sat there listening in silence as he depicted scenes of murder and rape, of looting and pillaging and the heart-rending image of hundreds of thousands of refugees, women and children mainly, now fleeing for their lives. Something would have to be done, Bono decided. The result would be a TV link set up between the Zoo TV tour and the war-ravaged city, beginning with a show in Bologna on 17 July. This was essentially a substitute for a proper U2 show itself in Sarajevo, which, Bill Carter persuaded Bono, would simply be too much of a security risk at that time. Nevertheless, argued Bono, there would be great publicity for the city's plight as a result of U2's interest and, eventually, he pledged, a concert by the band themselves there.

Meanwhile, back on tour, the Fly had now metamorphosed into the even nastier Mr MacPhisto, his name an obvious but telling hybrid of the earthly figure – Mephisto – that the Devil assumes in the legend of old, and a certain well-known fast-food burger chain fronted by a clown. Bono certainly got up to some devilish tricks in his new on-stage disguise. One which grabbed the headlines worldwide was Bono/MacPhisto's attempts at the end of the show each night to bombard (the first) President George Bush with calls via his sat-phone. Egged on by the audience, Bono would repeatedly speed-dial the White House until he got through to someone, explained who he was and what he was doing, standing before thousands of American voters, and asked ever so politely if he could have a brief word with the President. Though he never got through to the man himself, this daring piece of authentic political theatre would actually introduce Bono and the band into the political arena as a possibly influential "wild card" in the forth-coming US presidential election between Bush and the leading Democratic Party candidate, Bill Clinton.

Aware of the impact it would make, footage of President Bush, specially doctored, was now even being used to open the shows, the President appearing to say, "We will, we will rock you" in imitation of Queen's Freddie Mercury. Remarkably, Bush actually retaliated in kind, insisting that "if Bill Clinton is elected *you too* [U2] will have higher infla-tion, *you too* [U2] will have higher taxes". But despite the old-school Republican's best efforts, much to Bono and U2's delight, in late 1992, it was the sax-playing, woman-chasing, none-inhaling dope smoker, Clinton – who *did* later take an on-stage call from Bono – who found himself on his way to the White House in Bush senior's place.

To be seen as rock'n'roll's first kingmaker even set Bono's usually dependably down-to-earth head spinning. "It is pretty dizzy," he admitted. "Just the kind of media overload we all experience and also the feeling that you can feel the ground beneath you giving way. There's a kind of confusion that is great for a rock'n'roll band to play with. We got very excited about working with all the stuff that was out there. I mean, a simple device like a telephone, that you would have on stage, is probably something that could not have occurred to Elvis. But, you know, I just think that in the Nineties it's just amazing – you can just pick up a phone, you can ring the White House ... or, you know, Allesandro Mussolini, the great dictator's grandchild, who seems to be carrying on in the old boy's shoes." Best of all, he added, while all that was going on, you could also have "seventy thousand people singing 'I Just Called To Say I Love You' on the [mobile] phone. Or play with televisions and beam in the advertisements, you know, whatever it is that day that happens to be going on."

A swiftly recorded stop-gap studio album, *Zooropa* – recorded "on the run" between three different studios in Dublin (Windmill Lane, Factory and Westland), the band flying back to carry on working on the album between tour legs – had been issued, in July 1993, to commemorate the tour. A more "lateral" collection than any they had released since *Rattle and Hum*, one typical highlight included country music legend Johnny Cash singing lead on the superb final track, 'The Wanderer'. Cash had become friendly with Bono, Larry and The Edge when they had joined him on stage in Dublin the previous February, and said he would be "honoured" to sing on their album. Unlike its over-achieving predecessor, which had spawned five hit singles, the second U2 album of the Nineties was a comparatively laid-back affair with few tracks that suggested themselves as obvious hits. Bono knew better, however, and the first single from the album, the haunting 'Stay (Faraway, So Close)' hit the UK Top 5 in late 1993.

Interestingly, the album named The Edge as co-producer – the first time a U2 member had been so credited on any of their records – alongside the increasingly in demand Irish club DJ mix-master, Flood (real name: Mark Ellis) and a returning Brian Eno. "When we start records," Bono explained, "Edge is a slow starter. He's not quick to be enthused about a project. But at the end, when everybody else is fading, he's the guy who's up all night for weeks. I mean, I'm allergic to the studio after a few weeks." Therefore, he said, by naming their guitarist as one of the producers on the new album, "we wanted to acknowledge the baby-sitting that Edge does".

Having the guitarist in the studio hot seat for some of the time was also, reckoned Bono, what had made the album so fast and easy to make. "One of the things that worked about this record is that it was so quick. Edge is so good with the screwdriver, but we didn't give him much time to use it – which was great. He had more of an overall picture because he wasn't so taken up with the details." Modest to a fault, The Edge himself tended to put his instant success at the controls down to simple "beginner's luck". Whatever it was, it brought yet another new dimension to the ever-evolving U2 sound. Eno's spontaneous experiments were still much in evidence, and the dank air of Hansa Studios still clung over everything like a mist. But The Edge had helped bring the band back to the boil in the studio again – got them playing again simply as a band. Jetting in between shows, they still retained all the fizz of playing together on tour and they were firing off each other as they hadn't since the first album, quickly and easily, no messing around. Or at least, not much. As such, the results spoke for themselves: the material may have been less reliant on musical fireworks, but there was a renewed zestfulness about much of the singing and playing, turning even the most apparently downbeat moments into quietly smouldering hymns of hope and joy.

Nothing sounded like an obvious hit, yet it all fell into place perfectly when listened to with the right ears, Bono argued. So different was it, in fact, from what currently passed for the norm in the then grunge-obsessed American rock market, that Bono was both delighted and astonished when *Zooropa* went on to win the Grammy that year for Best Alternative Album. Not bad for a band who had been part of the ruling rock establishment for ten years at that point. But, as Bono commented wryly when collecting the award: "I'd like to give a message to the young people of America. That is, we shall continue to abuse our position and fuck up the mainstream ..." Cue: thunderous, if confused applause from the profoundly mainstream invitation-only audience.

At root, said Bono, the new U2 album was his and the band's attempt to tune into the energy that surrounds a band on tour "and stay up during the break in the tour [recording] rather than come down to earth again. This time we said: 'OK, we're up on the moon so let's stay here and make a record.' But that was our choice, to coast on that feeling rather than risk falling. So, in essence, the album could be seen as a substitute 'hit' for us, between tours. But it remains to be seen whether it will be as much of a 'hit' with everyone else!" He added: "I am also conscious that there is a part of me that doesn't want to come home. Part of me wants to stay on the moon. But as to whether I am addicted to that feeling, I honestly don't know. I can't give you the answer to that ..."

He paused, then continued. "When we came off the Zoo TV tour we thought we could go into a decompression chamber and sort of come out the other end normal. We thought we could live a normal life and then go back on the road this summer. But it turns out that your whole way of thinking, your whole body has been geared towards the madness of Zoo TV. So our feet didn't touch the *terra firma* when we got back to Dublin. I met Edge and asked if he was feeling any better. He said he wasn't, so we decided to put the madness on a record. Everybody's head was spinning, so we thought: 'Why not keep that momentum going – instead of standing on dining tables at nine o'clock and throwing fruit around the restaurant?'"

He recounted the story of a friend who had asked him recently: "How does your ego stand being in a band, how does it survive being a rock'n'roll star?" Bono was taken aback. "I thought that was one of the smartest things anyone had ever spotted about rock'n'roll. People think it's the opposite, that it pumps up your ego. I think it explodes your ego. It blows it out into fragments and that's why so many people who do what I do are so fucked up. So what U2 decided to do, with *Achtung Baby!* and the [Zoo TV] tour, is to explode our egos – publicly. Blow them up, in the billboard sense and in the sense of saying: 'Look, these are all the things we are.' So when I say that rock'n'roll is ridiculous in the sense that people like U2 are paid so much money to do all this, to play in a playpen, I mean it!"

New *Zooropa* tracks with a more experimental edge such as 'Numb' and 'Daddy's Gonna Pay For Your Crashed Car' clearly owed a huge debt to *Low*-era David Bowie, with their windy synthesisers and melancholic world view; as did the sinisterly Germanic parody of 'Achtung Baby' (the title track of their previous album, mysteriously included here). Whatever their immediate musical influences, however, for Bono the songs would always remain crushingly personal. He described the weirdly compelling 'Daddy's Gonna Pay For Your Crashed Car' as the sort of song that "could be about dependency or something more sinister". Despite the futuristic soundscapes conjured up by The Edge's treated guitars, at heart, insisted Bono, "It's an electronic blues – my Robert Johnson thing. Flogging the soul to Satan."

Similarly, he said, the chillingly hypnotic 'Numb' was "a kind of arcade music, but at base it's a dark energy we're tapping into, like a lot of the stuff on *Achtung Baby!*. And, here, I use my Fat Lady voice that I used on 'The Fly': there's a big fat mamma in all of us! But you need that high wail against the bass voice because the song is about to overload, all those forces that come at you from different angles and you have no way to respond. It's us trying to get inside somebody's head. So what we're trying to do is re-create that feeling of sensory overload." In which case, it has to be said, mission accomplished.

Other new tracks, however, such as the anthemic 'Stay (Faraway, So Close)' and 'The First Time' were as simple-sounding as demos, reflecting The Edge's own growing desire to return the band at least momentarily to something very much resembling straightforward high-energy rock. "Iggy Pop was very much an influence in terms of the way he'd make up songs in performance," Bono revealed. As such, he said, tracks like both the aforementioned tracks and 'Dirty Day' were "really U2 in its most raw state". The recording sessions had been so spontaneous that songs from *Zooropa* were only introduced gradually into the live set as and when they'd been learned. By the tour's end in December all but two numbers from the new album had been performed in the set.

It was the ever-expanding U2 stage show, however, that remained the real talking point at this stage of the high-stakes game the band was playing. With a stage set now so elaborate that it took forty-seven trucks to carry its 450-ton weight and more than 250 roadies to assemble it at each venue they performed in, this was now officially the greatest, certainly most successful, travelling show on earth. The question, as Bono knew only too well, was what would happen once the signal to receive Zoo TV was finally shut down for good? The answer was to come all too soon: a final show in Sydney, in late 1993, which would be broadcast live to forty-seven countries around the world, before the tour finally wound up in the suitably futuristic splendour of the newly opened Tokyo Dome on 10 December. This would be deliberately followed by a prolonged period of self-enforced inactivity. Even for Bono. "How did I de-Zoo myself?" he later mused. "I turned my television off. It was simple. My white dot has receded out of view. There was nothing left. The transmission had well and truly run its course."

It would, however, take them some time before they felt they had finally come down to earth from the tour. Bono and Larry were fortunate, in that they had their growing families to help cushion the crash landing. The recently divorced Edge was less fortunate, though he was slowly putting the pieces of his personal life back together. Adam, meanwhile, had become engaged in the last year to the supermodel Naomi Campbell, with a big celebrity wedding ceremony scheduled for Valentine's Day 1994. This was broken off at the last minute. Adam, it seemed, just wasn't ready to settle down yet. Bono quietly despaired for his friend but what could he actually do? Besides, with the ordeal of a world tour finally behind them and the media spotlight mercifully pointing elsewhere for a brief while, it was time for Bono to get his own family in order. Above all, it was time to put his devilish on-stage alter egos away, and spend some time being Mr Hewson again, happily married father of two. Mr MacPhisto, as he later jokingly told one journalist, had "gone to bed, covered his head and won't get up till Monday".

Looking back, Bono said, it was only now that it was finally all over that he felt he knew who the bizarrely clad MacPhisto really was. "I'd often found the sort of neon-light aspect of sex very funny, the leather and lace aspect. It wasn't a sexuality that I particularly related to, but it does seem a dominant sexuality. It's the one used to sell the products, and it's the one on every corner, and so I got into it, and it's great! It's just something I'm trying to understand, and I understand it a lot better having dressed up as a con man for the past year."

The tour had still been in progress when, in September 1993, Bono was able to reaffirm his elevation into the very top rank of world singing stars: he accepted the invitation to duet on a new updated version of 'I've Got You Under My Skin' with Frank Sinatra. Ol' Blue Eyes was on the point of enjoying one last career revival in the shape of his much-acclaimed *Duets* album, featuring the old master duetting with a host of other contemporary and classic stars. But while Bono was immensely flattered – astonished, in fact – he admitted in private that he was secretly apprehensive about the sheer scale of the task he was being asked to perform. "I don't know what I can do with that [song]," he grimaced. "I'm not going to croon it next to him. I might talk. I want to spook it up, because those Cole Porter songs are spooky. I don't know if you heard that 'Night And Day' thing we did [for the *Red Hot & Blue* charity album] but that's where we connect with Cole Porter. They're spooky, fucked-up songs of obsession. Some people perform them so fruity it's like whoa! [But] these are really dark pieces of work."

He went on to recall how jazz great Miles Davis had been a keen admirer of Sinatra's unique way of phrasing his vocals, and his impressive breathing techniques, and that it was reading that comment that had turned Bono on to the work of the legendary crooner, whom, he confessed, he'd now been to see in concert some half-dozen times. "We met him in Vegas," he later recalled. "We went backstage, and we were hanging out with him. It was like Rent-A-Celebrity, and we were like gypos, just the knackers." Their only real connection, said Bono, was that great leveller: music. "Larry was talking to [Frank] about Buddy Rich, who'd just died, and he didn't want to talk about anything else. He came alive! You got the feeling that maybe not a lot of people talk to him about music, and maybe that's what he's more interested in."

Despite his initial misgivings, Bono agreed to work with Sinatra on what would be, though nobody knew it then, his last album of substance. However, the reality of how they eventually recorded their "duet" was hardly what Bono had pictured in his mind when he'd first been approached with the idea. Then he had imagined standing shoulder-to-shoulder with the grand master of the mic as the two of them traded vocal punches; the reality, however, could not have been more different. Far from hanging out with Frank in the studio, Bono was obliged to record his vocal parts for 'I've Got You Under My Skin' at Dublin's STS Studios, during a quick break in touring in September, and without actually having the pleasure of Sinatra's company. That came, instead, in November, when Sinatra invited Bono over to Palm Springs, California, where a video for the song was now being shot. Never slow to seize an opportunity, while he was in Palm Springs with Sinatra, Bono pitched the idea of him recording a new song Bono had specially written with Frank in mind.

It was called 'Two Shots Of Happy, One Shot Of Sad', a wonderfully evocative song in the classic Rat Pack, Sinatra style, which U2 would themselves eventually perform publicly for the first time in 1995, as part of their contribution to a special TV tribute for Sinatra's eightieth birthday. Sadly, he died just three years later and it was left to Bono to record his posthumous tribute version of the song.

Shortly after his adventure with Sinatra, Bono also co-wrote (with old pals, Gavin Friday and Maurice Seezer) and recorded two tracks for the soundtrack of *In the Name of the Father*, the critically acclaimed film telling in docudrama form the story of the Guildford Four, a group of Irishmen whose false convictions and imprisonment for terrorist attacks in Britain in the Seventies had recently been overturned after many years of struggle by the families involved to see justice finally done. Bono's contributions were the film's title track and another song used elsewhere as part of the film's backdrop, entitled 'Billy Boola'; while the Bono-penned 'You Made Me The Thief Of Your Heart' was spectacularly performed on the soundtrack by Sinead O'Connor, who also starred in the film alongside Daniel Day Lewis.

After a lay-off – over a year, in fact, the longest period of inactivity in the band's career – when U2 finally returned to the fray as a collective, in the summer of 1995, they were motivated once again by images. As such, the first sign of renewed life was 'Hold Me Thrill Me Kiss Me Kill Me', the theme song – also released as the band's new single – for *Batman Forever*, the third movie in the successful series, originally devised and directed by Tim Burton, updating the classic DC Comics' superhero. To accompany what would be their first single for two years, and help boost the film, 'Hold Me Thrill Me Kiss Me Kill Me' was also given a clever video with a hyper-animated Bono intercut with shots from the film of the Caped Crusader himself in action. As a result, it became their biggest hit at home in Britain since 'The Fly' four years previously, reaching Number 2 that summer (Number 16 in the States).

Batteries evidently recharged, the newly three-dimensional, more obviously flesh-and-blood Bono had now grown a sandy-coloured beard, leaving him looking like a cross between Rasputin and a more hirsute Elvis Costello. Only the Fly's wraparound shades remained, and they had turned from terminally black to a sunnier, more see-through gold tint. But it was his collaboration with another bearded legend, Luciano Pavarotti, that was to make U2's next big headlines, when the world-famous opera tenor agreed to appear on a special one-off album Bono was especially keen for the band to make.

As such, although the rest of the band was all fully involved, the finished album was very much a joint venture between Bono, The Edge and long-time collaborator and producer Brian Eno. Titled *Original Soundtracks 1*, it would be composed of musical pieces, Bono earnestly explained, some long and full-blown, some barely more than snippets of musical "conversation", inspired primarily by films and images chosen completely at random; specifically, in the case of the album's most famous track, 'Miss Sarajevo', footage of the Bosnian war. Just one plank in a much larger project, Bono also served as executive producer on a remarkable documentary film, released around the same time as the album, that gave a chilling portrait of Sarajevo under siege at the height of the war. Also titled *Miss Sarajevo*, it would later win a string of prestigious awards, including the International Monitor Award, the Golden Hugo, and the Maverick Director Award at the Newport Beach Film Festival.

To accompany both album and film, the band released the 'Miss Sarajevo' single – featuring the unmistakable voice of Pavarotti – though not as U2 but under the assumed name of the Passengers. Bono had originally intended this to be the new U2 album, but apart from his and The Edge's unmistakable contributions, tied in as it was as well to the film, the record company execs argued that the concept lay outside the accepted U2 career path and therefore it would not be appropriate to market it as a fully realised new U2 album. Bono, to his credit, took their point on board and agreed to release it instead as a "one-off" project. Besides, the singer quickly realised, renaming themselves the Passengers wouldn't fool anyone; there would be no secret made of its true origins. Whatever they called themselves, Bono and The Edge's magical interaction with Pavarotti was so beautifully done that it produced one of the surprise hits of the year. So popular did it immediately become on radio and TV, in fact, that at one point it was actually quoted in betting shops across the UK as a 12/1 contender for the Number 1 single that Christmas. (It eventually reached Number 6.)

Commercially, *Original Soundtracks 1* made less of an impact, reaching Number 12 in Britain and only a paltry Number 76 in America. As Bono later laughingly recalled: "Brian Eno has been our producer for many years and it was really nice to be in a band where he got to take the shit!" More seriously, he said: "It's a very unusual record that we've just made with Brian. He has an extraordinary musical imagination and we've learned a lot from him over the years. Usually, he takes the role as irritant, he's some-body in the studio who stirs it up and has to make it work. This time around he didn't have any other responsibilities other than just being right on it, and we are happy to be in his backing band. There is some interesting material and it's a real trip of a record. It won't be for everybody and this is not a rock record," he warned. "It's a sort of late night on a fast train." The lead single, 'Miss Sarajevo', "is about a beauty pageant", he added. "You know, the song's not saying: 'Things are really bad in Sarajevo, please give us some money and I'll take a cut.'"

By the start of 1996, however, all eyes were now focused on the next venture proper from a group which even when they were doing little continued to dominate the world rock scene. As The Edge told an audience of critics and peers during his acceptance speech of a merit award at the 1995 *Q* magazine awards: "We've been away. We needed a break. We're back.

We've got some work to do. We've got some songs to write. You'll be seeing us soon."

The final U2 album of the Nineties, *Pop*, would – inevitably, perhaps, given the more experimental areas the band had found themselves working in over the past seven years – prove to be another hugely daring, yet remarkably successful demonstration of just how far they could take the basic U2 template and remould it in their attempts to reinvent themselves. Sessions for the new album finally started taking shape in Dublin, in January 1996, with Flood back at the mixing desk. The band liked working that way. It meant they didn't have to leave home and could come and go more easily, and they could write and mess around with sounds as and when the mood took them, rather than when the studio clock said so.

Three months later, they were ready to shift the scene over to the rather more plush (and considerably more expensive) surrounds of Miami's South Beach Studios. The deadline to hand the finished masters over to Island had originally been 1 July, but it had already been agreed that that was never going to happen. One of the problems, in terms of the sheer time everything was taking, was their exploration of yet another new way of working, bringing in DJ Howie B, a DJ and remixer with whom they'd also worked on the *Original Soundtracks 1* album. Knowing that Howie was deeply immersed in the worlds of acid jazz, trip-hop, techno, drum'n'bass and lounge, to name a few, for some weeks Howie would be regularly invited to the studio, where the band would encourage him to play them a wide sample of cutting-edge contemporary dance records in the hope that it would spark their interest and send them spinning off into a new direction musically. Their aim, explained Bono, was not just to try and understand and even enter into the cloistered worlds of the dance clubs, but to allow the more innovative sounds of the modern-day dancefloor to infect and influence them. Along with Howie B, Nellee Hooper – another veteran of the techno-pop world who had produced Björk's earliest, groundbreaking solo albums, which Bono had been very taken by – was also on hand to aid in the new production process. Hooper had also worked his unique electronic wonders with such diverse and critically acclaimed artists as Soul II Soul, Massive Attack and Madonna. He had also previously helped out by co-producing the 'Hold Me Thrill Me Kiss Me Kill Me' single with Bono and The Edge. Indeed, the main problem this time seemed to be not with where to find the inspiration but with having too many new ideas to know what to do with them all. Even as the original July deadline came and went, U2 already found themselves with enough new raw material for at least two albums' worth of music, albeit still in an unrefined, as yet unreleasable form.

But if the rumours emanating from first Dublin then Miami warned of a new immersion into the world of techno and dance, behind the scenes, as time went on and they gradually began completing the tracks, the band themselves began to see what they were doing as more of a logical musical progression from where they had just gone with their two previous boundary-blurring albums. Despite the rather kitsch and knowingly "ironic" images employed to promote the *Pop* album when it was eventually released early in 1997 – the video for the first single, 'Discotheque', was a sharp but affectionate parody of Seventies' disco group the Village People – The Edge, for one, saw no incongruity in this and the true meaning of an album he genuinely felt underlined the depth and integrity of U2's music. "Ironically," he said, despite all appearances to the contrary, *Pop* was "probably one of our most spiritual records. Even though it's dedicated to the moment, in a weird way it became a very spiritual record. I don't quite know how that has happened. It wasn't really our intention. Maybe when you pare things down to their most essential [elements], you are almost at a very religious spiritual level." Whatever the true source of the feelings their new music engendered, U2 fans certainly found no discrepancy in it, and 'Discotheque' would top the charts in thirteen different countries, including Britain.

U2 officially announced the release of *Pop*, their first album since 1993, in February 1997. The unlikely venue was a K-Mart store in a run-down area of downtown New York. Unlike its immediate predecessors, *Pop* would not be hailed unanimously as a classic by the critics, and once again, as with *Rattle and Hum* nine years previously, U2 would see the decade out with an album that polarised critical opinion. Humming and hawing from the media notwithstanding, such was the band's commercial clout that *Pop* became an instant squillion-selling hit anyway, reaching Number 1 in twenty-

Brian Eno (below) and his Canadian cohort,
producer, writer and multi-instrumentalist
Daniel Lanois (left).

Back-stage in Arizona, US, in April 1987, U2 talk to their manager, Paul McGuinness.

The Berlin Wall is
demolished, November 1989.

Salman Rushdie appears at a U2 concert, August 1993.

Bono as the Fly on the 'Zoo TV' tour, 1992.

U2 launch their 'PopMart' tour at a K-Mart store in New York, 1997.

Bono with manager Paul McGuinness in London.

Wim Wenders directed
Bono's film, *The Million
Dollar Hotel* (2000).

Bono and Ali arrive with their daughters Jordan and Memphis Eve at Sarajevo
for the film festival, August 2000.

Bono at the iPod
press conference in
California, US, 2004.

The odd couple: Bush and
Bono at the Oval Office,
Washington, 2002.

Bono finally meets Nelson Mandela at the Laureus Sports Awards in Monaco.

Bono, The Edge, Larry Mullen and Adam Clayton pose at the Grammys, 2005.

(From left) Bill Clinton, Bill Gates, Thabo Mbeki, Tony Blair, Bono and Olusegun Obasanjo at the G8 and Africa session at the World Economic Forum, Switzerland, 2005.

seven countries, including both Britain and America, and notching up sales of just under five million copies in its first four weeks of release alone – unprecedented, even by U2's own standards.

The low-key store location was chosen specifically for the announcement, because the tour to support it was to be called PopMart. "I can't quite remember how we got the idea of taking a supermarket on the road," joked Bono. "But I remember it made a lot of sense at the time." A clear attempt to try and out-dazzle the spectacle of the previous Zoo TV tours, the new PopMart tour show famously featured what was then the largest TV screen in the world (170 x 56 feet), a hundred-foot Golden Arch, a twelve-foot stuffed olive (on a hundred-foot-long toothpick, natch) and a giant mirrorball in the shape of a ten-foot-tall "lemon", out of which the band would emerge each night, Spinal Tap-like, on to the glittering, revolving stage. A fantastically complicated show, in terms of cues and prompts for all manner of sophisticated electronic gadgetry, nobody was ever really sure how much was meant to be tongue-in-cheek and how much was to be taken seriously, least of all, it seemed some nights, the band themselves. When it was finally over, more than a year later, Bono swore blind he would never do anything like it again. But then he always said that at the end of tours ...

The 1997 PopMart tour would fill sixty-two stadiums across North America, Europe and Britain, starting, appropriately enough, Bono felt, in Las Vegas, the spiritual home of fake western glitz and giant-sized everything. Everything about Vegas was up for sale and ready to go. It was almost too perfect, said Bono. "We believe in trash," he announced boldly. "We believe in kitsch, and that's what we're up against." Nevertheless, he conceded, "despite these mirror-balls, these stadium tours, I'm always gonna be the fucker with that white flag as far as [the press is] concerned. We're still the bleedin' hearts club," he concluded playfully, "our music is still painfully, insufferably earnest. We just got really smart at disguising it." The phrase "many a true word is spoken in jest" springs to mind here.

As if to underline the point, the opening track of the album, 'Discotheque', sounded like a straightforward challenge to most conventional U2 fans; on the surface, it was a musical car wreck that, in Bono's words, "[mixed] metal and dance in a cheesy hybrid. When we were recording that, we had the whole studio in mirrorballs and disco lights." He took pains to deny, however, that the song was anything to do with drugs, as some commentators had suggested, claiming instead that it was more "about the pleasures of the flesh". It was also extremely catchy, becoming U2's third UK chart-topping single. Elsewhere, 'Do You Feel Love' was an old-fashioned groove-based rocker draped in the fairy lights on an electronica dance mix. Similar in many ways to 'Even Better Than The Real Thing', in that it successfully combined both "old" and "new" elements of the quintessential U2 sound, the idea for 'Do You Feel Love' originally came from an improvised recording made at an early session in Dublin with Howie B, and taking Naked Funk's 'Groove Sensation' as its starting point. 'Mofo', another bubbling concoction of old and new U2, was accurately characterised by Gavin Friday ("consultant poptician", according to the sleeve credits) as "Led Zeppelin after taking an E". 'If God Will Send His Angels' was a title that had been hanging around waiting for Bono to turn it into a fully fledged song since the *Zooropa* sessions. While the delightfully ethereal 'If You Wear That Velvet Dress' came out of yet another late-night improvisation between Bono and Nellee Hooper, though even his impressive armoury of computers couldn't disguise the unashamed romanticism of the song; like an old Irish folk ballad given flash new twentieth-century garb.

Beyond the obvious dance and techno influences on *Pop*, there were also echoes of earlier, pre-punk times. 'Staring At The Sun', which would reach Number 3 in the UK when it was released as the follow-up single to 'Discotheque', appeared to owe more than a little to 'Soul Love' from Bowie's seminal 1972 *Ziggy Stardust* album, while 'Last Night On Earth' was built around a swelling, Beatlesesque chorus that would have put even those arch Beatles copyists Oasis to shame. The latter also brought U2 another Top 10 hit when it, too, was later released as a single.

'Gone', meanwhile, with its clearly more spiritual lyrical overtones, was verging almost on Verve territory in its apparent yearning for some sort of emotional catharsis. Or as The Edge ventured: "There are many layers to that song and there is another level to it which I haven't figured out yet." While 'Miami', a determinedly disco-free return to the more

Zeppelin-like psychedelic blues first evoked on *The Joshua Tree*, was another Edge favourite; inspired, he said, by a band trip to Florida one day during a break from recording at South Beach in April 1996. "It's sort of creative tourism," he deadpanned. More in keeping with the overall mood of barely concealed desperation that dominates so much of the album, musically and lyrically, was the driving, densely textured 'The Playboy Mansion' – a dark song, said Bono, about those who would treat "prosperity like a religion", looking down on an increasingly shrinking world where money and power were now the new gods.

'Please', a deceptively light-sounding song that would also become the fourth single from the album was, in fact, claimed The Edge, "one of the most intricate pieces of music we've ever written". But perhaps strangest of all was the hauntingly atmospheric closing track, 'Wake Up Dead Man', which began with a musical backdrop full of spaghetti-western portent, in the midst of which Bono addresses his anger and confusion, his frustration and sheer desperation to Jesus personally, until he is almost screaming at him, this so-called son of a God he now admits he has begun to believe may not even be there to hear him any more.

Amid a cacophony of thundercloud guitars and swamplike rhythms, Bono lets it all out: *"I'm alone in this world / And a fucked up world it is too!"* he bellows. Not originally intended for the finished album but recorded as a potential B-side for one of the singles, it was an awestruck Gavin Friday who pushed Bono hard to reconsider. So impressed was he by the tape Bono had played him, that Friday finally persuaded him to use it when he suggested it might make the perfect incongruous end to a determinedly left-field album. Bono agreed and thus was born one of the finest moments on *Pop*. How apt that it started out as a mere throwaway ...

The critics, by and large, saw things somewhat differently, however, and *Pop* was generally panned for being, of all things, over-ambitious. Meanwhile, with new, more authentic, refugees from the UK dance scene such as the Prodigy, the Chemical Brothers and Underworld all scoring their first major international hits that year with their own trailblazing mix of dance-rock, Bono and U2 found themselves pilloried in the music press, most ludicrously of all for being bandwagon jumpers, an idea Bono refuted strenuously. "If some snotty little anarchist with an Apple Mac and an attitude thinks he invented dance music and the big rock group is coming into his territory, that's ridiculous," he shook his head. "It's been a long time since there's been a dance movement, particularly in the US. To have hard-core dance on white [rock] radio would be crazy. It would be so good!"

According to Bono, what the mealy-mouthed critics were missing was the fact that, as he now saw it, rock had surrendered all of its rebellious nature long ago; now U2 and everyone else would be obliged to look elsewhere in order to maintain that elusive "free spirit" in whatever choice of music they made. "White-bread rock has, for me, lost its sense of adventure and seems very tired in comparison to hip-hop," Bono said, laying down the gauntlet. He openly admired and respected what bands like the Prodigy, Chemical Brothers and Underworld were doing in that still uncharted zone between dance and rock, he said, even going so far as to suggest that he would dearly love to have at least one of those acts open some of U2's future dates. Underworld, in particular, he claimed, were "really taking this DJ-culture thing to another plane".

The PopMart world tour was typically lavishly staged, though they attracted more press opprobrium for ticket prices of up to $53 [approximately £30] on the US leg of the tour. Bono, however, remained unrepentant, citing the huge costs involved in mounting such a state-of-the-art show in a different city every night. "If you're going to play big places," he pointed out, "and you don't want people to be in the back of a muddy field, like they were in the Seventies, you then have to try and do something special to make these 'events' in the full sense of the word, and you've got to spend to do that. We want to make, as they say in Ireland, a show of ourselves. We're working round-the-clock to put [the show] on, and we have two hundred people on the road, or whatever it is. It's madness! And I'm not sure we could do it again."

There was one special date for which tickets would prove priceless, however. A distraught Bono had lost his voice on the eve of the band's history-making concert in Sarajevo back in the summer of 1995 – a date with fate Bono had again pledged to make when he visited the ruined remains of the city just weeks after the war ended. As a result, U2 had allowed many of their shows since then to be broadcast to

Sarajevo via satellite. It wasn't until October 1997, just as the PopMart tour was reaching its zenith, that they were finally able to keep their promise and give Sarajevo a proper full-on U2 show of its own. As the band hit the stage that night, Bono yelled "Viva Sarajevo!" and the ground started to shake with the sound of stamping feet. Almost two hours later, as the show closed with a spine-tingling 'Miss Sarajevo', images of the 1993 beauty pageant flickering on the big screen, irony was no longer the order of the day. This was about straightforward human emotion.

Standing on stage in the stadium originally built for the 1984 Winter Olympics – and since battered almost to bits by Serbian artillery – U2 seemed, for a moment, to have united all of Bosnia. The only explosions, for once, were on stage as 45,000 people of all religious and cultural backgrounds mingled freely again, along with several thousand off-duty NATO troops, all joined together in a unique celebration of an occasion that would have been thought impossible just a couple of years previously. Earlier in the day, when Bono and the others were formally introduced to the new Bosnian President, Alija Izetbegovic, Bono had told him that the band's message "is banal, a simple one: that music is beyond politics". Certainly the show that followed that night seemed to be the proof of that.

The PopMart tour officially closed in April 1998 at the Johannesburg Stadium in South Africa in front of an ecstatic, mixed-race crowd of over 67,000. Less than two months later, however, just as the band should have been burrowed away with their families and friends back home in Dublin, U2 would take time out to head north of the border, where they performed a special benefit show in Belfast, in support of the Referendum for Peace in Northern Ireland. Bono, with his "mixed" religious background and ever-expanding political consciousness, had been especially keen for the band to lend their name to a campaign to reaffirm the Good Friday peace agreement, support for which had been dwindling in recent times as the political enmity between the two sides threatened to drag on for ever. "We're here to try to convince some of the people who have real concerns, genuine concerns, about the peace agreement, still to vote yes," Bono told waiting reporters. "Because to vote no is to play into the hands of the extremists who've had their day. Their day is over as far as we're concerned. We're on to the next century here." The show that night, in front of two thousand jubilant fans at Belfast's Waterfront Hall, was predictably emotional. Later in the year, Bono would also represent U2 by lending his voice to a charity cover of Lou Reed's 'Perfect Day' for that year's BBC national Children in Need campaign.

By the beginning of 1999, however, Bono was ensconced with the band in their own recently purchased and outfitted Dublin studio with old friend Daniel Lanois. The album they were now intent on producing would not emerge until 2000, yet the world's press were already camped on their doorstep eager for news. Larry took time out to tell the door-steppers that "everything has changed … all of a sudden, pop music has become pretty big".

The message, however obliquely delivered, seemed to be that electronic experimentation was to be left behind with the old millennium, and that it was time for Bono and the boys to chart another new course for U2. Millions of fans could only watch and wait ...

CHAPTER FIVE 2000

More so than the passing of a normal New Year, the advent of the millennium was cause for millions of people around the world to take a closer look at themselves in the mirror; to try and take stock of where their lives were leading them. Where had they been? What had they done? Where were they going now, and what would they find there? Or would the "millennium bug" (the supposed inability of twentieth-century computers to adjust to the twenty-first-century double-digit date setting of 00 which it was feared would lead to a complete breakdown in services) be the end of civilisation as we know it? These were the questions occupying the minds of many as midnight swung around on 31 December 1999 and a whole new century dawned.

Paul David Hewson was no exception. Not only was he acutely aware of entering a new time-frame in human history, he himself would be reaching a significant milestone in his own journey through life: on 10 May 2000, Bono would be forty-years-old – the traditional halfway point in a man's life and the open swing-doors to middle age. A time when intimations of one's own mortality become ever more apparent: the deepening lines of the face, the first hint of white in the beard, the extra "tiredness" that comes with being in your forties, even the experience of watching one's own children rapidly growing up. There is great joy to be found in witnessing these things from a fortysomething perspective; and there are tinges of regret, too. The future, no longer a rainbow at the end of which lies the metaphorical pot of gold, now appears to be disturbingly finite, like coming to the end of a long dark alley and finding only a wall. Too late to turn back, you wonder what else to do ...

Bono's way of dealing with this possible mid-life crisis was to busy himself, both personally and professionally, as never before. He and Ali had two more children during this period, one born either side of the millennium. Both were boys this time, the first – named Elijah Bob Patricius Guggi Q (known to the family as Eli) – born in August 1999, and the second – John Abraham – in May 2001, famously described by his father at the time as "looking like a thug".

But even these momentous events did not seem to slow Bono down for long. By contrast, they appeared to have the opposite effect on him, and when he wasn't in the studio working on the new album, Bono spent most of 1999 publicly addressing some of what he now saw as the major threats to the planet his children would be growing up in – a subject we will explore more fully a little further on. Meanwhile, Bono's seventeen-year marriage to Alison appeared to be stronger than ever. Wherever Bono was in the world or whatever he was doing, behind the scenes, Ali has always been very much the anchor in his life. Not the kind of wife to sit at home, tending to the family as they all await the patriarch's return from his latest adventures overseas, Ali was a fiercely intelligent young woman determined to enjoy a life of her own, independent and entirely separate from that of her husband's more glitzy professional career. Utterly unlike the stereotypical rock wife eager to share the spotlight's glare, Ali stayed as far out of the public eye – at least where her husband was concerned – as possible. After they were married in 1982, instead of slavishly following her new husband around on the road, as many would have chosen to do, Ali had wisely decided to remain in Dublin, where she became an honours student at the University College, taking a degree in political science, before embarking in the late Eighties on raising a family.

Ali had decided early on: there might be periods when her husband was away from home for months at a time, but her ability to stand on her own two feet would never be called into question. Even Bono was surprised by his wife's strength and resilience. For example, when Bono once called her family on the phone from the United States to ask them to keep an eye out for her in his absence, Ali's reaction was to place her own furious call to her husband, where she told him exactly what he could do with his "help" then slammed the phone down on him. She let a suitably contrite Bono stew a few days, however, before flying out for a brief and enjoyable on-the-road reconciliation. Needless to say, he didn't make that mistake again.

Indeed, if anything, it has often been the other way around in their relationship: it is Alison who has been the one who provided unstinting support to her husband. Happy to back Bono privately in his efforts to raise awareness for various causes – including that memorable trip to Ethiopia with her husband in September 1985, when they spent three weeks as voluntary unpaid aid workers – Ali also had her own charitable commitments and causes, which she championed in her own right, an array of commitments that would continue to grow over time. In 1993, for example, she had visited the gruesome, melted-down nuclear reactor in Chernobyl, in the Ukraine, as part of an official foreign delegation. Having witnessed at first hand the grotesque and multi-faceted forms of suffering the 1986 catastrophe had caused the children of the region (from a terrifying array of radiation-related cancers to the babies born with grotesque disfigurements), she ventured back to the Ukraine a further seven times over the next ten years.

As a result of her unflinching commitment, in 1995, an independent production company named Dreamchaser approached her to help produce *Black Wind, White Land*, a documentary film they were planning on the story of Chernobyl and its mind-bendingly horrific aftermath. This involved spending three weeks there, which Ali courageously agreed to do. Screened to huge critical acclaim by RTE in Ireland later that same year, *Black Wind, White Land* also went on to achieve a more global audience as several other high-profile TV stations broadcast it over the coming months, resulting in the film eventually being short-listed for a prestigious Irish television award. As well as filming the TV documentary, Ali also lent her weight to the Chernobyl Children's Project (CCP), founded by Adi Roche, after an international appeal in 1991 from doctors working against the odds in the equally disastrously affected neighbouring former Soviet republic of Belarus.

In 1996, Ali went a step further and actually brought three of the orphaned children she had encountered on her latest visit back with her to Ireland for medical treatment. One, Lena, would be fortunate enough to remain in Dublin after being adopted by an Irish couple; while Ali would herself become godmother to another, Anna Gabrielle. In 2000, Ali also helped organise a high-profile fashion show in Dublin to raise further funds for the cause. The Chernobyl Children's Project was also the subject of another, more recent award-winning documentary film, *Chernobyl Heart*, which won the Oscar for 'Best Documentary Short Subject' in 2004.

"It is a very great honour for the [CCP] to be involved with a documentary that is on the short-list for the Academy Awards," said founder Adi Roche. "Our hope is that the publicity gained from this great achievement will help to once again highlight the plight of the victims and survivors of the world's worst environmental disaster." Alison Hewson's involvement in the rehabilitation of the children of Chernobyl remains ongoing.

Ever inquisitive and permanently on the look-out for other ways to express himself, Bono also found new ways of doing this as the years went by. In 1989, he gamely entered into the world of poetry, when he agreed to appear as one of the guest speakers at Dublin's Abbey Theatre, in an evening dedicated to the works of the famous Irish poet, W. B. Yeats. Invited to participate in this role as a much-lauded lyricist in his own right, Bono, as usual, had gone the extra mile and had actually set two of Yeats's poems to music specially for the event. Looking for music from the period the poems were set in also sparked a new and abiding interest in discovering more about the rich heritage of Irish traditional music, which he had hitherto, he confessed, "almost deliberately ignored".

The mid-Nineties would find Bono attending a number of literature festivals in his guise, in 1995, as one of the newly appointed patrons of the UK Year of Literature – a status he was "honoured" to share with the likes of Ireland's Poet Laureate, Seamus Heaney, legendary American playwright Arthur Miller, and Bono's new friend, the controversial author Salman Rushdie. A similar event held the same year in Ireland, at Cuirt in County Galway, also saw Bono introduce celebrated US beat poet Allen Ginsberg on to the stage. Like a great many of the Seventies "poets" who would put their words into rock songs, Bono was a great admirer of Ginsberg's most famous poem, "Howl" – like a rock song without music, he always thought. In one of his last major public appearances outside America before his death soon afterwards, Ginsberg would also later feature in the promo video for U2's 'The Last Night On Earth' single.

Meanwhile, attending yet another literature convention at Swansea University in October the same year, this time it was Bono himself who was billed as the evening's star turn.

In front of a packed 1,200-seater theatre, Bono stood up and announced that he was there not as the singer of U2, specifically, but simply as someone who aimed to help promote literature and raise awareness of human rights. He added, jokingly, that he felt he'd always had a hard time getting "the English" (*sic*) to accept lyrics as literature. "They somehow look down on them," he said. "It's as though, because lyrics are not written in books, they are a lower form [of art]." (Four years later, when Bono was introduced to the Pope, he would present him with a book of poetry by Seamus Heaney.)

Back in Dublin, family life for the Hewsons, initially at least, had always been something to be grabbed between tours. "Normal" married life was a concept Bono and Ali had been forced to redefine for themselves, making up their own ground rules as they went along. Fortunately, while Bono was away on the road, Ali was busy with her own life, first with her studies, then her own career. In those days, absence really did make the heart grow fonder. And besides, as a free agent until the children came along, Ali was still able to join her husband on his travels from time to time. However, as both she and he were to find out, the arrival of children changes everything, even for millionaire rock stars. No longer just husband and wife but now parents, too, the long separations could no longer be so easily managed or brushed aside. Perhaps also having seen The Edge's marriage fold under the strain, Bono and Ali now set increasing store on ensuring they had enough "quality time" together with their daughters. Windows would be built into the touring schedule to allow this to happen. In late 1997, for instance, Ali and the girls flew to Miami, where the band were playing, for the family to enjoy some time together. When this kind of venture involved the girls, both now of school age, missing their studies, Ali would ensure the learning process continued, bringing books and specially prepared lessons so that they did not fall behind even by a week from the rest of their classmates.

Bono, Ali and the children, now boosted by the inclusion of four-month-old Eli, spent Millennium Eve in an even more exotic location: as the guests of another high-profile couple, President Bill Clinton and wife Hillary, at the White House, where more than three hundred and fifty guests had gathered to mark the passing of the twentieth century. After a lengthy but enjoyable formal dinner, replete with speeches and handshakes and endless photo opportunities, Bono moved on to the nearby site of the Lincoln Memorial, where a 300,000-strong crowd enjoyed a gala concert in which he participated, getting up on stage to guest with ex-Fugees rapper, Wyclef Jean, a recent musical collaborator and friend.

The connection between Bono and Bill Clinton had first been made back in the summer of 1992, when U2 had lent their weight to the Rock the Vote campaign, a Clinton-backed project aimed at encouraging young people to take seriously their right to vote and actually exercise that option at the coming presidential elections that year (at which Clinton was standing as the Democratic candidate; his opponent, the incumbent President Bush). Clinton, then plain Governor of Arkansas, had previously called the band on a coast-to-coast radio talk show and thanked them for their "service to democracy". "We don't suggest who people vote for," insisted Bono, "but we do suggest that they vote." Fascinatingly, the future president also thanked the band for making *The Joshua Tree* album, telling them: "You made me feel like I had a place in rock music, even at forty-six." Bono's well-timed response prompted laughter from New York and Little Rock. "Well, Bill," he deadpanned, "if we got you into it we must have done something wrong!"

Bono and Clinton would actually meet face to face for the first time a few weeks later, in Chicago, where by chance both the band and the presidential candidate were staying in the same hotel. Initially, however, Bono's request for a quick meeting with the Governor appeared to be rebuffed. But none of the candidate's aides had actually bothered to ask him whether he wanted to meet the singer and when Clinton found out he immediately rebuked those responsible and ordered them to arrange a meeting with the U2 singer for the very next day. When they did finally get together the following afternoon, the connection between the twinkling-eyed Clinton and the furrow-browed Bono seemed to be immediate. Far from discussing the finer points of *The Joshua Tree*, subjects up for discussion that day ranged from Irish access visas – "Ireland's supposed to have a special relationship with America," Bono complained to the future president, "but we need special visas, whereas the UK doesn't"; film director and creator of *Star Wars*, George Lucas; educating US children with computers; and only then, finally, music. "The nickname for [Clinton] by his aides was Elvis," Bono later smilingly recalled, "and the odd thing was he was essentially on tour. What brought two very disparate entities together was the touring life – he was on the road too ..."

His circle of friends, both at home and abroad, rapidly expanding, someone else Bono developed a close bond with in the Nineties was playwright and author Salman Rushdie, whose acquaintance he had first made at the historic Wembley show in 1993 when Rushdie joined the band on stage – his first major public appearance for nearly five years. With his own vast experience of what it was like to dwell as a constant prisoner, to some extent, of fame, Bono felt he could appreciate to a certain degree some of the difficulties Rushdie must have faced, hidden away for so many years from prying eyes. The feeling of impermanence engendered by the constant moving from place to place surrounded by bodyguards – skipping from hide-out to hide-out under cover of dark. Being forced to live the half-life of an existence both in and out of the public eye simultaneously was a condition Bono felt he could empathise with, to some extent at least. As such, he was quick to offer Rushdie his own personal support, starting with the Wembley "phone call", a symbolic public re-emergence for the author (who had first been to see the band perform at Earls Court in 1992, while still incognito), and continuing with his taking up of Bono's offer to come and spend some time at the singer's Killiney home (where some newspapers now claimed he had been a secret resident for some time). Later on, as their friendship blossomed, they even found themselves beginning to collaborate on ideas together, including one of Bono's most famous recent songs: 'The Ground Beneath Her Feet', on which Rushdie provided most of the lyrics, Bono the tune.

It all came about when Rushdie told the singer of an idea he had for the next book he wanted to write, to be called *The Ground Beneath Her Feet*. Rushdie gave Bono the title and some already penned suggestions for lyrics and challenged him to find a tune to fit them. At first, Bono admits he was nonplussed. But inspiration finally struck during a meal break in the sessions for what would later become the *All That You Can't Leave Behind* album. Working fast, Bono and producer Daniel Lanois quickly came up with a simple voice and acoustic guitar arrangement to the tune Bono suddenly had bubbling inside his head, then The Edge sat down with the cans on as they played the track back and added a razor-edged electric riff to counterpoint Lanois's plangent steel guitar. When they were finished, Bono was convinced they had fashioned another diamond out of the dirt. The rest of the band, however, was not so sure, and eventually rejected it as a track for the album; the general consensus seeming to be that it was a nice tune, but just another ballad (or "salad", in band parlance).

Disappointed but, as usual, unbowed, Bono later reclaimed the song as his own when the band agreed to record it for the critically acclaimed 2000 movie *The Million Dollar Hotel*. Bono was credited as both "co-writer of the story and producer – even though I don't know what that is", he claimed mysteriously. "I'm also writing a few tunes for the soundtrack, I'm hoping to bring the band in on the soundtrack as well, if they can fit it into their schedule," he added with just a hint of sarcasm. Meanwhile, producer Wim Wenders later described the fractured nature of the song Bono and Rushdie had written as the perfect choice for the movie as "it so perfectly grasped its spirit". (Interestingly, and almost certainly as a result of this later critical acclaim, the British and European versions of the *All That You Can't Leave Behind* album would feature 'The Ground Beneath Her Feet' as a "bonus" track. It was also the first time U2 had ever recorded a song featuring "outside" lyrics.)

Meanwhile, back on the home front, a stark reminder of what can happen when showbiz couples allow their pursuit of celebrity drastically to overtake their personal lives came with the ghastly death from an alleged drugs overdose, in September 2000, of Paula Yates, estranged wife of the Hewsons' long-time friend, Bob Geldof. Bono returned from the States where the band was on tour to join mourners at the funeral at the modest Kent church where Paula was to be laid to rest. As part of the ceremony, Bono essayed his own heartfelt musical farewell to her when he joined former Squeeze pianist Jools Holland (also, famously, Paula's co-presenter on *The Tube*, the groundbreaking Eighties TV show that first made her famous) in a solemn but emotionally cascading rendition of 'Bullet The Blue Sky'. Earlier that day, Ali and Bono had issued a joint statement in which they were quoted as saying that "our thoughts are for the [couple's] four girls. It is their tragedy more than anyone's. We know Bob is a great dad. They are a strong family, but still our heart breaks."

Even when away with the band for months at a time, Bono would always make a point of staying in close touch with home. Ali may not have appreciated such close attention in the earliest years of their marriage, but with three children to look after now and another on the way in 2001, Bono knew his wife needed his support, wherever he was, and however much she bravely pleaded to the contrary. As if to prove the point, it was while Ali was expecting their second son, John Abraham, that Bono took to using his satellite phone on stage again, stopping the show each night of the 2001 Elevation world tour to call her and ask how she was getting on, in a more domestic variation of his earlier Zoo TV antics. He would round off this section of the show by proudly sere-nading her with 'All I Want Is You', one of the tracks from *Rattle and Hum*. It wasn't his first musical message to the love of his life, of course; there had been many others in the past, most notably, perhaps, when he composed 'The Sweetest Thing' for her after committing the cardinal sin of forgetting her twenty-fifth birthday during the recording sessions for *The Joshua Tree*. (Proceeds from the release of it as a single were donated to Ali's own preferred charitable cause, the Chernobyl Children's Project.)

Despite the seeming ubiquity of his image, popping up everywhere these days it seems from the political pages of *The Times* to the reviews section of the *NME*, compared with most celebrities of his stature, Bono has rarely found himself mired in the kiss-and-tell tittle-tattle of the gossip columns. Occasionally, of course, the tabloids have tried to ensnare him in some typically made-for-page-three melodrama, but they have rarely, if ever, succeeded. The only time they came close to revealing anything remotely controversial about Bono was in the run-up to the 2001 Brit Awards – the high-profile, televised UK music business equivalent of the American Grammy awards show. In the week leading up to the televised show in London, the *Sun* ran a story suggesting that Bono had been seen flirting with Andrea Corr, lead singer of Irish soft-rock group the Corrs, over dinner at a West End restaurant. Bono, understandably, was not amused. He may have had dinner with the beautiful lead Corr but to put a sly slant on the meeting was out of order, particularly as there was no foundation for the claim, he said. How did they define "flirting" anyway? Eating with your mouth closed and laughing at someone's jokes? A still irate Bono used the post-Brits party to take the *Sun*'s then pop columnist, Dominic Mohan, to task about his paper's coverage. A startled and clearly off-guard Mohan agreed to straighten out the matter forthwith and his encounter with the U2 singer, along with his heartfelt testimonial to his wife – "She's a great woman" – was duly printed the next day.

Another aspect of Bono's life, which rarely gets much of an airing in public, is his own incredible personal wealth. For if it is true that Bono has shown not only extraordinary ingenuity but an apparently bottomless commitment in helping to raise hundreds of millions of dollars for countless good causes over the years, it's worth noting that he has also proved commendably astute when it comes to his own private business affairs. Like the rest of the band, Bono and Ali now live in the exclusive Dublin suburb of Killiney. Apart from owning several properties around the world, he and U2 also, at one time or another, reputedly shared interests in several plush Dublin addresses, including their own hotel, studio complex and club. In 2001 it was revealed that Bono had recently bought a sixteenth-floor luxury penthouse apartment overlooking New York's Central Park, a suitable venue from which to lobby the United Nations, no doubt.

In a further effort to stabilise their lives as far as possible, the band have also owned their own recording studio in Dublin for many years now. Purpose-built for them, their original Hanover Quays complex, situated on the banks of the River Liffey, included a large, stage-size rehearsal room, fully functional luxury living quarters and two state-of-the-art recording studios. Well-appointed and discreet, the only drawback in their earliest days there was the constant phalanx of river cruisers coming in too close in an effort to spot the band through the panoramic windows the builder had thoughtfully installed in the riverside walls of the building – a problem the band eventually solved by mooring a motley collection of old boats and tugs alongside the banks of the studio, to prevent other vessels getting close enough to provide any real distraction. More recently, however, the Hanover Quays complex has been earmarked by the local council for demolition, with plans already in place for the original site's re-development as a luxury riverside apartment and office block. As a result, 2005 has seen U2 forced to relocate their operation, though stubbornly refusing to move too far. Their new studio now resides less than a mile up river – in another new tower-style complex.

That said, Bono is, understandably, quick to play down his own wealth. He doesn't want his personal fortune – which some estimates put in excess of £50 million – to be used to cloud what he sees as the real issues. "We have two ways of dealing with our wealth," Bono had declared back in 1989. "We have what U2 does as a group – decisions that are made collectively about income – and we have our own personal responsibilities. Both we keep secret, and while that doesn't absolve us from all the guilt of having a lot of money in a society that doesn't have much, at least it makes us feel we're doing something worthwhile with that money. There are still contradictions to be tackled – but if I choose what I'm going to tackle in a day, I mustn't put it before being in a band making music." He paused to consider. "You know, it's almost harder to give away money than to earn it because of the responsibilities involved."

Nevertheless, he still remembered his early days in Ballymun, the grey, now tower-blocked streets where he grew up with his pals in the Lipton Village of their collective imagination. He found himself thinking of those days more, for some reason, since the children were born, and he would find himself some days gazing around at the nine-bedroom

Victorian-style mansion he and his family now reside in, in County Dublin, and wondering quite how he had managed to get there: from his mother's death, to joining the band, to … this. It wasn't as simple as that, of course – nothing was – but that's what it amounted to. Would Paul Hewson have found the fire within, the unrequited yearning, the eternal sense of injustice, to become Bono if Iris had not died that awful day in 1974? He didn't know.

Bono has also shown remarkable determination over the years to keep his family as far away from the spotlight as possible. Indeed, the last time Bono really wore his heart on his sleeve in public was when his father, Bobby, died in the summer of 2001, after a long struggle with cancer. The last few shows on the European leg of the Elevation world tour became highly emotional occasions as Bono paid lengthy tribute to his beloved dad from the stage each night. The increasingly distraught singer had been flying back to Dublin whenever the schedule allowed him to spend a few snatched, precious moments with his father, who lay slowly dying in hospital. At Manchester's MEN Arena on 12 August, the first date of their latest sell-out UK tour, Bono introduced the song 'Kite' with the words: "This is for my Dad, Bob Hewson. He's only got a few days left in him." It was the first time he had spoken publicly of his private torment.

Mercifully, Paul, as he had always remained to his father, was able to be there with Bobby when, nine days later, he passed away in the early hours at Dublin's Beaumont hospital. Rousing himself, Bono bravely flew to London later that day to join the rest of the band for their scheduled show at the Earls Court arena. As Bono came on stage that night, he knelt in front of the 17,000-strong audience and made the sign of the cross. Introducing 'Kite', he said: "I wrote this for my kids, but now I think the old man wrote it for me." As a source close to the band later commented: "Bono was determined that the show must go on – he was determined not to let anyone down." Nevertheless, it was one of the hardest performances he'd ever had to give; how he got through it he didn't really know.

Inevitably, and despite his son's best efforts, Bob Hewson's funeral in Dublin on 24 August was turned into a mass media event, the church where the funeral was held at Howth surrounded by TV cameras and newspaper photographers. Doing his best to ignore the undignified mêlée outside, speaking to the assembled mourners during the hour-long mass, Bono paid tribute to what he described as his father's "beautiful tenor voice ... I want to thank him for giving me this voice," he said with a choke. He then joined with The Edge on acoustic guitar to sing a brand-new song he said he had written with his father in mind, entitled 'Sometimes You Can't Make It On Your Own', a beautifully haunting melody that would eventually appear on 2004's *How to Dismantle an Atomic Bomb*, as well as becoming the album's second hit single, early in 2005. Afterwards, Bono, older brother Norman and Larry Mullen acted as pallbearers, carrying the coffin out of the church and up towards the graveyard. They were comforted on the church steps by mourners including another new close friend of Bono's, the former Boyzone singer, now successful solo artist, Ronan Keating.

As for the rest of the things about his private life which Bono would rather remain hidden, or at least partially obscured from public view, the rampant but unconfirmed rumours of behaviour behind the scenes commensurate with the privileges he enjoys in his private-jet lifestyle – word round the campfire is that there's no smoke without fire. Or as U2 manager Paul McGuinness says of his principal client, "He certainly lives life to the full." But if the lamb does stray occasionally – and let's hope so, the thought of a saintly Bono never doing anything just for the hell of it would be too much to bear – it's never for very long. He has "too many beliefs that run too deep", he says, ever to allow himself to be held down by "the trappings".

Perhaps the most important thing to remember about Bono is that the sex and drugs were never what he was actually doing the rock'n'roll for. For him, great music was about something much more important than that. Great music was better than sex and drugs; great music could lift you up to the sky. And that's where Bono aspired to be: as close to heaven as he could get himself while still keeping at least one cowboy-booted foot on the ground. For at the core of Bono's beliefs lies his ongoing dialogue with God. His view on religion has changed over time, of course, from upstanding member of the flock to accusatory black sheep. Yet his basic beliefs appear never to have left him. In an early letter home he told his father how he felt his committed Christianity would help the band "rise to the top of the music business". Always touchingly (some might say cringingly) open about it in early interviews, to his credit he was equally forthcoming when, as the years slid by, religious disillusion set in – peaking with 'Wake Up Dead Man' from *Pop*, in which Bono openly rails against his Maker.

Latterly, the pendulum appears to have swung again. 'Beautiful Day', the memorable hit from the 2001 album, *All That You Can't Leave Behind*, shows the singer's anger maturing at last like old wine, name-checking the biblical white dove that brought a twig of hope to Noah's Ark. The rest of the album evokes a similarly redemptive mood, going so far on the track 'Grace' to summon forth the New Testament spirit of *agape*. That is to say, love without condition, or true charity. Or, put yet another way, the kind of love only a parent, perhaps, can guarantee someone.

Despite an obviously sincere search for religious answers, wherever they might find them, Bono and U2 still found themselves at odds with the Catholic Church in Ireland, a situation that became clear right from the outset with the band's open support for birth control. With all forms of contraception banned in Ireland, U2 had lent their support for birth control advocate groups as far back as the late Seventies, when they played a benefit gig in a Dublin car park supporting a protest movement against such ruinous laws. It was a theme they would return to more than once over the next few years, thereby incurring the opprobrium of the entire Catholic Church of Ireland. Undeterred, in 1992, the band made sure that "Achtung Baby" condoms were among the many items of merchandise on offer on their tour dates. The year before, they had also brought much-needed publicity and support for the Irish Family Planning Association when they were fined for selling condoms at a Virgin megastore in Dublin. The band offered to pay the £500 fine, they said, "because we feel the IFPA have much more important things to be doing than turning up in court. Furthermore, the group fully supports the IFPA's call for the law on the sale of condoms in Ireland to be changed." Contraception and the ready distribution of condoms remain high on Bono's agenda to this day, not just in Ireland but in Africa, and anywhere else in the world where religious ignorance or corporate barbarism has made them most needed.

Perhaps the defining characteristic of Bono the public figure, however, is the unexpectedly urgent energy he brings to everything he lends his name and/or image to. Now in his mid-forties, instead of turning the volume on the remote down a notch, he seems to be more active than ever, not just in the field of music but in the wider, much more strenuous world of geopolitics and financial power structures. Bono, it seems, doesn't just have a dream of the world he wants to live in; as far as he's concerned, he's actually got a map. All we have to do is follow him ...

More prosaically, U2 have also maintained their much-publicised links through the years with environmental charity organisation Greenpeace and prisoner of conscience champions Amnesty International, pledging long-term support to both organisations. "I still have very strong feelings about such matters," says Bono now. "All the prisoners aren't out and all the people who are starving aren't fed, so it goes on." Nevertheless, he also accepted that his first priority, as a musician, was simply that: to make music. As he put it, "You see, the first responsibility of a rock'n'roll star is not to be dull. I think it's part of the job to have jeopardy … It's cool to be concerned about the environment and have a political attitude but only if it brings you close to your real job as a firework," he concluded enigmatically. "So martyrdom is cool, you know, the business of getting up on the cross." Contrary to opinion, he said, "I don't think in the Eighties we were rock'n'roll. I think we were the loudest folk band. And now we're a rock'n'roll band and I know that the best way to make the same point is to be a bit smarter."

Live Aid had clearly had a profound effect on Bono, as had the trip to Ethiopia with Ali the following September. They travelled to the latter at their own expense, with no publicity, and worked for a month in a refugee camp that for security reasons was fenced in – an emotionally steely environment that Bono later likened to a Second World War concentration camp. Meanwhile, they mucked in, sometimes literally, with the everyday duties, many of which involved exhausting hours toiling in the hot sun. Seeing the suffering all around, living with it every day, gave Bono, now biblically bearded and with hair almost rivalling Ali's long locks, yet more cause to question his faith: "I felt more removed from Christianity," he later said, of his time in Ethiopia. "Not what it is but what it has become."

He also later told publicist B.P. Fallon, as recounted in his book *Faraway So Close*, that when he revealed he was a singer (doubtless an unusually humbling experience in itself) the camp authorities decided he would be more use writing songs for the children than shovelling dirt. "So I wrote and sang songs that were translated into Amharic, songs about all sorts of things – hygiene, health, growing food – anything the nurses and doctors wanted from us. We also wrote little short one-act plays, pantomimes really." Ali, he recalled, wrote a play about childbirth using a doll with a long umbilical cord attached. The result was that the children, by going round the camp singing the songs, actually educated both themselves and their parents. They were also happy songs that made people smile; an achievement in itself, said Bono, "because laughter is very important in these camps – it lifts the spirit of everybody". On balance, he likened Ethiopia to "a modern-day Garden of Eden: when you go there it's one of the most beautiful countries on earth, an amazing place. On every corner I saw Bob Marley's face."

He and Ali would also journey together the following year to the Central American country of El Salvador, a venture Bono feared might put his beloved wife and soul-mate in too much danger this time. "I thought: 'I don't want to get Ali into trouble, maybe she wants to go somewhere else.' I said, 'Ali, we can go anywhere in the world ...' But as usual she was up for whatever it takes. She's the one who finally said, 'Let's go ...'"

Their experiences there included seeing US-backed government jets overhead en route to attack locals, a group of soldiers shooting rounds above their heads: a nightmarish experience he would later attempt to re-create musically on 'Bullet The Blue Sky'. The shots fired above their heads had been a warning not to enter a so-called fire-zone, where a loose cordon is thrown around a "rebel area" and the population is told to leave before fire is "called down". "They laughed," recalled a clearly distressed Bono. "We didn't. I just felt sick." El Salvador was a dangerous place indeed, and a long, long way from more habitual haunts like Dublin, New York or Los Angeles.

As well as expanding his world view in the years since Live Aid, Bono has also, he confesses, given himself more time to consider what it really means to be Irish. Back in the early Eighties, people at their shows in Ireland had thrown money on to the stage when imprisoned IRA supporter Bobby Sands was going through his much-publicised hunger strike. "I thought that guy must be so brave," said Bono, though he admitted he kept asking himself why. "Why be so brave? Why die? There's something not right about this. People were going, 'Yeah! You're Irish!' But these people were seeing everything in black-and-white about Ireland and they didn't realise it was all in the grey. But they know better now, I think [and] we contributed to that understanding."

Whenever the Irish tricolours had been handed to him, as routinely happened at a lot of their early shows, instead of turning them away from the stage Bono would swathe them in his white flag, to make a point, however oblique and, more practically, to avoid any potential problems with crowd violence.

However, when in November 1987 news reached the band in their dressing rooms as they prepared to take the stage at a show in Denver, Colorado, of the Enniskillen bombing that claimed thirteen innocent lives, Bono found it hard not to send out a withering verbal volley to those who claimed they approved of "the struggle" going on north of the border.

In 1982, full of youthful enthusiasm, Bono had joined a committee in Dublin set up specifically to look into the affairs of the unemployed and young people, a short-lived venture which Bono quickly grew despairing of. As he recalled: "I was the only young person on the committee." But then Irish Prime Minister, Garret Fitzgerald, had asked him personally "and I respect the man very much. But they had another language, committee-speak, and it wasn't mine. They did some very good work, but I have to say my own contribution wasn't as vital as it could have been. I just felt that if they were going to talk about unmarried mothers, I wanted an unmarried mother to be there and talk."

He continued: "I wanted to put flesh and blood on to the statistics. It was all part of this personality crisis as to whether making music was really a waste of time, when we should have got on with the real problems." These days, he said, "I've come to terms with that." He realised, above all else, now that "U2 is what I do best. Pete Townshend rapped me on the knuckles and said, 'Leave the social work to old people like me.'" Advice Bono was happy to consider – and just as happy to ignore.

In 1986, Bono and U2 took part with the Pogues, Van

Morrison and several other high-profile acts in Self Aid, an attempt to raise money to alleviate the hardships of the long-term Irish unemployed. But the event attracted much criticism, and as the highest-profile individual involved, Bono was unfortunate enough to cop a great deal of the flak personally. However, since it was later estimated that some thirteen hundred jobs had been created as a direct result of the initiative, in retrospect the criticism seems to have been badly aimed.

At the same time, Bono knew he trod the line sometimes between preacher and pied piper; that anyone could wave a white flag. And he was also the first to admit that his knowledge of the Northern Ireland conflict was far from detailed. That didn't mean he couldn't be involved in the healing process, though, he said, he just had to be careful not to position himself and the band so far in one political direction they completely failed in their much larger overall objective, which was unity, pure and simple. Peace. As he observed in 1997, "I would hate to be the boring rock'n'roll pain in the arse who shoots his mouth off about subjects he doesn't know anything about. I understand that these situations are complex."

Growing up the son of a Protestant mother and a Catholic father, he reminded everyone, he knew exactly "how grey it is", the divide between the two sides. "I was always sitting on the fence," he'd famously said, with no clear idea of whether he was Protestant or Catholic, "working class or middle class". In fact, he said, as far as he was concerned, "There are no sides, and I think people know better now [and] I think we've contributed to that." Nevertheless, he conceded, "People in the South [of Ireland] don't fully understand the situation up North. I am conscious of that. So I won't shoot my mouth off about it. I'm just really excited about the cease-fire and I think there's people on both sides – from what little I know – who want to make a difference. I'm sure there's an old guard on both sides that are sticking their feet in, but they're part of the last century – we're on to the next."

When it came to credible religious and political role models, Bono pointed to what he saw as the shining example of the martyred civil rights campaigner and former church minister, Dr Martin Luther King, who, Bono claimed, "wasn't a passive pacifist, he was a *militant* pacifist". Bono denied, however, that he was attracted to such men because he saw himself as "a man of God myself". Quite the opposite, he insisted. "The real reason that I'm attracted to these peaceful men is that I'm the guy with the broken bottle," he declared. "I grew up that way and I despise violence, I despise the violence that's in me and that's why I'm attracted to men who have turned their backs on it."

Another such individual that Bono identified as worthy of being mentioned in the same breath as King, this time in the equally fractious context of the Northern Ireland conflict, was John Hume. "He has been working the same groove for twenty years," the singer explained. "He's the Martin Luther King of this moment, and I am sort of Old Testament and Californian enough to believe in atonement and karma, but I do think it is also very important for Britain, because Britain has a lot to answer for in this regard. I think people want to throw off that baggage and I think it's really important to start again and start afresh." On a roll, he added with a flourish: "I think it would be great for Prince Charles to come to Ireland and actually say there has been a terrible tragedy here and we are part of it and let's try to work our way out of it. Something like that would do. I mean, what else are royalty good for?"

As a result of such efforts, in November 1999, at the annual MTV Europe Music Awards, which were held that year before a sizeable crowd of industry bigwigs and genuine fans at Dublin's Point Theatre, Bono stepped up to accept the Free Your Mind award, in recognition of his work on behalf of a Yes vote (in favour of the Good Friday Agreement) in Northern Ireland. Mick Jagger, who presented him with the specially commissioned award, suggested in his introduction to the crowd that Bono was edging ever closer to sainthood. It was salutary, however, to remember how Bob Geldof's "sainthood" a decade before had reduced him almost to the status of a non-musician, and there had been tension behind the scenes when the band's preliminary work on their next album had to be put on hold while Bono completed his charitable obligations.

Indeed, Bono told *Billboard* magazine in late 2000 that, having recently handed a once-in-a-lifetime petition with an incredible 21 million signatures on it to UN Secretary General Kofi Annan, he felt it was "time to leave the business of saving the planet to those who are better qualified. It just landed in my lap, and I felt obligated as a human being to follow it through." He admitted, however, that "It definitely tested the patience of the band, who wanted this record [*All That You Can't Leave Behind*] to come out last year." Needless to say, that was one promise he didn't manage to follow through.

Despite the money, the fame, the power, with a blank canvas crucial to Bono's lyric writing, allowing him to target anything political, commercial or otherwise that may drop into his sights, one of the chief reasons, perhaps, why he and U2 have survived so long without having to face the most serious accusations of selling out, is because for years they steered clear of any direct commercial endorsements or advertisements whatsoever. As Bono once said, "It's horrible to see rock'n'roll stars doing it because they've got a shit-load of dough anyway. It's just embarrassing to see someone wrap their arms around a Coke can and kiss it for money when they don't need the money." It would be different, he said, if they really did believe in the products, as with the band's own endorsements of various instruments and bits of band equipment. "It's not a big deal ... I mean, people that provide your gear, your strings on your guitar [a band advertising those products has] always happened. So we don't want to get too sanctimonious about it. But it's just where you draw the line. Also, for young bands, I can't blame them, if they want to appear as a sponsored act and they have no money ..."

As for the idea of using songs on commercials, he added, it was important to remember that "you don't have to do it. I always thought that was the deal, you know, there is some kind of deal between you and your audience. I mean, they gave you the dough and say don't worry about where you're going on holidays and where you're going to live and all the rest, just give us the good music and don't do anything stupid." This stance appears to have softened in recent times, however. In 2000, 'Beautiful Day', the first single and one of the most memorable tracks from the then recently released *All You Can't Leave Behind* album, was surprisingly sanctioned by the band for use as the theme music for ITV's new Saturday-night football show, *The Premiership*. And of course, more recently, we have seen the *How to Dismantle an Atomic Bomb* album and accompanying lead single, 'Vertigo', promoted by a hi-tech TV ad campaign in which Bono and the band clearly endorse the new iPod in the most glamorously seductive way.

There were more than a few eyebrows raised when, in February 2005, Tony Blair entered the Labour Party spring conference in Gateshead to the strains of 'Beautiful Day'. Afterwards, a faintly appalled Bono instructed a spokes-woman to issue an official statement on the band's behalf pointing out that the choice of song in no way reflected U2's own political affiliation.

"We are flattered they like our tune but this is not an official endorsement of the Labour Party," the statement read. "We reserve the right to fall in and out with any political party and their policies. Mind you, every piece of airplay helps." Bono, of course, has always been someone who reserves the right to "change my mind at any second".

Besides, for him, he said, quaint concepts such as "rebellion" no longer had any real credence in rock music. "The whole idea of [rebellion and danger] is still rooted in the Sixties. What was dangerous back then is not at all dangerous now. The whole thing, this self-destruct thing, the whole sex and drugs and rock'n'roll, that's playing into the hands of the corporations. They just call it built-in obsolescence, you know, burn out some rock'n'roll star, find another one. That's all bullshit." On the other hand, he opined, rebellion, where it did exist, was now a much more sophisticated concept anyway. "To be subversive is not to smash up your hotel room," he snorted. "Your record company will be very happy about that. You know, if I wanted to piss in a cup here that might be very good for record sales but it is not dangerous or rebellious. I actually cannot believe that people still fall for the old shite. It's too easy, I can't believe that people are still plugged into that idea of rebellion."

The new way to express rebellion was from within. "The things of the spirit are what is really rebellious," he insisted. "That's what actually puts people's noses out of joint right now and not sex. Sex ... corporations are built on that, it sells Pepsis, sells Coca Colas, sells everything. We're shocked so easily, it's sad." He shook his head disbelievingly.

Another important long-term personal relationship in Bono's life which, despite the occasional falling out, he has had no trouble sustaining over the years has been his often love–hate relationship with first the music press, then the wider media in general. It's all about perception, he says, and he is right. Let's face it, love him or loathe him, one thing we can all agree on, Bono has the gift of the gab; his ability to fill endless column inches over the years with interesting quotes is an invaluable, if sometimes precarious, asset for a bunch of musicians not otherwise known for being particularly loquacious. Mainly, the fact that Bono was nearly always an interviewer's dream would be used to his advantage as the years passed and he tried to introduce his non-musical agenda to fans and non-fans alike. As a by-product, it also meant press attention was, happily, deflected away from his family and more personal life, and over the years Bono has become a master at making sure that the media spotlight stayed firmly on the topics he, and not they, were most comfortable with, and considered most "valid".

As a result, the UK music press of the mid-Eighties had often highlighted a pretentious element in U2's early music; bracketing them for a time alongside what they saw as equally preening products of the late-Seventies new wave such as Simple Minds, their similarly mullet-haired Eighties stadium-rock contemporaries. But even the notoriously tough UK music press would find it increasingly hard over the years to knock the band as they rose to ever greater heights while making it abundantly clear that they retained a social conscience, as well as a genuine sense of adventure with their music. Even someone like Paul Morley, then the star writer of the *NME*, who had gone out to interview them in the early days and might have been expected to find fault with their every pronouncement, returned instead to file a hugely approving feature for the paper punningly headed "Eires Apparent".

By 1987, the crucible of Live Aid and the fifteen million copies they had sold of their first post-Live Aid album, *The Joshua Tree*, meant U2 no longer had to worry what the guttersnipes in the music press were saying, but Bono, always seeking the last word, insisted on keeping the dialogue going, as he still does today with the music press. In truth, however, the band was now into bigger things. TV and radio adored them, and the journalists following Bono around searching for the Big Interview came less from magazines such as the *NME* and *Rolling Stone* and more from broadsheet newspapers such as *The Times* and the *Telegraph* and upmarket monthly magazines such as *Esquire*, *GQ* and *Vanity Fair*.

There were also the inevitable occasional hand-wringing, angst-ridden colour supplement articles along the lines of "U2 have just earned $26.2 million, yet they still wear ripped jeans ... is their stance as conscience-stricken saviours the genuine article or a marketing scam?". But Bono's willingness to fight his corner, when access to the singer was offered, almost always led to his usual robust defence. Most journalists thought they were coming to interview one of those insufferably pompous rock stars and were taken aback to find someone quite different; not only their intellectual equal, but someone with genuine commitment, and even more important, real reach. This was one rock star who not only said he wanted to get involved in helping solve the world's problems, he actually went out and did it. Whether you bought into his stance or not, you had to admit: it was certainly something new to write about.

As for the infamous British tabloids – the attack-dogs of what was once Fleet Street – with precious little gossip to trot out, their take on Bono and his band has varied over the years, often depending on a particular paper's own political allegiance. By and large, though, looking at the wide range of cuttings the band have picked up over the years, you would have to say that the tabloids have always been largely supportive of U2. The *Sun*'s then pop columnist, Dominic Mohan, in particular, was one of the first to grasp that favourable coverage of this insanely popular group could only add to copy sales. That said, not all the newspapers were always as keen to jump aboard the U2 bandwagon. For example, the *Daily Mail* seemed deliberately to go against the grain in their vitriolic review of the band's otherwise hugely acclaimed 1993 Wembley concerts with the savage headline: "U2's message to the world: Loud, cool and totally meaningless". But then, by that point, neither the peace-espousing Bono nor his band were likely to appeal to the *Mail*'s hardcore constituency of mainly elderly, right-wing readers. More in tune with their audience was a paper such as the *Guardian*, which could always be relied upon to give U2 a push, especially when good works were involved, as with the story they ran in 2002 headlined: "Pro Bono – how an Irish rock star won the ear of the world's most powerful man".

These days, of course, the cause that most concerns Bono

the political activist centres on the plight of the troubled people of Africa, a tragic, complex situation, encompassing aspects of Third World debt and simple human justice, and the fight against the ever-growing AIDS epidemic. In 2004, Bono and U2 had visited the headquarters of Archbishop Desmond Tutu's Truth and Reconciliation Commission in South Africa, at a special ceremony where they were introduced personally to Tutu, who began the meeting by inviting them to join him in a communal prayer. Afterwards, in more upbeat fashion, he took them upstairs and said, "Look, I have a few people who would like to meet the band," before taking them inside a large room in which sat around six hundred specially invited guests of the Archbishop. "Ladies and gentlemen," Tutu told them, "I have for you, to sing a song, U2!" Bono was momentarily taken aback. Nobody had said anything about singing a song! "We had no instruments, nothing!" he later recalled with a smile. "We just looked at each other, just like rabbits [caught] in the headlights. The only thing I could think of singing was 'Amazing Grace', which turns out was appropriate; it is a story of grace interrupting karma. If Nelson Mandela's story is the most inspirational for their liberty, this is for our liberty."

Speaking after he had returned from South Africa that summer, Bono said he believed that Archbishop Tutu had created "one of the most inspiring stories of the last fifty years to have come out of South Africa", an achievement to rank alongside that of Nelson Mandela, adding that in the Truth and Reconciliation campaign Tutu had "created a model that you could apply to the Middle East, to Northern Ireland, to Bosnia. It's the most extraordinary thing to see relatives of murdered protesters standing in front of the people who shot their wife and ask them questions like: 'Do you remember a woman wearing a green dress, she was waving at the time when you shot her.' And then with tears rolling down their faces, both of them often, the victims and the perpetrators, start talking. Just to get to the truth, not to get to a result that puts people behind bars. I think that it is the most extraordinary jump in human consciousness that I've heard about in a very long time."

Bono also took the opportunity to highlight the example of AIDS activist Zackie Achmat as "the third inspiring story", he had been told during his visit. As he explained: "[Achmat, who was himself HIV positive] went on drug strike and refused to take ARVs, whilst his fellow AIDS activists were not getting them," due to the fact that there were simply not enough effective medicines to go around and a horrific "pecking order" had been introduced. Bono continued: "They took the South African government to court and won on the issue of generics. But he put his life on the line. That's the extraordinary thing, to be sitting, as I have, and hearing committees of activists, the heroes sitting around in their canteens discussing who is going to go on the drug treatment and who isn't."

Appalled by the catch-22 situation the people of Africa now found themselves in, Bono rightly believed these were choices no human being should have to make. As he angrily pointed out, "These drugs cost fucking nothing to make after research. At a time when people do not think that we are such a benign force in the world, we are letting people die for the stupidest of reasons: money! It is so fucked up!"

That we could all agree on. But what was there anyone could do? Bono thought he had the answer to that one, too. "The pharmaceutical industry needs to get faster at dealing with this emergency," he said simply. Not in a purely altruistic sense, he added. You had to be realistic. "I don't think we should expect the pharmaceutical industry to behave like a charity. That's not what they are in. We shouldn't be shocked when commerce refuses to offer philanthropy." He did, however, believe that it was "up to the governments to put pressure on [the drug] companies". Let them still sell their precious drugs; but force them to do so at prices the people who need them – the impoverished Third World – could actually afford.

Easier said than done, of course, as Bono was the first to admit. But surely a start had to be made somewhere. A line drawn in the sand. He knew it was the bigger picture that counted most, which is how he had first become involved in the campaign to end Third World debt, the chief cause of the impoverishment of such countries. His first public statement on the subject could not have been better staged. In February 1999, Bono had decided to use his appearance at that year's televised Brit Awards ceremony in London to generate further much-needed publicity for his newly adopted cause. Having been presented with the Freddie Mercury Prize for "outstanding charitable works", Bono said a brief thanks then took the silver award and leapt from the stage with it in his hand. From there, he immediately ran over to the front row of the audience, where he graciously re-presented his Brit to the veteran heavyweight boxing legend Muhammad Ali, guest of honour that evening. It was a gesture, explained Bono afterwards, intended to highlight a new campaign he and figures such as Ali had agreed to represent, an organisation set up in order to try and persuade the most powerful governments in the world to cancel Third World debt, beginning with significant cuts – now. They called this new operation the Jubilee 2000 project, a coalition of eventually more than ninety pressure groups, headed by some of the most famous faces of the day – including Bono as its most vocal public figurehead, and Ali as the organisation's international ambassador – demanding that Western governments cancel debt repayments by the new millennium.

The catalyst for Bono's involvement in this radical new project had been Jubilee 2000's creator, Jamie Drummond, who had been depressed by the discovery that, while Live Aid had helped save countless lives, the people of Ethiopia ten years on were faced with such a ruinous mountain of debt which, in terms of annual repayments, constituted over two and a half times the money raised by the historic event itself. Outraged, Drummond determined that the music industry should once again take a lead, and pursued Bono to become the organisation's chief spokesperson. The connection was made by Richard Constant, a lawyer for Island's owners

Universal Music Group and a mutual acquaintance, and in 1998, after listening attentively to what Drummond had to say, Bono agreed to come on board immediately.

The Brits, he said, had simply given him his first real chance publicly to articulate his concern. "It is the desire of most people's hearts," Bono declared earnestly, "to do something for people who don't have much. Since Live Aid with Bob Geldof there hasn't been a co-ordinated attempt to do something about poverty. We raised two hundred million pounds with Geldof, but Third World countries pay that much every week in debts. Every one pound we send to Africa, they owe us nine pounds." It was a shocking, shameful statistic, he said, and one that had, frankly, rarely been considered before outside hard-line political circles. Now Bono, as was his way, was bringing the argument out into the streets, via the TV, press and radio, via any means he damn well could.

That said, Bono's Brits appeal had met with a mixed response. While the Prodigy's Keith Flint would be moved enough to go out and get the words "Drop the Debt" tattooed on his back, Blur singer Damon Albarn, for one, was less impressed by what he saw as a pop star "preaching" at an awards ceremony. "Bono is very well-meaning," said Albarn, "and has probably got a very good heart, but the idea of them and a thousand people, all tanked-up, all toasting this kind of great sentiment – the level of hypocrisy in all standing up for Third World debt to be abolished – it's profoundly Western."

Profoundly Western or not, undeterred as ever, that June

would see Bono and The Edge join over thirty-five thousand demonstrators who had gathered to protest and present a petition outside the G8 summit then being held in Cologne. The highlight of what was a generally civilised if agitated affair came when Bono and Radiohead's Thom Yorke stood on the steps of the building together with German Chancellor, Gerhard Schroeder, where they jointly presented him with the petition signed by more than twenty million people. As a result, the demonstrators were at least partially rewarded for their huge efforts by the hurried announcement of a new debt-relief programme: the so-called "Cologne Debt Initiative", which, it was said, would provide seventy billion dollars' worth of new debt relief for impoverished Third World nations. "It's just a token. It's what they can afford to do without really trying," said an unimpressed Edge. But the publicity value of even this relatively small victory was invaluable and, partly thanks to Bono, the campaign continued reinvigorated and with a renewed sense of what could actually be accomplished.

As a follow-up, in October that same year, Net Aid staged three simultaneous charity concerts at Giant's Stadium in the USA, Wembley Stadium in the UK and a smaller, invitation-only concert in Geneva, Switzerland. The event's specially composed theme song, 'New Day', was performed by the band at Giant's Stadium and simultaneously broadcast in London and Switzerland (and via the internet). Featuring such stars as Bono, Jewel, Sheryl Crow, Adam Duritz, Michael Stipe, Wyclef Jean, Mary J. Blige, David Bowie, the

Eurythmics, Robbie Williams, George Michael and Bryan Adams, the three concerts broke the record for a live cyber-cast, as well as being broadcast live simultaneously on the satellite channels MTV and VH1.

Bono's involvement with the Jubilee 2000 Drop the Debt campaign, and its pledge to come up with real solutions, would also eventually lead to him becoming a co-founder, in 2002, of DATA (Debt, Aids, Trade, Africa). DATA was to be another energetic new organisation that would work to raise awareness about, and hopefully spark international response to, the various crises now swamping Africa. Namely, the problem of unpayable debts, the apparently uncontrolled spread of AIDS, and the widespread misuse of blatantly unfair trade rules.

More eager than ever, it seems, not to let any opportunity to spread the good word pass him by, in March 2002, Bono was even to be seen again back in the White House. Not with his old sax-playing pal Bill this time, though, but with his former nemesis, President George W. Bush, the son of the man Bono had once stalked telephonically from the stage during the Zoo TV tour. Little wonder then, perhaps, that the presidential staff now affectionately dubbed him "the Pest". The photo opportunity was to accompany the announcement of a $5,000,000 rise in US aid to Africa, which Bono's cease-less lobbying had helped put through. An occasion of some note, not just for the money it raised or for the priceless publicity value, but one, nevertheless, that had somewhat alarmed the ever vigilant Edge. As Bono later recalled: "Edge was pleading with me not to hang out with the Conservatives [or the Republicans]. He said, 'You're not going to have a photo with Bush?' I said, 'I'd have lunch with Satan if so much was at stake.'" The issues, Bono had decided, were simply much "bigger than whether it makes me cringe or not. So the band might cringe, I might wince, but I went to Washington to get a cheque and [later] I'm going back to get a bigger one ..."

The idea behind getting to meet Bush was simple, said Bono: to progress Jubilee 2000's arguments about writing off Third World debt on a political level rather than take the easy way out with another Band Aid. And why should it always be the ordinary people who supported such events who were asked to dig deep for the money? Wasn't it the turn of governments to take a humanitarian stand? Without them, whatever U2 or any other entertainers did would only ever truly be a "band aid" in every sense. With the American government even partly on board, however, real long-term solutions could be found for these problems. Besides, the suggestion of another concert, whenever Bono had even tentatively brought the subject up with Bob Geldof, had always been swiftly dismissed. "I said it's not going to work," the ex-Boomtown Rat revealed. "These are very dry, empirical, economic arguments, and it needs something different. The main thing [Bono has] got is access because of his fame, and the only route I was prepared to go was one that would move the political agenda along. It's embarrassing and pathetic," concluded Geldof, "that people who have celebrity have access, but if that's the case let's fucking use it, you know?"

Bono agreed. With that end in mind, the two singers would later spend a weekend together as the guests of honour at Chequers with UK Prime Minister Tony Blair and Chancellor Gordon Brown. However, it soon became clear as they tried to advance their arguments that they were, in Geldof's memorable phrase, "pushing at an open door", and Bono later joked to friends that he and Geldof had even organised a "good cop bad cop" routine. "Geldof rages at the injustices served by the West on Africa, while Bono comes in politely and asks what we're all going to do about it." They half-jokingly called the concept "Sabbath economics", the idea that every seventh day you stop consumption and exploitation, and every forty-nine years you write off debts and free slaves. "It's the opposite of globalisation and Bono got very excited," revealed Jubilee 2000 organiser Ann Pettifor afterwards. If only the PM and his stone-faced Chancellor had felt so passionately.

Nevertheless, Bono's latest charm offensive would staunchly refuse to recognise boundaries. To the surprise and confusion of many, he controversially invited US Republican Senator Jesse Helms – who once famously stated that homosexuals were "weak, morally sick wretches" and blamed drug abuse and violence in America on Satan's direct involvement in the music industry – to be his guest at a U2 show on the 2001 Elevation world tour. Whatever point he was making – forgiveness? Tolerance? A new chance of understanding? – Bono seemed to have proved it when the eighty-year-old

Helms later claimed to have been turned into a U2 fan that night. "It was the noisiest thing I ever heard," Helms was later reported as saying. He added that he had also been impressed by the crowd: "moving back and forth like corn in the breeze". As if to prove an even more personal point, Bono also took the opportunity to take the elderly politician to task over his wayward views of the gay community. Standing in the dressing room after the show actually quoting some of the scriptures to Helms, Bono reminded him that "two thousand, one hundred and three verses [of the Bible] pertain to the poor, and yet Jesus speaks of judgement only once – and it's not about being gay or sexual morality but about morality". Bono later claimed that, to his credit, Helms had stood there and listened patiently and, at the end of it, appeared to be "really moved. He was in tears. Later he told me he was ashamed of what he used to think about AIDS."

There was, of course, no small irony to be found in the sight of a multi-millionaire showbiz personality pleading the case for the poor and needy, and this certainly wasn't lost on the painfully self-aware Bono, yet you got his point. "I'm uncomfortable being a rich rock star, doing this," he confessed. "I'm unhappy with that juxtaposition, I would love not to be doing this [espousing good causes], for somebody else to do this who was not as compromised as me." Nevertheless, he admitted that he still worked night and day to master his brief, even, when he had to, "going to bed with World Bank reports" to ensure he was as clued-up as the advisers and civil servants who surrounded the world leaders and international powerbrokers he was now regularly rubbing shoulders with. As Geldof put it, "For a summer [Bono and I] had high-level tutorials until we knew this boring shit backwards. Bono's an exceptionally clever man – the pop star of record. He's charming, he's persuasive, and the politicians can go home to their daughters and say: 'I had a meeting with Bono today.'"

It seemed that Bono's example had also spawned a new rock star with a conscience in the shape of Coldplay vocalist Chris Martin. In one of his first major interviews in America, Martin told *Rolling Stone* magazine that what he and his own band had learned from Bono and U2 is that "you have to be brave enough to be yourself. It's amazing," he pointed out, "that the biggest band in the world has so much integrity and passion in their music. Our society is thoroughly screwed, fame is a ridiculous waste of time and celebrity culture is disgusting. There are only a few people around brave enough to talk out against it, who use their fame in a good way." Coldplay intended to follow U2's example, he seemed to suggest, and speak out regardless.

Martin said he also appreciated the ultimate lesson the four members of U2 had taken so long finally to learn: that "the band is more important than any of their songs or albums. I love it that [U2] are best mates and have an integral role in one another's lives as friends. I love the way that they're not interchangeable – if Larry Mullen Jr wants to go scuba diving for a week, the rest of the band can't do a thing." He also drew comparisons with his own situation in the fact that, "U2 – like Coldplay – maintain that all songs that appear on their albums are credited to the band. And they are the only band that's been around for twenty years with no member changes and no big splits."

As a result of such endeavours, today Bono can count among his friends such illustrious and diverse names as Bob Dylan, Brian Eno, Luciano Pavarotti, Sting and Trudie Styler, Quincy Jones, Tina Turner, Björk, President Bill Clinton, Jack Nicholson, UN Secretary General Kofi Annan, Nancy and Barbara Sinatra, Bruce Springsteen, Salman Rushdie, Sean Penn, David Bowie, Van Morrison, Sir Bob Geldof, Phil Joanou, the late Johnny Cash, Billy Corgan, William Gibson and Muhammad Ali – and that's barely scratching the A-list. Yet he really does remain the kind of person who likes to stop and chat on the street with anyone, from the poorest peasants of the South African shanty towns to the smart-arses of Dublin's O'Connell Street.

Almost inevitably, some of his many friends also became musical collaborators along the way, and Bono's outgoing nature led him to work with a great many other great singers, too – not least among whom was the late Roy Orbison, a former Sun Records label-mate of Elvis Presley and Jerry Lee Lewis. The legendary balladeer had first called on U2 during the same 1987 US tour leg on which they had filmed much of *Rattle and Hum* and – when the cameras weren't around – Orbison had asked Bono if he had any material that might be suitable for him to record, as he was about to start work on a new "comeback" album. Bono was bowled over by the request. A long-time admirer of the silverlarynxed legend, he was also aware that Orbison was then on the crest of a genuine comeback as one-fifth of the Traveling Wilburys – along with Bob Dylan, George Harrison, Tom Petty and Jeff Lynne – and, through the million-selling success of that project, had been offered his first major solo recording contract for many years.

As a result, unlike Frank Sinatra, who sadly never got time before his death to record Bono's offering to him, 'Two Shots Of Happy, One Shot Of Sad', Orbison was delighted to be able to incorporate a new Bono song into his repertoire, and, in September 1988, the pair worked closely together in the studio as the number quickly took shape. Sadly, "the Big O", as he was known to his most ardent followers, would die of a heart attack, aged just fifty-two, a matter of two months later and therefore, sadly, was not around to enjoy the massive success of his now posthumously released "come-back" album. A great pity as it was a fine album. Bono felt particularly honoured that its title, *Mystery Girl*, had been taken from the song Bono had written specially for Roy, and the track that became the album's big hit single, the positively lush 'She's A Mystery To Me'.

Another major Roy Orbison fan was Bono's youthful muse, Bruce Springsteen, whose famous 1975 *Born to Run* track, 'Thunder Road', had famously referred to *"Roy Orbison singing for the lonely ..."* The circle was arguably completed therefore when, in 1999, Bono was invited to induct "The Boss" (who had, in his turn, previously had the honour of inducting Roy Orbison) into the US Rock'n'Roll Hall of Fame, at a special ceremony in New York. Tellingly, Bono's speech to the televised assembled throng that night said as much about his own musical youth, as it did about his mentor's music.

He began by explaining to the audience how, "In 1974, I was fourteen [but] even I knew the Sixties were over. It was the era of soft-rock and [jazz] fusion. The Beatles were gone, Elvis was in Vegas. What was goin' on? Nothin' was goin' on. Bruce Springsteen was comin' on, saving music from the phoneys, saving lyrics from the folkies, saving leather jackets from the Fonz ..." Bono began singing a refrain from one of Springsteen's earliest, most romantic songs, 'Sandy': "Now the greasers, they tramp the streets and get busted for sleeping on the beaches all night, and them boys in their high heels, ah Sandy, their skins are so white ... Oh Sandy, love me tonight, and I promise I'll love you for ever ..."

There was a pause while he let the laughter and applause die down, then he continued in more serious vein. "In Dublin, Ireland, I knew what he [Springsteen] was talking about. Here was a dude who carried himself like Brando, and Dylan, and Elvis. If John Steinbeck could sing, if Van Morrison could ride a Harley-Davidson," that would be Bruce Springsteen, he suggested. "It was something new, too," Bono went on. "He was the first whiff of Scorsese, the first hint of Patti Smith, Elvis Costello and the Clash. He was the end of long hair, brown rice and bell-bottom [trousers]. It was the end of the twenty-minute drum solo. It was good night, Haight-Ashbury; hello, Asbury Park ..."

Again, he had to wait for the applause to die down before

he could continue. "We call him the Boss," Bono concluded, at length. "Well, that's a bunch of crap. He's not the boss. He works for us. More than a boss, he's the owner, because more than anyone else, Bruce Springsteen owns America's heart."

What he was too gracious to mention, of course, was that Bono also now owned a piece of America's musical heart. You could be sure, however, that, like all his other passionately discharged duties, including the occasional lingering glance in the mirror when he thought no one else was looking, it would remain a responsibility he would take extremely seriously.

Oddly, considering the degree to which they obviously looked forward to the challenges of a new millennium, the first years of the twenty-first century would find Bono and U2 returning with increasing ardour to their musical roots. Discarding the costumes and elaborate stage sets that had characterised their Nineties output – the postmodern angst and inverted, cyberpunk songs – they appeared to satisfy themselves with simply being a rock band again. Not that this would curb Bono's off-stage political enthusiasms, of course, but at last, it seemed, they had figured out how simply to have straightforward fun with their music again. Along with all the stage props went the hi-tech trappings that had swamped all their Nineties albums, to a greater or lesser extent. In their place strode a new, leaner, more musically muscled band that appeared more relaxed than ever before with the simple business of being a group again.

As if signalling this newfound sense of fun, they readily agreed to appear, alongside co-star Steve Martin, in the special 200th episode of *The Simpsons* animated TV show shown that year. Happy to send themselves up, suddenly they appeared to have the whole caboodle in the right perspective.

When, in September 1999, during a break from recording in Dublin, he and Bob Geldof had visited Pope John Paul II, in Rome, as part of an official delegation from the Jubilee 2000 campaign, Bono memorably swapped his sunglasses for one of the Pope's rosaries. "The Pope's legged it with my goggles," he joked afterwards.

Bono wasn't the only one now enjoying the fruits of his success. In March 2000, Dublin acknowledged one of their own when Lord Mayor Mary Freehill conferred the Freedom of the City on U2 and their manager Paul McGuinness; all five crucial "elements" of the band, as Bono saw it, being honoured for both their musical achievements and their tireless extracurricular work for good causes. "I'd have thought people would be sick of U2 by now," Bono commented wryly in his acceptance speech. "It's still so moving to come home and see the amount of goodwill towards us." The band rounded off proceedings with an impromptu concert before thousands in Dublin's Smithfield market square.

With over thirty hit singles and ten chart albums to their name, there had been much talk over recent years of a U2 "Greatest Hits" collection of some kind, but so far neither Bono nor the rest of the band had ever felt the time was right. The Nineties had been a time of relentless pushing forward, with precious little interest in the idea of suddenly looking in the rear-view mirror. Indeed, it might be argued that the main thrust of U2's musical mien in the Nineties revolved around their determination to move their music as far away as possible from everything they had done before.

Now, having made their statement, re-establishing them-selves, as they saw it, on a new and higher plane from which to gaze down at the rest of the rock world, and, not least, with the impending end of a whole millennium to consider, suddenly the time did seem right for some sort of retrospective U2 package. As usual, however, this was to be no ordinary, clumsily thrown together "Greatest Hits" confection. Instead, the band opted to present a collection of material chosen specifically to reflect their earliest years as recording artists. By carefully cherry-picking from their first recording decade, the eventual album, *Best of: 1980–1990*, released in time for Christmas, in 1998, was not only a huge worldwide success, it also shrewdly left the door open for a follow-up companion release on the Nineties. The equally shrewd addition of a "bonus disc" with the official album, containing a collection of all the various B-side tracks from their earliest singles, was enough to satisfy long-time fans who owned all the other material already, and helped propel the collection to Number 1, U2's seventh UK chart-topper, while the stand-alone album, which for some reason is listed separately by the *Guinness Book of Hit Albums*, peaked at Number 4, having had the wind somewhat taken out of its sales by the more tempting double-disc collection. But only somewhat. By the end of 2000, almost twelve million copies of the *Best of: 1980–1990* album had been sold around the world, making it the band's most commercially successful album since *Rattle and Hum* twelve years before.

The *Best of: 1980–1990* album was also promoted by the release of the single, 'The Sweetest Thing', one of Bono's earliest love songs to Ali, and hitherto tucked wastefully away on the B-side of the 1986 'Where The Streets Have No Name' single. With all monies raised from the newly released single earmarked to benefit Alison's preferred charity, the CCP, the Kevin Godley-directed video to 'The Sweetest Thing' was particularly fascinating, almost surreal, seeing the band parading through the streets of Dublin in carnival style and featuring a supporting cast that numbered at least one elephant, several excessively muscle-bound firemen, plus a sprinkling of the band's celebrity friends: the world champion Irish boxer (and then recent conqueror of Chris Eubank) Steve Collins, along with the entire cast of Irish boy band, Boyzone, whose lead singer, Ronan Keating, saw himself, he confessed, as something of a Bono protégé. (The concept behind the video, Bono later explained, was to include as many of Ali's favourite things as possible.) As a result, 'The Sweetest Thing' reached Number 3 in the UK charts that Christmas.

Meanwhile, if, as many had suggested over the years, Bono's wide-screen lyrical vision and ever more elaborate video shoots had alluded to any serious movie-making pretensions, 2000 was the year they were proved right and those dreams became, briefly, a reality. Ten years after the agreement was signed, Bono's first film venture, *The Million Dollar Hotel*, finally "wrapped". Co-produced and directed by the fabled film-maker Wim Wenders (whose earlier movie,

Paris, Texas, Bono had found deeply affecting), and with a screenplay written by Nicholas Klein (based on an original story by Bono) and a cast headed by Mel Gibson (whose own production company was financing the film), the film is set in a seedy downtown area of Los Angeles where the love story between Tom Tom and Eloise unfolds at a run-down and faintly eerie hostel, the sardonically named Million Dollar Hotel. With an unexpected death in one of the guest rooms comes the involvement of FBI Agent Skinner, a man clearly with issues of his own to deal with, played with expertly dark comic timing by Gibson.

Mel Gibson had read the original script several years before after Bono had pressed a copy upon him one night at a U2 show the actor had attended. As one of Hollywood's most bankable superstars, Gibson was used to people foisting their "killer scripts" on him, but as it was Bono, he agreed to take a look. Bono was a singer, not a film-maker, though, and Gibson admitted later that he hoped what he was about to read wouldn't be too bad. Instead, he was surprised at how good it was, calling Bono up a few days later and telling him how much he "really liked it".

Bono later explained how the original idea had come to him while standing with the band having their pictures taken on the roof of the Frontier Hotel, in LA – aka the Million Dollar Hotel, to locals – during the *Joshua Tree* tour of America. "Myself and The Edge were on the roof," he recalled, "we used to hang out a lot downtown [there], there were some great clubs. Everyone goes to bed in LA really early and we were looking for a smaller community to play with and we found one downtown, which was kind of nice for us. So we kind of knew this area."

He recalled how it had been photographer Anton Corbijn's idea to take them up on to the roof to take some shots of them. "Myself and The Edge were up on the roof of the hotel, finding it kind of hard to believe that it was called the Million Dollar Hotel. And that's the funny thing about America, isn't it – the poetry of the place names. Words seem to fall out of the sky [there] and it seemed like the name of a book or a play or a movie already, just waiting to be written. The first clue we had was that if you get to the edge of the roof, there's about a ten-foot jump to the other building and Edge was convinced he could make it. He said, 'If you have faith, if you believe you can do it, you can do it.'" But Bono didn't believe and, thankfully, neither man felt compelled to put the guitarist's theory to the actual test.

Wim Wenders's involvement, the ultimate catalyst for Gibson's company to get the movie green-lighted and into production, stemmed from the video he had also previously directed for U2's *Red, Hot & Blue* AIDS charity album contribution, the cover of Cole Porter's 'Night And Day'. Even so, Bono admits that he was still nervous of approaching the legendary auteur and at first shrank from the task of even broaching the subject with him. "I didn't think maybe that he'd go for it," he said. "But, in fact, he has an unusual eye on America … you can see it in *Paris, Texas*, you can see there is a love of the landscape there. And we needed to have somebody to bring a fresh eye to downtown Los Angeles, to not shoot it like a jeans commercial."

Bono was credited on the final film as both co-writer of the original story and co-producer, even though, as he cheerfully admitted, "I don't really know what that is. I'm also writing a few tunes for the soundtrack, I'm hoping to bring the band in on the soundtrack as well." Writing for film was, he agreed, quite a step on from the business of merely writing songs for a rock group. For example, he said, "The idea of writing in the third person is a real break for me. A lot of U2 songs are in the first person, that's why they play well live. They're not story songs, we don't do story songs really. So I wouldn't mind a break from that."

As for the subject matter itself, it was important, too, he felt, that neither the film nor the accompanying music try to glamorise the gutter-level life they were trying to depict. Nor did they wish to paint things too black. As Bono explained: "It's easy for rich rock stars and the like to romanticise a place like downtown LA, and I've seen the suits stepping over bodies on their way to the banks [there] and it seems so heartless sometimes." He continued: "The hotel [in the film] is populated by all kinds of people. There are deadbeats and people who were put out from mental institutions and set up there. And then there are just good people getting on with their life, decent people who have come to Los Angeles and want some inexpensive accommodations. And you see some dignity, some real dignity and humour from the locals ..."

Dismissing as too fanciful the link some critics made

between the aimless hobos that totter about the film and Bono's more youthful Lipton Village collective, the true meaning of the film, he seemed to suggest, was actually mirrored in the way in which it was made. "To come right into the heart of film-making in America," he said, "to go to downtown LA and to miss Hollywood, to an area that people don't come to when the sun goes down and to find some beauty in downtown, in the Million Dollar Hotel, to find some light, some colour ..." That, in a nutshell, was what it was all about, he said.

The official *Million Dollar Hotel* soundtrack album was released in March 2000, just a month after the film's much-publicised première at the Berlin Film Festival, an event Bono made sure he attended. While the soundtrack album was not credited to the band as such, in truth, much of the material on it had, Bono acknowledged, emerged from several different U2 recording sessions, jams or just fragments of out-takes that had been amassed over the years, small moments discarded by the band that he had quietly pocketed, feeling subconsciously that there might yet be a time when such stuff would come in useful. As a result, six songs of the sixteen tracks eventually included on the *Million Dollar Hotel* album were performed by Bono and/or various members of U2. 'Stateless', for example, one of their most infectiously bluesy tracks since *Rattle and Hum*, had originally come out of a loose soundcheck jam on the last tour. While the blissfully shady 'Dancin' Shoes' and the unashamedly romantic 'Falling At Your Feet' were the products of some inspired last-minute Bono rewrites on the guitar with producer Daniel Lanois. And of course, there was 'The Ground Beneath Her Feet', the aforementioned Salman Rushdie collaboration and possibly the most evocative moment on an album brimming with mood and changing temperatures. The last of the six songs and often the least considered, was 'Never Let Me Go', a sublimely moving jazz number featuring the silky, melancholy skills of ace trumpeter Jon Hassell, who received a co-writing credit for his trouble. The rest of the mainly instrumental tracks on the final album were nimbly credited to the Million Dollar Hotel Band – in reality, Bono and co-conspirators Lanois and Brian Eno. These were all recorded at U2's own Hanover Quays Studio in Dublin and produced without over-elaboration by Hal Willner.

At the end of the day, after the completion of yet another outside project, however interesting or successful, it was now decided that no more should get in the way of Bono and the band concentrating on the main event: the completion of what would be the first all-new U2 album of the new millennium. If you had a million dollars to invest, at this point, there was no hotel yet built that would yield the profit expected from a good new U2 album.

With most of the basic tracks for the new album recorded at their own Hanover Quays Studios throughout the latter part of 1999 (often at the same time as Bono was laying down tracks for his film soundtrack album), and finally completed during the early months of 2000, U2's first new album for over three years was released worldwide in October 2000. Titled *All That You Can't Leave Behind*, this was to be the most refreshingly straight-ahead, song-based U2 album since *The Joshua Tree* nearly fifteen years previously. The connection was no coincidence, either, as Bono and the band had taken the decision to bring back the dream production team of that golden era, in Brian Eno and Daniel Lanois; persuading them to reunite in order to attempt what Bono was beginning to view more and more as the musical and spiritual successor to that era.

As such, *All That You Can't Leave Behind* was also destined to become U2's most internationally successful album since *The Joshua Tree*, topping the charts in thirty-two countries, including Britain, where it became their eighth Number 1 album – achieving a record first-week sale of over 164,000, outstripping *Pop*'s opening weekly sale by over 12,000 copies, and placing U2 just short of the UK total of Number 1 albums shared by Abba and Queen, and with a more than reasonable expectation of eventually overhauling the total amassed by both the Rolling Stones (ten) and the Beatles, still standing proud at the top of the pile with thirteen Number 1 albums to their credit.

Adding the icing to the cake was the fact that *All That You Can't Leave Behind* was also their biggest-selling album in America since the mid-Eighties. As in the UK, the new album had achieved record first-week sales, raking up almost 430,000 copies. Privately, Bono was delighted by the news – and not a little relieved. The three U2 albums of the Nineties

– Achtung Baby!, Zooropa and *Pop –* may have been the most musically adventurous, daringly experimental albums of the band's now quarter-century career, but they were also the most challenging in the sense of effectively alienating a significant section of the mainstream audience that previous more straight-ahead albums, such as *The Joshua Tree* and *The Unforgettable Fire*, had achieved for them in America. All three Nineties U2 albums had been significant US hits, of course, but not on the same scale as *The Joshua Tree* or even the critically derided *Rattle and Hum*. Moreover, while their Stateside tours still played in the largest venues, the band was no longer always able to do multiple nights in every city they played, one of the main commercial drivers behind their decision to promote the PopMart US tour as a 'one-night-only' attraction.

The arrival of the *All That You Can't Leave Behind* album reversed that trend practically overnight. Eventually reaching Number 3 in the US charts – their highest chart position in the US for a new U2 album since *Rattle and Hum* – the real success of the new album was that it single-handedly re-established U2 as the driving force behind mainstream arena rock in America in the new millennium. Shows on the subsequent world tour began each night with a public quote from Psalm 116 of the bible, and ended with a shower of hallelujahs and exhortations; the mix of rock and politics momentarily subsumed by the intense white heat of some serious religious fireworks.

The opening track, and first single from *All That You Can't*

Leave Behind, was 'Beautiful Day', a track which in many ways exemplified the positive overall mood and simple, upbeat vibe of the album. The Edge wound the clock back by reclaiming from his guitar collection his trusty old Gibson Explorer, that fearsomely angular "axe" he'd wielded to such simple yet dramatic effect so often in the early days. "Because we were coming up with interesting and innovative music I felt I had a licence to use some signature guitar tones," he explained in his usual understated style. "Bono was particularly uncertain about it," he revealed, "but it really stood up."

Indeed it did. 'Beautiful Day' was another one of those special songs that blissfully just emerged sometimes – "when we're not looking" – from a studio jam when the band kicked ideas about, hoping to open the locked floodgates of inspiration with just a word, maybe, or phrase, or simple guitar lick. Sitting Buddha-like behind the mixing desk, listening to the band noodling around in the studio, Daniel Lanois claims he suddenly had a vision. As he put it, amid the musical chaos he could suddenly see "Bono singing about beauty in the midst of flying pieces of metal and mayhem … like a hymn". Suitably inspired, it was also Lanois who would persuade Bono to try using what was originally a throwaway line in the middle of the jam as the chorus and opening line of the new song, a suggestion that fired Bono up and caused him to rethink the whole thing, eventually recasting the song so that it went beyond a simple, if moving crescendo and turned into a gloriously over-the-top anthem for the new millennium. Or as Bono later put it: a sort of "heavy-metal hymn" for the new century. It would also go on to become another Grammy winner for them when it won Best Single at the annual awards show in LA, in February 2001.

Another highlight from the new album, the hauntingly evocative 'Stuck In A Moment You Can't Get Out Of' – also destined to become another sizeable hit single for the band in January 2001 – was said to be inspired by the life of Paula Yates, the late wife of Bob Geldof. Bono had also known INXS singer, Michael Hutchence, the man for whom Yates had famously left Geldof a few years previously. Bono confessed that he and Hutchence had once discussed the concept of suicide. At the end of it, he revealed, they had both come to the same conclusion: that suicide was, ultimately, the coward's way out. There was, therefore, the sense that Bono's later grief at Hutchence's bizarre, unexplained death (he was found asphyxiated in an apparently wanton act of sexual self-immolation, in his suite at the Ritz Carlton hotel in Sydney, in November 1997) was tinged with puzzlement and disappointment. Yates, of course, had also died, not long afterwards, of an alleged heroin overdose, leaving behind her estranged husband and tragically bereft children, her baffled and distraught circle of genuine friends to try and pick up the pieces; to try and explain what had happened to her. To him. To them. All of which Bono somehow managed to convey in a few starkly drawn lines, accompanied by a guitar melody dripping with pathos.

Another great track destined to become a Grammy award-winning single was the emotionally stirring 'Walk On', a wonderfully rousing moment dedicated to imprisoned

Burmese opposition leader Aung San Suu Kyi – a fact which was enough to get the album officially banned by the Burmese government. (Aung San Suu Kyi had been under house arrest since 1989 when she was elected to office as the leader of Myanmar – formerly, Burma – prompting a military junta.) As a result of Bono's efforts to shed light on her nightmarish plight, she had actually been granted the Freedom of the City of Dublin in March 2000, alongside U2, Bono again using a public event to dictate his own, more meaningful agenda. Whatever his motivation, however, 'Walk On' was simply a beautiful song.

Just as in the old days, the album ended on an almost prayer-like note with 'Grace', the spiritual counterpart, perhaps, to the moving 'MLK' from *The Unforgettable Fire*, and, further back still, the angry-sounding '40', from *War*. Bono, it seemed, hadn't done with talking to his Maker just yet. Musically, however, 'Grace' had Eno's eclectic fingerprints all over it. A fittingly ghostly, yet yearningly tangible moment to end an album overspilling with flesh-and-blood, three-dimensional concerns, if *All That You Can't Leave Behind* rocked like a bitch, 'Grace' was its final reminder that beyond the fire and brimstone lay only still dark waters, impenetrable floods of emotional entanglements that not even Bono could accurately describe sometimes. He just knew they were there and wanted, needed, to let them out as best he could.

And of course there were also those songs Bono was now equally famous for that dealt more directly with real-life stories. For example, there was the elegiac 'When I Look At The World', widely interpreted as a homage to Ali and her tireless work on behalf of the beleaguered children of Chernobyl; and the solemnly straight-faced 'Peace On Earth', a song Bono later revealed was written on that dreadful day in August 1998 when the Omagh bomb, which claimed twenty-nine lives, also dealt a cruel and devastating blow to the Northern Ireland peace process he and the band had done so much themselves to promote. "In Dublin, when they read out the names of the people who had died on the six o'clock news, the city came to a complete standstill," he recalled with a shudder. "People were weeping. Not only was it the destruction of lives, it was the destruction of the peace process which had been held together with sticky tape and glue and tacks and a lot of faith." That such a song could co-exist on the same album as 'Beautiful Day' said much both for Bono's emotional resilience and the sheer depth of the band's musical range.

Elsewhere on the album, 'Kite', its title a simple but clear metaphor for the way life's different winds can blow you off course, no matter how well-intentioned your journey, also took on the mantle of a personal statement by Bono on the nature of mortality that had clear connections to the painfully slow death of his father, Bob, as well as taking on the aspect of a rumination on his own parenthood (a fourth child, John Abraham, was also now on the way). Indeed, Bono later recalled how his eldest children, Jordan and Eve, had been the original catalyst behind the song. He had taken them down to the seaside near their home for the day, he explained, to fly a new kite he had bought for them, and get some fresh sea air into their lungs as they "communed" with the landscape. The girls soon grew bored, however, with the kite always getting stuck in the sand and asked to go home and commune with their PlayStations instead!

The experience of trying to get the infernal contraption aloft was not wasted on Bono, however, as just a cursory listen to the finished track will confirm. Later, singing the song at Earls Court on the day his father's life fell from the sky, it was clear the song was about the deep emotional scar left by Bobby's death, something that would take a long time – possibly for ever – to heal. "In Ireland we have this thing called keening at funerals," Bono told *Q* magazine in November 2002. "Women wail, it's almost an African-type response to death. I guess I did my grieving for my father keening in front of twenty thousand people singing U2 songs [at Earls Court]. They really carried me, those songs and my three mates. After the shows I felt a lot better."

Fortunately, the rest of the promotion of the album wasn't so testing for Bono personally. Certainly an old-school leg-kicker like 'Elevation', with its wall-of-sound guitars and archly postmodern 'Fly'-era lyrics, was no problem to blast out at any time. The studio version included input from producers Richard Stannard and Julian Gallagher, who were then better known for working with the likes of Kylie Minogue and Brit boy band 5ive. Inevitably, this unlikely connection was first suggested by Bono after he, Gavin Friday and Maurice Seezer had recorded a blistering cover of

T. Rex's glam-rock classic 'Children Of The Revolution' for inclusion on the *Moulin Rouge* film soundtrack, which Stannard and Gallagher had also worked on.

In October 2000, just as *All That You Can't Leave Behind* prepared to hit the shops, U2 played yet another rooftop gig, this time on top of the Clarence Hotel in Dublin where BBC TV's *Top of the Pops* filmed them for a special live performance of 'Beautiful Day'. The single promptly entered at the top of the UK singles chart the very next week. It also reached Number 21 in the US charts the following month.

February 2001 also found U2 playing one of the more intimate shows of their recent career when they decided to play a 'semi-secret' gig at London's small Astoria theatre in the heart of town. As a result, traffic in the capital's adjacent Tottenham Court Road had ground to a halt within minutes of the show being announced as, in scenes reminiscent of their traffic-stopping antics in Los Angeles some fourteen years before, Bono and U2 were once more at their anarchic, attention-grabbing best. Tickets for the gig, which was aimed just as much at the world's media, had been distributed free to hard-core fans and competition winners, but those unfortunate enough not to have secured tickets were happy to pay scalpers up to £800 on the night for the privilege of being able to say they were there. Lucky names (plus one) on the guest list that night included Bob Geldof, Mick Jagger, Kylie Minogue, all of Oasis and various members of All Saints, Radiohead, Ash and Massive Attack, not to mention the authors Will Self and Salman Rushdie.

Madonna had recently played an almost identical invitation-only gig at the Brixton Academy in south London and, in one critic's view, "got away with half an hour of waffle, merely because her audience were delighted to be there". Mindful of the sceptics waiting in the shadows with sharpened knives, Bono and the band decided simply to go for it, showcasing their new album almost in its entirety, adding only comparatively recent hits like 'Until The End Of The World' and 'Mysterious Ways' to the set, plus a handful of equally unexpected numbers from their earliest days, such as a ferocious '11 O'Clock Tick Tock' and an incandescent 'I Will Follow'; songs that were older than many of the fans in the audience. The reaction from the crowd that night was ecstatic. Satisfyingly, critical reaction was equally positive. The review that ran in the *Telegraph* was typical of the range of reaction in the broadsheet press: "Bono, part Elvis Presley, part Joe Strummer, part Dublin urchin, still has charisma," it concluded.

A similar situation pertained at the televised annual Brit Awards show that year, too, where U2 were honoured for their Outstanding Contribution to the British Music Industry as well as picking up the Best International Group accolade. Always glad to be there at British music's most glitzy night of the year, but never more so than with this, their tenth full studio album in twenty years, the band also got up on stage that night, bringing the famously staid crowd of industry insiders to its feet with a raucous mini-set comprised of eye-wateringly powerful versions of 'One', 'Beautiful Day', 'End Of

The World' and 'Mysterious Ways'. It was a performance that set the seal on what was, everyone agreed afterwards, U2's night, pure and simple. "This is the year for hip-hop and R&B," Bono announced to the assembled throng as the band stepped up to receive the much-coveted award for Best International Group, "but they've given the award to a sort of guitar band with soul and attitude."

The band were presented with the Outstanding Contribution award by Noel Gallagher of Oasis, who told the crowd: "This award goes to a bunch of guys who have made an outstanding contribution to my record collection, your record collection and probably even the record collections of the cool people from Brighton. From the Republic of Ireland, please be upstanding and show some respect for ... U2!" Cue: thunderous applause.

The plaudits rolled Stateside, too, as 'Beautiful Day' won in each of the three categories it was nominated for at that year's Grammy awards show at the Shrine Auditorium in Los Angeles. "It is an unusual emotion I feel now," Bono said as he picked up the tenth Grammy of his and the band's career. "I think it's called humility." Just as they had at the Brits a couple of weeks before, the band also played live that night, thumping out 'Beautiful Day' for the benefit of an estimated global audience of over 175 million TV viewers.

Only rapper Eminem, who also collected three Grammy awards, could rival Bono and U2 that night, but a generous acceptance speech from the Irishman also graciously name-checked soul diva Macy Gray – who, he told the crowd, he believed should have won Record of the Year – as well as Radiohead and the Red Hot Chili Peppers, two bands who would be conspicuous additions to a star-studded bill when U2 returned to Dublin to headline Slane Castle again that summer.

In the aftermath of such a comeback, Bono conceded that he and U2 had succeeded in sustaining a career way beyond even his expectations, previously considered boundless. "There is a certain contour to a band's career that people expect to see," he mused thoughtfully. "You do your best work early on and then you burn out. Maybe we're just lucky, but it doesn't feel like we've started burning out yet."

He was soon matching actions to words as the Elevation 2001 (as it was dubbed) world tour kicked off in March of that year with a huge show in Florida. In a nice touch, volunteers from Greenpeace, Amnesty International and Drop the Debt were all approved as fellow travellers on the tour, handing out literature, selling T-shirts and generally raising aware- ness. From Bono's point of view, it would put a human face on what was now, in reality, an entire corporation. "We're a gang of four and a corporation of five," said Bono, including manager Paul McGuinness in on the deal. The reason they had made it, he said, was simple. "The thing that separated us from temporary, sophomoric, white-bread fucking art students is the thing that puts us in with hip-hop. Taking care of business, as Elvis Presley described it, is the thing that marks how much artists care about what they do. When rock stops trying to communicate on the level of the mass media, it becomes progressive rock; it becomes solipsistic." It becomes, in other words, everything that rock purports to despise: something safe and shapeless. No buzz at all. And if Bono knew anything it was that without the buzz, the vibe, the spirit, you didn't have anything at all.

The 2001 Elevation tour would eventually, by its final shows in December that year, gross more than $104 million. Or put another way, with one hundred and six shows on the itinerary, approximately a million bucks a show, suggesting that business had never been better for the U2 "corporation". According to *Billboard*, the top grossing shows of the tour were their four-night sell-out stint at Chicago's United Centre arena, where more than $6.4 million was taken over all four nights.

Back home across the water, the Slane Castle show in August 2001 represented the first performance from U2 in Ireland since the PopMart tour had taken over Lansdowne Road football stadium for the day four years previously. It also marked the twentieth anniversary of the band's first ever appearance there, when they supported Thin Lizzy and the much-missed Phil Lynott. But if the air seemed thick with memories for Bono as he wandered around backstage that day, the show itself was nothing if not forward-thinking. Special guests included the Red Hot Chili Peppers, Coldplay, Kelis, JJ72 and Relish. As a result, all eighty thousand tickets for the Slane show had sold out within forty-five minutes of going on sale months before, some fans having camped out for two days or more to make sure of their place at the front of the queue when the box-office finally opened. Indeed, there was such an overwhelming demand for tickets that the band were forced to schedule a second show at the fabled old castle for the following weekend. (McGuinness, anticipating just such an eventuality, had had the foresight to pre-book the venue for a second weekend.)

Welcome though the addition of the second show was, by common consent it was the first Slane show that had been the one to be at. Afterwards, Bono and the band agreed that it had been as good as U2 had ever played in their home country. And of course there had been an added poignancy in the fact that Bob Hewson's funeral had taken place in Dublin just the day before. When the second show was over, however, Bono was able to reflect better on the wider implications. It had been almost twenty years to the day since they'd first played Slane, he observed, at a time when they were in the midst of a spiritual crisis that was threatening to tear the band apart. But of course they had eventually weathered that storm, as they eventually had all the other storms that had come their way in the years since. Bono knew his faith in himself and his band, and their own collective belief in a higher power – fate, luck, God, dog, call it what you will – was now enough to weather any storm life could throw at them. Even something as mind-blowing as 9/11 ...

What was reported as "arguably the most emotional concert U2 have ever played" took place in late October 2001, when Bono and U2 took to the stage at Madison Square

Garden, New York, just six weeks after the 9/11 attacks had razed the twin towers of the World Trade Center to the ground, sending thousands of innocent men, women and children to their deaths, and signalling the start of President Bush's War on Terror and the beginning of a whole new era of international sabre-rattling and domestic paranoia. The reds were no longer coming; now it was the rag-heads. As such, the show at Madison Square Garden would prove to be a much-needed catharsis for the capacity crowd, whose response to the band Bono likened afterwards to the kind that perhaps only the Beatles had previously enjoyed at Shea Stadium in 1965. "It was New York on a night out and we were just the excuse," he explained modestly, adding: "It was great to be that excuse!"

With their latest globe-straddling jaunt behind them, Bono and U2 viewed the onset of 2002 as a good time to recharge those no longer quite as youthful batteries. June 2002 proved to be a particularly joyful time for The Edge, who got married for the second time. The lucky lady was Morleigh Steinberg, his companion of the last ten years, with whom he had already had two children. The couple had met when Morleigh became the belly dancer on the Zoo TV tour in the mid-Nineties, after the guitarist had been divorced from his first wife, Aislinn, in 1995. In a rare concession to the assembled press corps, and in order to cause the minimum of fuss at their friend's wedding, Bono and Ali allowed photographers to snap them arriving together at the ceremony, smiling as happily as ever. The wedding took place at a hotel near the band's holiday homes at Eze, in the south of France. Other famous guests who had flown in specially for the occasion included Lenny Kravitz, Dave Stewart and the legendary Hollywood actor Dennis Hopper.

Meanwhile, back in Britain, Bono was surprised to learn that he had topped *Q* magazine's recent list of the most powerful people in the music business, ironically beating Universal Music chief Doug Morris – in effect, the boss of U2's own record company – into second place. Rapper Eminem was voted third. "We wanted to reflect the biggest movers and shakers on and off stage," said a *Q* spokesman. Even so, Bono had never seen himself as some sort of music biz Mr Big character, and he took the whole thing with a pinch of salt.

Four Christmases after the release of their first chart-topping greatest-hits compilation, *Best of: 1980–1990*, U2 repeated the exercise in November 2002 with the ostensible follow-up, *Best of: 1990–2000*. As before, a double-disc augmented by all the various B-sides to their many singles throughout the period was unveiled a matter of days before the regular single-CD release, and, as before, pent-up demand for the harder-to-find tracks from the diehard U2 fans sent the double-disc version of the album soaring to the top of the UK charts, stalling just one place short of the Number 1 position thanks to the debut album from latest boy-band sensations Blue. The regular album release, however, didn't make it into the Top 30 at all, peaking at a disappointing Number 37, suggesting, perhaps, that much larger numbers of the more instantly collectable double-disc title had also been pressed up this time around. However, a new single, 'Electrical Storm', released to raise excitement about the new compilation, did reach Number 5, and the enterprise was considered a resounding commercial success.

Another reason for the single-disc album's relative commercial failure may have been down to the sheer proximity of so much of the material. Making a best-of out of your last three albums is not necessarily the way to bring long-time, or even relatively new fans through the doors. Which is a shame, as both single- and double-disc versions of *Best of: 1990–2000* tell their own story of the latter-day U2 musical adventure. As *Q* magazine astutely put it in its review, the album "soundtracks an era of warring factions, wayward experimentation, supermodel-assisted hedonism and, finally, a kind of peace".

In or out of the charts, on or off the road, it no longer mattered: everything that Bono did now was headline news, it seemed, from the sublime – being pictured in *The Times* shaking hands with Archbishop Desmond Tutu – to the ridiculous, like the coverage by the *Sun* of an incident in May 2003 when Bono reportedly paid a thousand pounds to have his favourite trilby hat flown out from Dublin to Italy, so that he could wear it on stage in a special charity concert with Pavarotti. Although the hat had its own first-class seat, it was moved up to the cockpit for safe keeping before being taxied to Modena, venue for Pavarotti's annual fundraising concerts. In the end though, for some reason Bono decided not to wear the hat after all, choosing instead to don what the *Sun* amusingly described as a "khaki back-to-front hat".

Another huge celebrity fundraising event to which Bono lent his name and presence that year was the special charity show hosted by Nelson Mandela in Cape Town, in November 2003. Billed as the "46664 Concert" (46664 being the inmate number Mandela had been forced to have tattooed on his arm during his thirty years as a political prisoner), Bono was also heavily involved in the campaign, also named after Mandela's former prison number, created to raise awareness of and bring much-needed publicity to the global HIV/AIDS pandemic, as well as helping to raise funds for the Nelson Mandela Foundation. The initiative was said to be the largest call to action for HIV/AIDS in history, and as the smiling Mandela walked on stage that night, a beaming Bono described Mandela, in a heartfelt introduction to the delighted crowd, as the "President of everyone everywhere who loves freedom".

The full list of international artists who performed at the Greenpoint Stadium in Cape Town that momentous day is long and impressive: Abdel Wright, Anastacia, Angelique Kidjo, Annie Lennox, Baaba Maal, Beyonce, Bob Geldof, Bongo Maffin, Bono, Danny K, David A. Stewart, Jimmy Cliff, Johnny Clegg, Ladysmith Black Mambazo, Ms Dynamite, Paul Oakenfold, Peter Gabriel, Queen, the Corrs, The Edge, Watershed, Youssou N'Dour, Yusuf Islam, Yvonne Chaka Chaka and Zucchero.

The Edge and Bono had been joined for their brief set by

both Beyonce Knowles (of Destiny's Child) and former Eurythmic Dave Stewart to perform 'American Prayer'. Youssou N'Dour then joined them on stage for the rousing '46664 Long Walk To Freedom', one of several brand-new songs written specially for the five-hour show. 'American Prayer', Bono later explained, might just as easily have been called 'African Prayer' or 'Irish Prayer'. At heart, he said, it was about asking "churches to open their doors, to give sanctuary that breaks the stigma that goes with being HIV positive. If God loves you, what's the problem?"

Another welcome and fascinating aspect of the show was that international stars were encouraged to team up with local musicians. Thus, the Corrs shared the stage with Ladysmith Black Mambazo, Peter Gabriel duetted with Yusuf Islam (the former Cat Stevens) and white South African singer Johnny Clegg, while Youssou N'Dour also joined Annie Lennox for a spine-tingling 'Seven Seconds', the former Eurythmic singing the part Neneh Cherry had performed on the original. Fittingly, Bono and The Edge returned near the end of the show to play 'One': a wondrously evoked song about the universally inclusive nature of love in a sometimes bleak and seemingly fragmented world, it had never sounded so apt as it did echoing around the massive Greenpoint Stadium that night. When it was over, they were joined on stage by Anastacia, Beyonce and others to perform Dave Stewart's specially composed freedom song: 'Amandla'. It was a movingly lovely image to be left with at the end of an unforgettable occasion, and many in the audience openly wept as the number reached its dizzy sing-along climax.

To commemorate that fact, the concert was later released on three separate CDs, entitled *46664 Part 1: African Prayer*, *46664 Part 2: Long Walk To Freedom* and *46664 Part 3: Amandla*; while March 2004 also saw the award-winning 1995 film *Miss Sarajevo* released on DVD for the first time, complete with some fascinating extra footage, including the original unused half-hour documentary and a never-before-seen interview with Bono dating from the first time film-maker Bill Carter met the singer and the band on tour in America, plus the first satellite link-up between Sarajevo and U2's Zooropa tour in Bologna, Italy.

Recognition for such tireless public efforts was swift to follow. In February 2003, Bono was nominated for the 2003 Nobel Peace Prize, the second year in a row he had actually been nominated for the prize – the most prestigious award of its kind in the world. In 2002, he had lost out to former US President Jimmy Carter. This year he was up against such diverse rivals for the prize as Pope John Paul II, French President Jacques Chirac, the governor of the US state of Illinois (who had famously spared all inmates on death row), and a Cuban dissident.

"We have a total of a hundred and fifty nominees so far, of which twenty-one are organisations," Geir Lundestad, the head of the Norwegian Nobel Institute, told reporters at the official announcement. Traditionally, the institute gives only the overall number of nominees and does not name them, but people and organisations whose names had already been made public elsewhere included Bono, the European Union, peace group Women in Black, Chinese dissident Wei Jingsheng, Cuba's leading dissident Oswaldo Paya, and the international human rights group Global Witness.

Mr Lundestad confirmed that Bono had been nominated again for the prize because of his work as an outspoken fundraiser for Third World problems in recent years, not least his involvement in the Drop the Debt campaign – specifically, his work as the public face and voice of DATA which, with heavyweight funding from the Bill and Melinda Gates Foundation, George Soros' Open Society Institute and the Centre for Global Development, had been instrumental over recent years in wiping out millions of dollars of international debt owed by Third World governments. Mr Lundestad added that he was pleased to note that the growing fears of an imminent US-led war on Iraq had apparently not distracted from the peace efforts being made both in Baghdad and elsewhere in the world. "The range of nominees is very wide," he said encouragingly.

But if Bono would again miss out on the big one – the prize eventually went to Shirin Ebadi, the Iranian lawyer, judge, lecturer, writer and activist, whose struggle for the rights of women and children in Iran had brought worldwide attention to the problem – he was also fêted that same month with the MusiCares Person of the Year award, at a sumptuous ceremony held at the Marriott Marquis Hotel in New York. In attendance that Friday night was the usual broad cross-section of famous figures from the worlds of both pop and politics. Hosting the event was Ashley Judd, and comic relief was provided by *Saturday Night Live*'s Jimmy Fallon, who had great fun sending Bono up for winning so many awards. Also attending the event were former President Bill Clinton, REM singer Michael Stipe and bassist Mike Mills, singer Fred Durst of nu-metal icons Limp Bizkit, soul legend Isaac Hayes, Hollywood superstar Robert De Niro, and many others. Music stars past and present also paid special tribute to the band, with Norah Jones, Sly Dunbar and Robbie Shakespeare, No Doubt, Elvis Costello, Black Rebel Motorcycle Club, Patti LaBelle, Mary J. Blige, Wynonna with B. B. King, and Garbage all performing cover versions of various U2 classics. Highlights included Sly and Robbie performing 'The Sweetest Thing', together with Gwen Stefani and No Doubt; Norah Jones doing a sublime job of singing 'Stuck In A Moment You Can't Get Out Of'; Elvis Costello bringing tears to Bono's eyes with his rendition of 'Kite'; and last but hardly least, Garbage's supersonic performance of 'Pride (In The Name Of Love)'. Fittingly, Bono himself closed the show with three songs – an extraordinarily moving version of the Sid and Sinatra classic 'My Way', followed by 'Night And Day' (accompanied on guitar by The Edge), and what was then the latest U2 single, 'The Hands That Built America' (from the Oscar-nominated Martin Scorsese film *Gangs of New York*).

Meanwhile, the next U2 album had long been scheduled for a summer 2003 release, but as time passed no confirmatory news emerged from within the closed doors at Hanover Quays. November 2002's *Q* magazine included a feature during which journalist Tom Doyle was played two new recordings the band had just made, titled, respectively, 'Original Of The Species' and 'Sometimes You Can't Make It On Your Own'. A year later, however, the band was still nowhere nearer completing what would be their last ever recordings at Quays.

Remarks made by manager Paul McGuinness in a BBC Radio Five Live interview the following spring suggested a November 2004 release date for the album – and so it would prove. He had also hinted to the *LA Times* that U2's 2005 world tour would be largely conducted in indoor venues where "the logistics are much more controlled. Now that high ticket prices indoors are accepted, if you're going to take the audience to a big outdoor event, you'd really have to be doing something very, very good, and we would take that responsibility very seriously. If we decide to go outdoors, it will be because it's worth doing something on a grand scale."

The finished, much-fussed-over new U2 album, had laboured under the working title of *Vertigo* throughout the long weeks and months they had worked on it in the studio. Now Bono suddenly had a change of heart. Or rather, he'd had a better idea. The new title for the album, *How to Dismantle an Atomic Bomb*, shared the apocalyptic associations of earlier nuclear-headed U2 albums such as *War*, *Under a Blood Red Sky* and *The Unforgettable Fire*. The aim this time, however, Bono declared, was "to make our own

Who's Next, where every track mattered [and] I think we've done that. This one," he concluded with a satisfied smile, "feels like a very special record."

Tellingly, perhaps, back in the production hot seat after an absence of twenty years was Steve Lillywhite, no less. The now veteran studio king had just renounced a career as a music business mover and shaker to quit as Mercury Records UK joint managing director and return to the job he liked best, closeted away behind the studio glass, making rock-'n'roll music. Though they'd been separated at the time, the loss of his wife, the singer Kirsty MacColl, in a freak boating accident in the West Indies, in late 2000, may also have been significant in his life-changing decision. In any event, the now middle-aged producer was clearly happy to be involved with his favourites again.

"It's the first time I will have gone in to actually start a record with them in twenty years," Lillywhite told *Billboard* just before the sessions began in Dublin. He went on to explain that, apart from the albums he had made with the band in the early days, behind the scenes he had also worked on some of the early material from *The Joshua Tree*, *Achtung Baby!* and *All That You Can't Leave Behind*. "But this will be the first time I've really set up the mikes and done everything for a long time," he conceded. "I've heard some great songs. The Edge is playing some really great guitar."

As for his more recent past as a record company executive, "I've had two great years, and I've loved a lot of it," he said, but in the end he had come to the unavoidable conclusion that he simply "wasn't that made out for getting up early in the morning", adding that, "that's what twenty-five years of producing records" did for you. "I got more and more of an urge to be in the studio [again], so I decided it was best that I return to that."

That said, Lillywhite's return to the U2 fold had not, in truth, originally been part of the plan at all; his late arrival on the scene was the result of a complicated series of discussions and events that meant, unbeknownst to the general public, that the tracks for *How to Dismantle an Atomic Bomb* were actually recorded twice. In fact, the new album's original producer had been Chris Thomas, whose previous client list included such luminaries of the pre- and post-punk rock firmament as the Sex Pistols, INXS, Roxy Music and Pink Floyd. Indeed, most of the serious recording with Thomas had taken place not at the Quays but at a rented studio on the French Riviera.

Holding album sessions on the Mediterranean, Bono later claimed, was designed to stimulate creative inspiration. "We've tried pretty much everything to make it feel like it's not a studio that we're working in," he said. In point of fact, their choice of recording studio in Nice reflected more the fact that all four members now had private holiday homes in the region. The Edge and Bono's families shared a villa, while Larry and Adam had their own palatial dwellings east of Nice. "Bono wanted us all to share a place," Larry later recalled, "and I told him straight: I'm happy to come here but I'm not living in the same house as you!"

Speaking exclusively at the time to *Uncut* writer Stephen Dalton, Bono went a step further, describing the album in his usual florid style as "punk rock made on Venus", dominated, he claimed jokingly, by guitars that went up to a Spinal Tapesque Number 11. As for the choice of new producer in Chris Thomas, Bono merely cited the fact that Thomas had worked as a studio engineer on both the Beatles' *White Album* and Pink Floyd's *Dark Side of the Moon*, before going on to produce *Never Mind the Bollocks ... Here's the Sex Pistols*. "And the first four Roxy Music records that are really hard to get your head round," Bono pointed out. "I think he's on three of them." He added that they had "particularly wanted him to work on the guitar sound. It's a guitar-driven record. It's got a lot of big, big tunes. You know? Remember tunes?"

When questioned on the subject of the band's unexpected break with the Eno/Lanois "dream team", Bono insisted that it was purely for musical and not personal reasons. Or as he tactfully put it: "They ... um, they don't really like the loud music!" he chuckled broadly. "Eno's not on it, but Daniel's coming in to play – his tour's ending in Dublin and I think he's going to sit in, as we musos say." He added: "I would love Brian [Eno] to be on it because Brian was on those Roxy Music records too, we shouldn't forget that. And it *is* otherworldly ..." The Edge, as ever, had his own highly personal take on things, describing the new music they were making with Thomas as "raw rock'n'roll ... a band in its primary colours of guitar, bass, drums, voice and a lot of vitality and energy".

According to Bono, the new album would be dominated, as never before, by The Edge's guitar playing. "It's made by a man who is really sick of the sight of his singer shaking hands with dodgy politicians," he quipped. "When you have got as much spleen and suffused rage as The Edge has, I think Number Eleven was the only way to go." He continued: "People forget just how extraordinary a guitar player he is. Everybody else is just replaying the blues again and again, it's just [recycled versions of] Muddy Waters and Robert Johnson. But this is someone who, in the colour spectrum, *owns* a few colours. In the same way as great [jazz] musicians like Miles Davis, or great guitar players like Sterling Morrison [of the Velvet Underground] – there arc great players who *own* something."

It all sounded great. So what went wrong? Sessions had gone on with Chris Thomas throughout most of 2003. Nevertheless, at the end of it, they were claiming that, in Adam Clayton's terse words, "We didn't gel for whatever reason" with Thomas and the decision was made over the Christmas break to let him go, scrap everything they had recorded with the producer in France over the past year – and simply begin again. Record chiefs from London to Los Angeles were dismayed by the news but, forced to count to ten before commenting, decided they could only back the band in its revamped plans. If the band wasn't happy with the album, they couldn't put it out anyway. It was back to the drawing board, it seemed, for everybody involved, as the map for 2004 was hastily redrawn.

Back in their own studios in Dublin, this time with the more reassuring presence of Lillywhite at the controls, work in the New Year convened with renewed vigour. But while the sessions assumed a pleasing new forward momentum, as late as July 2004, just four months before its release, Bono was still busy canvassing opinions as to mixes and running orders from the steady stream of diehard U2 fans who kept a mostly lonely vigil outside the Hanover Quays complex. Even the morning postman was used as a sounding board because, as Bono explained, "Working here is like being marooned on an oil rig. We can get cut off."

Nevertheless, things seemed to be reaching some sort of apotheosis when suddenly disaster struck the same month, when The Edge's unmastered copy of the album's so far completed eleven tracks was mysteriously stolen, in a strange echo of the lost tapes from the *Achtung Baby!* sessions all those years before. This time they discovered it had been taken from The Edge's bag while he was taking part with the rest of the band in a photo shoot with Anton Corbijn. Edge was beside himself when he found out what had happened. Doing his best to look on the bright side, Bono joked that he was just glad he wasn't the one putting his foot in it this time. "It's the sort of thing I would do," he laughed.

But the distraught guitarist was inconsolable. "A large slice of two years' work lifted via a piece of round plastic," he said disgustedly. "It doesn't seem credible but that's what's just happened to us ... and it was my CD." Paul McGuinness took a deep breath and tried to remain calm. "It would be a shame if unfinished work fell into the wrong hands," he said with typical understatement. Inevitably, the disappearance prompted fears (eventually proved unfounded) that all eleven tracks would reappear for sale on the internet.

Earlier that summer, Bono had taken time out from working on the new album to entertain Tony Blair at his Killiney home, during a lightning visit to Dublin in May. The British Prime Minister later thanked him publicly for the hospitality he had been shown in the Hewson household, going so far as to declare his host to be "a top man". Other house guests during the year had been soul music's foremost couple, rapper Jay-Z and singer Beyonce Knowles. This had been a particular treat for thirteen-year-old Eve, a big Destiny's Child fan, but Bono had to laugh when he over-heard his daughter telling a friend about how her dad had been "boring the arses" off his guests talking about Africa! (But then, both Bono and Beyonce were veterans of the 46664 concert, so perhaps Dad could be forgiven a little pros-elytising around the home hearth on that occasion.)

Later that year, as part of the planned promotion for the forthcoming album, U2 got involved in something they had always previously made a very public point of avoiding: a commercial tie-in. That autumn, just as the new U2 album, *How to Dismantle an Atomic Bomb*, was about to hit the streets, Apple would be announcing the launch of its new iPod U2 Special Edition: a black model of its new sound carrier with a bright red click-wheel which held up to five thousand tracks and would retail in American stores for

$349. As part of the cross-promotion, U2 agreed to appear in a specially shot iPod television commercial, accompanied by the release of a first-of-its-kind digital box set containing more than four hundred pre-loaded U2 tracks on it, both old and new. As yet another themed link in what would be both Apple's and U2's most spectacular ever worldwide launch, the first single from the new album, 'Vertigo', was initially made available for download exclusively via Apple's own on-line iTunes Music Store. As a result, the track immediately ascended into the service's Top 10 within twenty-four hours of becoming available. Within a week it was officially the most downloaded selection in the memory banks of the entire iTunes Store.

Meanwhile, fans could also buy the digital box set, entitled *The Complete U2*, containing all of the band's existing albums from the iTunes Music Store. Bono told reporters after he and The Edge had performed two songs from the new album at a special showcase performance, that, contrary to rumour, U2 had not been paid millions to appear in the iPod ads; in fact, he said, they had been paid nothing at all. The band and Apple would simply share the profits, he said. "It's a horizontal relationship rather than a vertical one," he explained. "If they sell, we will make [money] on the products that we put out together. If they don't sell, we won't."

Even the usually hard to impress Edge said he saw the partnership with Apple as the beginning of a wholesale transformation in the distribution of music towards an almost exclusively on-line phenomenon. "We wanted to find an innovative way to redefine the distribution of [our] music," he told reporters at the press conference for the launch. "We see it as the next step for the music business." Indeed, Bono had even gone as far as threatening to release the new album on-line via Apple's iTunes Music Store if the band's worst fears had been realised and tracks from the stolen CD had been either leaked illegally on the net, or turned into CD bootlegs.

Back in the real world of record stores and fans rushing in to buy, the sales target set by the record company bigwigs for *How to Dismantle an Atomic Bomb* was a staggering eleven million. Or put another way, the same number of albums its hit-laden predecessor had sold. By reaching Number 1 in over thirty countries, as it had done in the weeks leading up to Christmas 2004, it could be said to have achieved its benchmark. There seemed to be a lack of diversion, too – less musical introspection, more straight-ahead rock – that suggested the band were equally keen to recruit younger fans of bands like Guns N' Roses and Bon Jovi, whose stars had waned in recent years.

'Vertigo', the first single and original title track, was of course the perfect album opener. The video for the single, shot on location in a remote part of the Delta de L'Ebre, on the Spanish coast, hit a snag when a major sandstorm hit the beach the first day of the shoot and wrecked thousands of dollars' worth of camera equipment. As Bono later recalled: "We had every kind of freak weather condition you can imagine – the rain, the snow and the sandstorm." Video director Martin Fougerol was on the verge of calling the whole shoot off and saving the rest of the equipment when, after hours of battering them, the storm suddenly diverted away from them again. As The Edge later recalled: "It was pretty crazy stuff. We thought we were going to have to return to Dublin without a video. It got pretty tough out there. Bono and I were sharing a tent and we couldn't come out for at least six hours."

Not that you would know any of that from seeing the spectacular resulting video, featuring the surreal sight of Bono and the band performing on the surface of a remote river basin. (In order to achieve the effect, crew members had had to dig a huge moat around the outer perimeter of the shoot, offering protection from the sandstorm until filming could be completed.) Bono was right, too, when he said the result was well worth all the problems. As he explained: "We've made all kinds of videos over the years with uneven results. High-concept, story, abstract ... But we've never done a video that has a graphic arts background and this is what ['Vertigo'] is." He went on: "There seems to be so much clutter everywhere. Turn on music television and there's big cluttered sets, people walking round with clutter around their necks, great cluttered award shows ..." This, he concluded, "is our attempt to empty the frame".

Other highlights from the new album included the haunting 'Miracle Drug', a plaintive cry which somehow recalled 'Where The Streets Have No Name', and 'City Of Blinding Lights', a full-on Bono love song (to Ali?) to rank with any of his best for U2. While two other tracks on the album, 'Sometimes You Can't Make It On Your Own' and 'One Step Closer', are so clearly linked to the loss of Bono's father, Bobby, that they make painful if beautiful listening. The former, in particular, is possibly the finest, certainly the most poignant, one-on-one ballad Bono has ever accomplished. Never had he sounded so old before, or so vulnerable. Questioned by *Q* magazine, he admitted "a bomb went off [in my head] when my old man died and I had no idea how to deal with it. If I'm honest, I've been running away from it for the past two years."

He couldn't deal with the fact of his father's death, the manner of it, the injustice. He felt left with a sense of bafflement and loss, of weariness and regret, that culminated in a curious "lost weekend" he described in Bali when he flew out "for a drink ... got on a plane, went for two days, came back. I was sitting in a beach bar when I got there thinking, 'What am I doing here?'" He responded by throwing himself into his work, musical and otherwise, "taking on more and more projects. But eventually you have to turn and face yourself. That's come to an end now with finishing this [album]. Literally, in the last week, I've felt a sense of putting things to rest."

Yet, as *Classic Rock* magazine suggested in their review of the album: "Didn't U2 once stand for something more?" The inference was that, while Bono and the band may have rediscovered their roots, ditching the postmodern and getting back to the punk, did that mean they had stopped asking questions, too? Certainly, the musical twists and turns were relatively few and far between this time around, the electronic fizz of 'Love And Peace Or Else' a rare exception in this more musically conventional setting, even being compared by some critics to Nine Inch Nails.

Meanwhile, the 'Vertigo' video was just one manifestation of a major marketing push estimated to cost their record company something in the region of £7 million, promoting the album they all intended to make U2's biggest to date. This included a worldwide TV advertising, poster and publicity campaign. As a source close to the group reportedly told the *Daily Mirror*: "This is the biggest money they have ever spent on promoting an album. They believe it is their best work ever and they want the whole world to know it's out there. The money will be ploughed into a huge publicity blitz, the likes of which no band have ever done before. Their last album was big but this is going to be even bigger. Fans won't believe what the band are planning." Bono was said to be "so hyped up ... [he] really wants to give it his best shot. The budget for the promotion has been signed off by the record company and it's all systems go for the return of U2."

As a result, and contrary to manager McGuinness's speculation the year before about playing only indoor dates, U2's 2005 world tour was scheduled to surpass every tour the band had ever done up till then, not just in terms of publicity but in variety of venue, capacity and, most important of all, gate-receipts. Unlike their last epic tour of 2001 (in which they ended up as the top-grossing act of the year in America), the new tour would include stadium dates, as well as their first major tours of Japan and Australia for many years. This time, it seemed, everybody was invited to the party. The plan was for the world tour to begin with a thirty-five-date arena tour of the USA, in the spring of 2005, followed by at least thirty outdoor stadium shows across Europe in the summer. The plan then was for Bono and the band to return to the United States for another thirty-five arena dates before heading off to Japan and Australia for about twenty more shows. With Paul McCartney also planning a 2005 world tour, and a possible Rolling Stones trek also slated for later in the year, U2 will have superstar competition to contend with out there, and they know it. Which is why being first 'out of the box' with an official announcement of their 2005 touring plans was regarded as a major media coup: the idea being that by the time the McCartney and Stones tickets were put on sale, most of the U2 tickets would already have been sold.

But trying to use the internet and cutting-edge ticketing technology to help them achieve this edge was not always as simple as that, apparently, as they discovered to their cost in January. U2 fans who had already paid for official fan club membership had been told that they would be allowed priority access to tickets for the tour, including the coveted low-priced general admission (GA) tickets that had proved so popular on the previous Elevation tour. Members had been mailed a personalised password with links to a webpage from which they could choose a specific show they wanted to see, and order tickets. Unfortunately, attempts to link to the page proved fruitless for a great many, thanks not least to the incredible demand. And when fans did arrive at a purchasing page most found the GA seats (on average about 1,700–1,800 seats in a normal 15,000-capacity US arena) had all sold out within minutes. All the more galling since manager Paul McGuinness had previously stated: "The best seats are the cheapest, and we want people to get excited."

Many other problems were encountered with the ticketing system throughout the early weeks of 2005. One disappointed and frustrated long-time U2 supporter named Emily Worth summed up the feelings of many disgruntled fans when she posted the following message on their official website, U2.com: "U2 backed out on a promise to their most loyal fans. We joined the U2.com fan club under the premise that we would have priority ticket buying. Well, I'm a member of the fan club, but [three] hours after the pre-sale began, I am still ticket-less. U2 have clearly not allotted enough tickets to accommodate the fan club members. This treatment is unethical and has hurt the people that have funded the band's career for the past twenty-five years."

Inevitably perhaps, this contrasted sharply with the views of Propaganda, the band's official fan club, which had handled ticket distribution for years, before closing down after the last shows of the previous Elevation tour. Back then, Propaganda would circulate a letter listing forthcoming dates which fans would then check off and return with money for the tickets. U2.com's attempt to use the much-reviled (by Pearl Jam) Ticketmaster to co-ordinate the sale led to predictable criticisms such as: "The band took a reliable fan-friendly service like Propaganda and replaced it with a poorly managed company." European fans encountered similar problems when tickets went on sale the same morning, with the band's official website, U2.com, obliged hurriedly to run messages of apology and appeasement.

In an open letter to fans posted on the U2.com website, Larry Mullen did his best to try and clarify the situation for long-suffering fans. He wrote: "This is not something that I would normally do, but I feel that I have to do something to redress this situation. There was a mess up in the way the tickets were distributed through U2.com for the Vertigo [tour] pre-sale. Some of it was beyond our control, but some of it wasn't. I am now in the process of figuring out a way of distributing the tickets for our intended return to North America in the fall. The only fair way of doing this is to give U2 Propaganda members, who are now U2.com members, priority in the queue. After that, people will be given priority in the order in which they joined.

"Many people who joined U2.com and didn't get tickets are understandably angry. They now have the option to get a full refund of their subscription fee. The idea that our long-time U2 fans and scalpers competed for U2 tickets through our own website is appalling to me. I want to apologise to you who have suffered that. If your U2.com pre-sale experience has left you disappointed, I hope this will go some way towards reassuring you of our total commitment to our audience. Slainte, Larry." He added a postscript: "By the way, a note to those so-called U2 fans who are quick to accuse U2 of unseemly behaviour, I've only got two words for you ..."

The tour, meanwhile, had originally been scheduled to kick off on 1 March 2005, in Miami, but was postponed after an unspecified "family illness" had apparently adversely affected The Edge. (The guitarist subsequently went to court to prevent newspapers printing more about this on privacy grounds.) "All of the plans are in total flux," a source close to the band told *Rolling Stone* in February. In the event, as I write (February 2005), the tour is now scheduled to start in San Diego exactly four weeks later. Sixteen North American dates will form the first leg of the tour, ending in Boston on 26 May. European dates are now due to begin in Brussels in June and conclude in Lisbon in August. Meanwhile, ticketing controversy refuses to go away, with touts recently found posting U2 tickets on internet auction site E-bay at several hundred per cent mark-up.

As U2 had spent most of 2004 rebuilding their new album, they did not figure in any of the nominations at the televised annual Brits Awards show, in February 2005, which was celebrating its twenty-fifth anniversary. The new album was released in time, however, to allow the band to be nominated for several awards at 2005's forty-seventh annual Grammy Awards ceremony in Los Angeles, hosted by Queen Latifah. Indeed, as I write, the morning after the show, Bono and U2 will be waking up to the fact that they have just added three more awards to their overall haul now of sixteen different Grammys over the last twenty years; winning in all three of the categories they were nominated for: Best Rock Performance by a Duo or Group with Vocal (for 'Vertigo'), Best Short Form Music Video ('Vertigo'), and Best Rock Song (once again for 'Vertigo').

Best of all, from a TV viewers' perspective, unlike the corresponding annual MTV Music Video Awards, the spectacular production effects at this year's Grammys didn't intrude upon the live performances of the various acts that had agreed to appear (including U2, Green Day, Alicia Keys and Tim McGraw). Not least, when U2 stepped up to perform their latest single, 'Sometimes You Can't Make It on Your Own', the band stood against a stark white backdrop with nothing to distract viewers from Bono and his song to his father. Later on in the show, Bono also joined Stevie Wonder and Norah Jones for a special charity performance of the old Beatles tune, 'Across The Universe', which was also made available to be downloaded on-line for just ninety-nine cents (approximately fifty pence), with all donations and proceeds going to benefit the victims and their families of the terrible tsunami disaster which had struck south-east Asia during the Christmas holidays.

Back in Britain, more good news had reached the band just hours before the Grammys started when word came down the phone line that the new single, 'Sometimes You Can't Make It On Your Own', had that day gone straight into the

UK charts at Number 1, hitting the top spot in its first week of release and marking the first time a U2 album had produced two Number 1 singles in the UK (bringing their total of Number 1 singles in the UK to six).

In the aftermath of this latest success, over the next couple of weeks Bono and the band are scheduled to fly to New York where, on 14 March, they are to attend their own long-overdue induction into the Rock'n'Roll Hall of Fame. (Artists and groups have to have been around for at least twenty-five years before qualifying for induction, otherwise U2 would surely have been in there long ago.) Other nominees this year are original rap star Grandmaster Flash and legendary singer-songwriter Randy Newman.

Of course, such events still continue to jostle with political matters in Bono's cross-laden calendar. He was asked to guest-produce an edition of *Today*, BBC Radio Four's flagship breakfast programme, in December 2004, praising Gordon Brown's commitment to cutting Third World debt when the Chancellor chose the programme to renew his call for a change in the way rich countries tackle poverty. "We shouldn't have to choose, as we are at the moment, between the temporary emergency relief that we are giving and the long-term tackling of the underlying causes of poverty," he said. "We need to be able to do both, and that's why we need something akin to the Marshall Plan of the 1940s, which is a bold effort at reconstruction, a very substantial increase in resources."

Brown also used the success of the recently released Band

Aid 20 single (a version of 'Do They Know It's Christmas' revamped for a new generation featuring contemporary stars, in which Bono had of course participated as one of the sole surviving members from the original 1984 record) as evidence of the "huge groundswell" of support from members of the public as well as faith groups. Bono also got former President Bill Clinton to grant the *Today* programme an exclusive interview, in which he revealed that in his experience it was easier for world leaders to talk about helping Africa *after* leaving office because donating billions to charity does not always lead to political popularity. "Poor people in other countries don't vote," Clinton pointed out prosaically. "So what we have to do is build a political movement which not only gets publicity but turns this into a vote-winning issue for a substantial number of people." The former President also insisted that one of the reasons he had agreed to Bono's request for an interview was, as he told Radio Four listeners, "because Tony Blair is genuinely committed to this", and had succeeded in building a majority within the UK Parliament to send money.

For all his very real politicking, however, behind the scenes, hanging out with the rest of the band backstage, Bono acknowledged that he still had "the greatest job in the world" to attend to – being the lead singer of the group called U2. To his credit he had yet to forget his statement of a decade before in which he had claimed boldly, "Anyone who needs fifty thousand people a night to tell them they're OK has to have a bit missing." The fact was, he said now, he never had come to terms with touring. "Concerts are everything for me, but basically, twenty-two hours of the day are hell, and two hours when you walk on stage are sort of heaven. But after you come back to your hotel room, it's a very lonely place. Even if your mates are just down the hall from you, some-times it's just a very lonely place."

Bono and U2 had turned their *Top of the Pops* performance of 'Vertigo' into a mini-free concert in October 2004, when they braved the rain at the BBC's west London Television Centre, and treated a four hundred-strong crowd to a set of new tracks and classics from a makeshift stage in the car park. Bono, dressed in leather jacket and cowboy hat, whipped the band through a rare version of 'She's A Mystery To Me', the song he wrote for the late Roy Orbison, before giving way to the more familiar Bo Diddleyesque beat of 'Desire'. The band then performed a track from the new album, 'All Because Of You', before Bono addressed the crowd directly at last and said: "This next song is about how we used to come to cities like London and New York when we were younger and naïve, and how over time our innocence has disappeared and how experience has kind of kicked in … especially when you're smoking forty cigarettes."

He continued: "We played this amazing show after September eleven and we remember all these blinding lights after playing 'Where The Streets Have No Name'. People were crying and it was an amazing thing to see." The band then ended the show with another new song, 'City Of Blinding Lights', Bono concluding with the words: "We'll see you next summer. It'll still be raining," before jumping off the stage and walking off into the mist.

Two months later in December the band had brought the streets of New York to a standstill while shooting the video for 'All Because Of You', the yet to be released third single off their new album. They performed the song live from a flatbed truck as they made their way through the city, followed by a crowd of several hundred as helicopters buzzed overhead. The truck's destination was a field beneath the Brooklyn Bridge where a temporary stage had been set up for them to play. When the U2 website revealed the location, local radio stations were able to broadcast the news, too, and New York fans showed up in their thousands.

When U2 did finally take the stage, they opened a forty-five-minute set with 'Vertigo' and continued with more songs from *How to Dismantle an Atomic Bomb*, including 'Miracle Drug', 'Original Of The Species' and a hairs-on-the-back-of-the-neck-raising 'Sometimes You Can't Make It On Your Own', which Bono, as was now his habit, dedicated to his late father. They then launched with unexpected gusto into a handful of more vintage hits, which provoked an even greater reaction – 'Beautiful Day', 'I Will Follow' and 'Out Of Control'. As night fell, Bono repeated his story about 'City Of Blinding Lights' and, with his back to the crowd, gave the skyline a round of applause.

Less well publicised in the last year or so was the fact that Bono recently joined a Silicon Valley-based venture capital firm that plans to invest in media and entertainment proj-

317

ects. According to a published report in the *Wall Street Journal*, in June 2004, the forty-four-year-old singer had joined the newly created Elevation Partners, based in Menlo Park, Los Angeles, adding that the new venture aimed to raise over $1 billion for new business projects over the next few years. Launched by fabled technology investor, Roger McNamee, and John Riccitiello, former president of videogame maker Electronic Arts Inc., the new Bono-backed venture also includes the shrewd presence of Fred Anderson, who retired in May 2004 as Apple Computer Inc.'s finance director. When approached for an official quote about their intended activities, officials from Elevation Partners declined to comment, citing Securities and Exchange Commission rules for venture capital firms in the midst of fundraising, according to the newspaper.

Another venture of a more personal and artistic nature involved Bono's involvement with a new edition of the Prokofiev orchestral classic, *Peter and the Wolf*. Bono had made a series of sixteen paintings to accompany a new recording of the classical masterpiece, aided, he was quick to point out, by his two young daughters, Jordan and Eve. The Bono family artwork comprised a serious of colourful illustrations for a contemporary interpretation of *Peter and the Wolf*. Prokofiev's original musical score had also been updated for the project by film soundtrack producer – and Bono's childhood friend – Gavin Friday (also now famous for his work on the corresponding soundtracks to *Moulin Rouge* and *Romeo and Juliet*). As such, it became a much-sought-after collection that, when later put up for charitable auction at Christie's in New York, in November 2003, had raised over $368,000, with all proceeds earmarked for the Irish Hospice Foundation.

"Hello, my name is Bono and I am a rock star," said Bono with a mock smirk as he addressed the packed auction room, before going on to praise the "angels" at the Irish Hospice Foundation for the care they had shown his late father during the terminal stages of his own illness two years previously. Two portraits of Bono's father, Bobby, carrying his Cleveland golf clubs, both went for $15,000 each, while a closer, more detailed study of the wolf's head was bought for $20,000 by U2 manager Paul McGuinness. The top price at the auction, however, after some heated bidding from the floor, was achieved by the $60,000 paid by Doug Morris, CEO of Universal Music Group (U2's record company) for a self-portrait of Bono as a child which the singer had self-deprecatingly titled "Baked Bean Boy".

At times, the auction became a rather zany affair. When auctioneer Bernard Willams called Bono "the Basquiat of the future", Gavin Friday joined him at the rostrum and promised to put his tongue in the ear of anyone who would be prepared to pay the $30,000 they were asking for one of the larger paintings, all mixed media on paper, the largest some five foot by ten foot. As an unusually modest-sounding Bono explained in his speech: "I asked my girls Jordan and Eve to help me with detail and a filigree of flowers. I painted myself in a corner as Peter. My [father] we made the grandfather, as he was to Jordan and Eve, my two daughters who loved and were loved by him." Then added: "The Wolf was ambition for things just out of reach …"

Delighted Irish Hospice Foundation director, Marie Donnelly, revealed to reporters that the hospice expected to raise a further million dollars from the sale of a limited edition of two hundred box sets costing five thousand dollars each, with each box containing fine miniature reproductions of all the paintings. A book and CD would also be made available on-line via an official website – peterwolf.org – with all proceeds, once again, benefiting the Irish Hospice Foundation. Afterwards, at the post-show cocktail party, Bono mingled with celebrity guests such as Moby, Elvis Costello, Michael Stipe of REM, Matthew Barney and the gorgeous actress Aimee Mullins. He then headed off for a private dinner at the ultra-fashionable Mario Battalis Otto restaurant before ending the night at très-chic early-hours nightclub, PM.

So what of the future? As long ago as 1988 Bono had stated his intention "to clog up the airwaves for some time to come. You know," he added cockily, "the sorta mega album then the mega silence is just too much of a cliché, at this point. You know, we put out the record and then we tour it around the world for a year and a half, and then we go to Barbados and have a holiday for another year and a half, and then we come back. That's so boring." U2, he had vowed, "intend to make music until people are sick of us".

One suspects that Bono knows he may never find what

he's really looking for, but it seems clear that his apparently endless search is set to enthral and entertain the rest of us for many more years to come.

INDEX